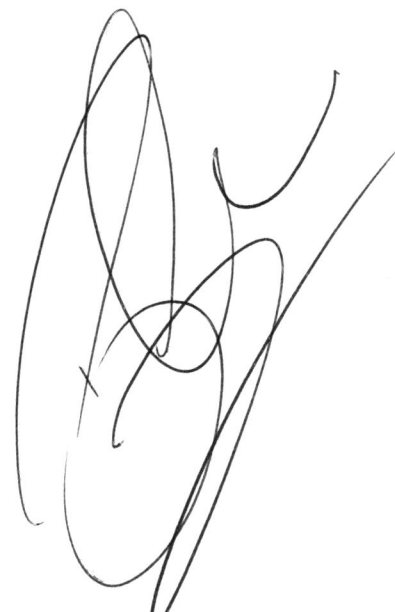

THE BEST OF BURNLEY
A Burnley FC Anthology

Compiled by Dave Thomas

THE BEST OF BURNLEY
A Burnley FC Anthology

Compiled by Dave Thomas

Vertical Editions
www.verticaleditions.com

Copyright © Dave Thomas 2018

The right of Dave Thomas to be identified as the author of this work has been asserted in accordance with the Copyright, Designs and Patents Act, 1988

All rights reserved. The reproduction and utilisation of this book in any form or by any electrical, mechanical or other means, now known or hereafter invented, including photocopying and recording, and in any information storage and retrieval system, is forbidden without the written permission of the publisher

First published in the United Kingdom in 2018 by Vertical Editions, Unit 4a, Snaygill Industrial Estate, Skipton, North Yorkshire BD23 2QR

www.verticaleditions.com

ISBN 978-1-908847-09-6

A CIP catalogue record for this book is available from the British Library

Cover design by HBA, York

Printed and bound by Jellyfish Solutions, Swanmore, Hants

Contents

Acknowledgements 7
Source Material 8
Introduction 9
1   John Haworth and the 1914 Cup Final 13
2   1932 Tommy Boyle is Taken Away 50
3   Burnley V West Ham, FA Cup 1964 69
4   1977 Brian Laws Joins Burnley..87
5   1982 And So to Doncaster 113
6   From the Big Time to the Bad Times 130
7   Roger Eli's Glorious Season 147
8   Owen Coyle Returns..169
9   Sean Dyche 193

Acknowledgements

I am indebted to Phil Whalley, Michael Calvin, Roger Eli, Brian Belton, Brian Laws, Mike Smith, Daniel Gray, Dave Roberts, and their publishers for permission to include their work.

Burnley Football Club for the use of photographs.

Karl Waddicor at Vertical Editions for his text amendments and coming up with the suggestion that we split all the material I had to make two books rather than one unaffordable, 400-page, 'heavyweight'.

Mrs T as ever for tending to my computer, still ailing after all these years.

John Gibaut for his tireless help with proofing.

Source Material

The London Clarets magazine: *Something to Write Home About*

Ray Simpson: *Burnley A Complete History*, Breedon 1991

Brian Belton: *The Men of 64*, Tempus, 2005

Ray Simpson: *The Clarets Chronicles*, published by Burnley Football Club

Mike Smith: *Broken Hero*, Grosvenor House Publishing 2011

Dave Roberts: *32 Programmes*, Bantam Press 2011

Brian Laws and Alan Biggs: *Laws of the Jungle*, Vertical Editions 2012

Daniel Gray: *Hatters, Railwaymen and Knitters*, Bloomsbury 2013

Roger Eli and Dave Thomas: *Thanks for the Memories*, Vertical Editions 2012

Michael Calvin: *Living on the Volcano*, Arrow Books 2015

Introduction

Burnley Football Club: a club with such a long and illustrious history, a founder member of the Football League, a club with an endless list of great players, a club that has won cups, trophies and titles. And as such, despite being a 'small' club, has inspired so much literature, either dedicated Burnley books, or books with chapters that have featured Burnley.

Two such books were the two *No Nay Never* anthologies that gathered together accounts of events and players in Burnley's story. The last one was produced in 2008 and now 10 years later there is enough material for another anthology, this one under the heading *The Best of Burnley*, and once again featuring the best of Burnley writing.

It begins with a piece and collection of articles by Phil Whalley about John Haworth and the 1914 Cup Final win against Liverpool in the early days of the club. There are strong arguments to support the view that Haworth was Burnley's greatest ever manager.

The descriptive, meticulous reporting and comprehensive writing style of the time (elaborate, complex sentences that seem to last forever) is typical of the age. Compare it with something from today's *Sun,* or *Daily Mirror.*

In some ways, the real history of Burnley Football Club begins with John Haworth. The club existed before him of course, but it was Haworth who put it on the map and it was his wonderful achievements that formed the beginning of the club's greatest chapters. The 1914 FA Cup Final victory and the Championship in 1920/21 were down to him. The word legend is overused. But it fits John Haworth perfectly.

Mike Smith's biography of Tommy Boyle is a masterpiece of painstaking research. Mike was kind enough to allow me to use material from his book as a sort of follow-on to the John Haworth chapter. Boyle was a key member of the 1914 cup-winning side. His story is quite harrowing. At his peak he was nigh on a household name but then his fame and fortune faded badly and he ended his days in a mental institution. Players that once 'had it all' and then ended up broke, with failed businesses or family problems, or mental breakdowns, are by no means a modern phenomenon.

The career of Harry Potts is already covered in *Harry Potts: Margaret's Story* but for this new book I came across a chapter about the FA Cup game at West Ham in season 1963/64 in a book by Brian Belton about West Ham's Cup triumph that year.

Although this volume does not look in detail at the life and times of Harry Potts, the cup-tie at West Ham in 1964 was one of the many games when he was in charge. In season 1963/64 it looked possible that Burnley might be heading for Wembley again when they got as far as the quarter-finals. I am grateful to Brian Belton for allowing me to use the West Ham versus Burnley chapter from his book *The Men of 64* which is the story of West Ham's progress to the FA Cup Final that year.

In this new book the chapter by Brian Belton about West Ham's cup triumph of 1964 adds to the Harry Potts story. Brian is a diehard West Ham supporter and has written several West Ham books. Brian Belton's chapter on the cup-tie is reproduced, a tie that was not without its controversies and as a consequence Bob Lord was far from pleased at the outcome.

Brian Laws joined Burnley as a young player in 1977. His career as a defender was distinguished and he was a firm favourite whilst at Burnley as a player, but John Bond eventually dispensed with his services. Brian Clough eventually signed him, a clear testament to his talent as a full-back. As a manager he had success in the lower divisions but when he returned to Burnley in 2010 to replace the departed Owen Coyle, it was an appointment perhaps doomed to failure from the start due to a number of factors, not the least of which was the utter deflation felt by several of the players when Coyle

Introduction

left them. In truth it was an appointment that had both players and fans scratching their heads. His book, *Laws of the Jungle*, left many questions unanswered about his time at the club, but the Burnley sections are included here.

In 1982 Laws was a star member of the side that won at Doncaster in the season that the club won promotion from Division Three to Division Two. The account of that game is mine. It was a memorable evening that I reminisced about years later in the resultant article.

When I first read *32 Programmes* by Dave Roberts, my first thought was, what a wonderfully simple idea, why didn't I think of that?

Dave and his wife made the momentous decision to move to the USA. 'You are not taking all your 1,134 programmes with you,' she told him. But she did allow him to take a very small collection of his favourites. If you want to know why the title is *32 Programmes* then you will need to buy the book. Two of them involved Burnley.

In 2012 I spent a very happy year with Roger Eli working on his book *Thanks for The Memories*. Roger's story is one of injury, bad luck, perseverance and how players are always at the mercy of any manager. One of the reviews described it as almost a text book on what can go wrong in a player's career and should be read by any young footballer trying to make his way in the game. Roger battled on and during one memorable season at Burnley he was named Player of the Year, and scored the Goal of the Season. He will be forever remembered at Turf Moor as one of the players who took the club out of the old Fourth Division after too many years in that basement. It is a pleasure to include one of the chapters from his book.

After a decade of exile in Scotland, Daniel Gray returned to England to re-acquaint himself with English football and football grounds. He describes *Hatters, Railwaymen and Knitters* as an affectionate search for the essence of not just football but England itself as he traverses the land and visits a number of places and grounds from north to south, from Carlisle to Ipswich. Burnley is one of them and provides a delightful chapter that is both illuminating and entertaining.

Finally there is a feature on Sean Dyche, the Burnley manager who masterminded two promotions to the Premier League. Written by Michael Calvin, the chapter comes from his book about managers,

Living on the Volcano, with chapters on the likes of Brendan Rodgers, Eddie Howe and Alan Pardew, chapters that range from the well-known to the not so well-known. A more absorbing book you could not wish to read. It leaves you asking the simple question: just why would anyone be a manager?

The question has been asked, where Sean Dyche is in the all-time list of Burnley managers. His record puts him alongside the very best, two of them being John Haworth and Harry Potts, both featured in this book.

Putting together a book like this is fairly easy; it's just a question of finding Burnley articles. It is great fun searching for them, and finding those books that do have a Burnley mention in them. Ready for the next volume is an obscure 1948 book written by the 1947 Cup Final referee; a game between Burnley and Charlton Athletic. The covers are falling off, it is battered and torn, held together by browning sellotape; but spotting little books like this in a tiny, dust-filled second-hand bookshop, is like finding treasure.

The hardest part is getting all the necessary permissions and contacting all the authors. All the books featured are still available either from Amazon or eBay. Ninety-nine per cent of authors make no great fortunes from writing football books. It's a fair bet they have other jobs as well to make ends meet, or are journalists, or, like me, enjoy the luxury of retirement so that writing is such a pleasurable hobby.

The chapters here in this anthology are just samples and it would be nice to think that they will encourage readers to go out and buy a copy of any of the books included.

Dave Thomas, October 2017

1

John Haworth and the 1914 Cup Final

Phil Whalley is a longstanding Burnley supporter, living in London, and the author of Accrington Stanley: The Club that Wouldn't Die. *He edits and produces the London Clarets Magazine:* Something to Write Home About, *a respected, scholarly publication that has been produced for many years. The excerpts that follow are from various Burnley newspapers of the time that Phil has used to tell the story of the 1914 Cup Final and Burnley victory when they were managed by John Haworth. They first appeared in* Something To Write Home About. *The newspaper reports of the day were written by reporters with the pen names Brunhilde, Sportsman and Brunbank. They remained anonymous. The* Burnley Express *and* Burnley News *were just two of the local newspapers with the reporters writing for all of them.*

Born in Accrington, it is John Haworth who lays claim to being Burnley's greatest ever manager. But because his achievements took place so long ago, his claim goes largely forgotten. Of course we know that Burnley won the FA Cup in 1914, and that they won the First Division title in 1920/21, but the man who took them to those achievements is rarely mentioned or remembered as often as Harry Potts, or Jimmy Adamson, Stan Ternent or even Owen Coyle. DT

***

From *Something to Write Home About*, the Magazine of the London Clarets. Article by Phil Whalley

'Let us kick off with the inspiration of it all. This was when I was stood as a youngster amid the mighty mass of people assembled near the town hall of Burnley to cheer home our Cup winners of 1914. That vast crowd was there, together with the City Fathers, to welcome the Cup to Burnley for the first time. The team came out on the balcony, and there was Tommy Boyle, the captain, holding the Cup in triumph as high above his head as he could in order that all those people should see it. Even I, as a nipper of six, could see it. How I thrilled!'

So wrote Bob Lord in his autobiography *My Fight for Football*. And on that balcony, up to which Bob Lord gazed with wonder and delight, would have been one of the men who had made it all happen. Perhaps more than most, he deserved to take some of the acclaim, to hold that world-famous trophy up high, and accept the congratulations of the people. I doubt he did as such a thing would seemingly have been wholly against his character. Even so, no one could have begrudged him his moment of public triumph if he had. His name was John Haworth and he was the manager who had guided Burnley to their first major trophy in their history.

Under John Haworth, Burnley Football Club set itself new and previously unattained standards that are commemorated to this day. By the time his tenure came to an untimely end, his place in the history of the club was assured. The rise of the club from Second Division obscurity to League Champions in 1921 had something of the rags to riches about it. Because of people like him and his achievements we know there is something special about the place.

Exactly what is it that makes Burnley special? Is it something intangible or are there rather more concrete foundations? Perhaps these foundations were laid by John Haworth with the great team that he constructed, a team roared on by proud townspeople. He broke the mould of mediocrity and anonymity and in so doing began the tradition of which we are now so proud. He changed the entire history of the club. He set in place the precious historical commodity of success. It was against his team's great achievements that the great side of the sixties measured their progress; just as we Clarets use the sixties and seventies as the yardstick for so many of the comparisons we make today. And, where John Haworth broke the mould was in wanting to be the best, wanting to take the club to a higher level, and setting out to actually do it with his astuteness and his tireless work.

He applied for the Turf Moor managership after the awful accident that befell incumbent manager Spen Whitaker in 1910. Their lives had crossed several times already and it is certain that they were both friends. Both were Accringtonians and both lent enormous enthusiasm and energy to amateur football. Neither men were especially good players but both discovered an aptitude for coaching and administration.

Raised in a sporting family, John Haworth received an Accrington education in the game but it was tinged with a hint of glamour; his uncle was an England international and much respected captain of the town's League club known as Th'owd Reds. Despite being by far the smallest town to foster a professional Football League club, for the first couple of seasons they cohabited comfortably with big city clubs like Derby County, Aston Villa, Notts County, Everton, Wolverhampton Wanderers and Stoke City. This courage to punch above one's weight shaped the early outlook of the young John Haworth.

It was perhaps the financial chaos that engulfed and wrecked Accrington FC in 1893 that in part inspired the young John Haworth to begin his career in football management. It was clear by this time, although only in his teens, that he would not emulate his uncle on the field of play. Demonstrating a firm grasp of reality that would always serve him well, John began to plan his path to pre-eminence as a manager. In 1894, at the sprightly age of 18, he took over the managership of Meadow Bank Rovers for whom he was playing. However, his target was to re-establish the professional game in his home town of Accrington.

Within three years he had disbanded Meadow Bank and merged it with Accrington Stanley. He was appointed to the committee and within three years was Stanley manager. For a team on the rise, the Lancashire Combination was the place to be offering the chance to compete against the likes of reserve sides from Everton, Blackburn Rovers, Oldham Athletic and Preston North End. In 1905/06 they had won the Championship twice and with Haworth still only 30 he was established as a very bright prospect. It was while he was at Accrington Stanley that he demonstrated his approach to management and motivation of players that would go on to transform Burnley. He believed in the power of money.

This is not to say that he held the view that man was essentially greedy and self-seeking, and that money was merely the most effective way of securing compliance. Instead it had a social and economic impact on professional football. It was a primary factor in the development of football as soon as families realised that football could pay regular working wages. Football was becoming more and more important to communities within the grey deserts of factories and terraced housing. The Saturday match was an entertaining diversion from the daily grind. In this world, the local lad made good on the football pitch was a true working-class hero, for he came from the same streets as the spectators. It was to these young men that Haworth offered an avenue away. A playing contract was a treasured prize. While everyone else took to the mill or the mine, the professional footballer took to different cobbled streets, not exactly paved with gold, but still shining with the promise of honour, adulation and a fair wage. Under John Haworth, the players of Accrington Stanley earned all three.

By 1910, Haworth had clocked up 13 years as manager of Accrington Stanley. At that point Burnley had made no impression on the Second Division. The Cup run of 1909 was a fading memory. Folk on the terraces were growing disillusioned. With the season as good as over by February and gates below 4,000 Burnley played out their remaining fixtures with minimal interest from the town. And then tragedy befell the Burnley manager Spen Whitaker.

On April 15th he set out by train to London to register a player. The events of the night are unclear, that is to say, how he actually fell out of the train. His injuries were horrific and he died in hospital unable to tell anyone what had happened. It was a terrible, terrible tragedy.

As sad as Spen's death was, Burnley FC had to face the future and appoint a new manager. The Board sensitively waited until the end of the season before advertising and received around 60 applications for the job. From this pack emerged John Haworth. He had no experience of League football, but had guided Accrington Stanley from amateur obscurity to powerful semi-professional status, picking up a number of trophies and championships along the way. He was cut from different cloth than Spen Whitaker. This time Burnley had gone for a more sophisticated manager of men, a man of the head rather than of the heart, someone capable of motivating players with a stick as well as the carrot – moreover someone who could use a combination of the two.

The Turf Moor that John Haworth found in July 1910 was certainly in a far healthier state than that which confronted Spen Whitaker in September 1903. However, the club was still in the Second Division and the finances were still precarious. Just as the Cup run of 1909 had lifted the club out of debt, the early Cup exit the following season, coupled with a poor League campaign and low attendances had dragged the club into the red once more. Burnley posted a financial deficit of £1,974 for season 1909/10 and the Board decided to decrease the players' wages. Eventually Burnley came to an agreement with their players (following a threatened player rebellion), but the episode did not go down well with a public hungry for success. The week after the team reported back for pre-season training a letter appeared in the *Burnley Express.* It expressed doubts about the team's ability to survive and it strongly berated the management.

The same author wrote again: 'I want my old team to regain its prestige, and it can only do this, in my opinion, by being composed of good men who will play for the honour of the club as well as the pay they derive from the game.'

At least no one could argue with that point and once again the town readied itself for the new season. As a sartorially elegant John Haworth lined up with his new team on the eve of the season, the Turfites were resplendent in their new strip of claret and blue. Haworth's first game in charge saw the visit of Lincoln City and the Imps were sent home pointless following a 3 – 1 defeat. This was followed by two home draws and an away win at Huddersfield.

His first season in charge was generally satisfactory. They had made 14th position their own in the previous two seasons. In 1910/11 Burnley had managed eighth position, losing only 10 games. With the benefit of hindsight, the season was particularly prescient for three reasons (four if you include changing the strip to claret and blue). Firstly in October 1910 a famous Burnley name established himself in the first team – Willie Watson. Secondly in January 1911, Burnley began to show some FA Cup form eventually reaching the quarter finals. Thirdly, thanks to that season's FA Cup run, John Haworth had some money in his pocket to try and alleviate the team's goalscoring problem. He caused a sensation by going to First Division Everton and returning with two forwards, one of them Bert Freeman, an England international only two seasons previously. It was quite a coup by John Haworth to persuade the Everton man to sign for Burnley. Perhaps this was the first indication of the 'address and finesse of the diplomat' heralded by the *Burnley Express* upon his appointment.

In August, 1911, the *Burnley Express* reported an epidemic of football fever in the air. The town had awoken to the fact that Burnley had at last made real progress in their quest to regain First Division status. As a new stand on Brunshaw Road neared completion, John Haworth sought to further strengthen his team, signing young winger, Willie Nesbitt from local Calderdale side, Portsmouth Rovers. In September, 1911, still only four weeks into the season he travelled with chequebook to Oakwell intent on the signature of Barnsley's much admired centre-half, Tommy Boyle.

Boyle had clearly decided the time was right to move on. The amount Barnsley received is unclear; reports vary between £800 and £1,150. It represented Burnley's biggest investment in one player. Boyle's impact was almost immediate as Burnley embarked on four straight League victories.

At the end of March with only five games remaining, Burnley were seven points clear of third-placed Derby. Promotion was almost secure. But then disaster struck with defeats in three days at Birmingham and Leicester. Chelsea stole in at the death to claim the second promotion place. Burnley had occupied a promotion place for most of the season, but had been pushed to third at the very last.

Failure to be promoted was a bitter disappointment to everyone in the town, but John Haworth could derive enormous satisfaction from what was only his second full season as manager. Perhaps most crucially of all he had succeeded in capturing the imagination of the Burnley public by raising the profile of the club through imaginative and bold signings. From a financial point of view this was something of a gamble, but the manager had bought quality players who still had years of playing ahead of them. They were investments rather than speculative risks. It was an astute and visionary policy – John Haworth was going to build a formidable side with a combination of home grown talent and high profile signings.

If Burnley's supporters had expected the team to carry on in 1912/13, where they left off the previous season, they were in for an initial let down. Despite being most peoples' favourites for promotion, if not for the title itself, Burnley had an inauspicious start. But, by March 12th, 1913, they were second in the table, and in the semi-finals of the FA Cup. On March 8th they had taken on Blackburn Rovers in front of 47,000 at Ewood Park with an estimated Burnley contingent of 20,000. To a man the Clarets were magnificent, defeating their First Division opponents 1 – 0 and going into the hat for the semi-finals for the first time ever.

John Haworth did not let this glorious Cup performance distract him from the main priority, promotion, and a League defeat with a poor performance to boot, this time at Grimsby was the prelude to more decisive activity in the transfer market. George Halley was signed from Bradford Park Avenue and for the first time the Burnley half-back line read: 'Halley, Boyle and Watson.' The FA Cup semi-final draw had been unkind to Burnley pairing them with Sunderland. A 0 – 0 struggle at Bramhall Lane preceded a classic replay at St Andrews which saw Burnley lose 3 – 2. Three wins and a draw in the next four games secured promotion with two games to spare. Promotion was greeted with euphoria in Burnley and the club held a special celebratory dinner.

Tellingly, the report of the dinner does not mention any speech from John Haworth, yet he was the one who perhaps deserved the most credit, nurturing the talent of Dawson, Mosscrop and Lindley whist strengthening the team in strategic areas with some master acquisitions. For the quiet man from Accrington, Burnley's promotion and the celebrations that followed were personal and typically restrained.

If the League achievements following promotion were modest and in the FA Cup there had been semi-final disappointment, the Cup run in the following season, 1913/14, took them all the way to the Final at Crystal Palace. The team retired to Lytham St Annes to prepare for the game, the opponents Liverpool. One player who did not feature in the FA Cup winning side was the legendary Bob Kelly. He emerged in the season after the Final having signed in November 1913 from St Helens Town. By this time Burnley had earned a reputation as big spenders. Although he was not in the Cup Final side, some brilliant performances in the reserves prompted his promotion to the First team in November 1914. He would go on to be the star attraction of a post-war Turf Moor when John Haworth would further cement his reputation by guiding Burnley to further honours including the never to be forgotten title win of 1920/21 and the sequence of undefeated games.

***

The Road to Crystal Palace

It is over 100 years since Burnley won the Cup in 1914. The following articles (again researched and put together by Phil Whalley and published in Something to Write Home About) *reveal just how feverish things were then, just as they would be today. Although the cost was prohibitive, and travel was difficult, time-consuming and uncomfortable, over 15,000 made the journey to Crystal Palace. After journeying overnight, many boarded chartered buses to see the sights of the capital and, as the kick-off approached, the route to the ground was a sea of claret and blue. Descriptions of the crowds, the fans, the partying and the revelry after the game destroy any stereotype Lancashire images of cloth caps and whippets. It may have been over 100 years ago but the day was much as it would be now; the press coverage, the excitement in the town, colours in every shop and home window, the sale of souvenirs and memorabilia, and the plans for travel. Then on the day there was the exodus from the town, the anticipation, singing, entertainment, the huge crowd and the sense of a great day out. The section entitled 'Doing the Sights' gives an insight into a social world long gone.*

Phil Whalley begins:

It could be said that Burnley's name was 'on the Cup' in 1914. Up to that point the Clarets had little of a Cup tradition and had only just lifted themselves back into the First Division. The 1913/14 season was, in league terms, a season of mid-table consolidation. Yet something special was brewing at Turf Moor. With promotion and a Cup semi-final behind them from the previous season's campaign, Burnley were fast earning a reputation for dynamic attacking football. Their dynamism on the field was matched by determination and vision in the boardroom. Under Chairman Windle, the men behind the scenes gave Manager John Haworth the resources to build a strong team, Burnley at one point acquiring the whole of the Gainsborough Trinity defence in one deal. The ambition was palpable – all concerned talked openly to the Press about their dream of bringing the League Championship to Turf Moor.

But FA Cup success came first despite a previously poor record in the competition. By 1911 Burnley were beginning to show promise. A better than average league campaign was supplemented by a Cup run to the last eight, which was halted by a defeat to the eventual winners Bradford City. After narrowly missing out on promotion in 1912, the Clarets finally made it to the top division the following season finishing runners-up to Preston North End. The season was notable for a significant Cup run to the semi-final. The first game against champions to be Sunderland was a draw and in the replay they went down 3 – 2 but only after a titanic struggle.

The following season was one of consolidation but it was in the FA Cup that this team would really distinguish itself. After a straightforward defeat of non-league South Shields in the first round, the Clarets were blessed with the luck of home draws for the next two rounds, although they faced First Division opponents on both occasions. Derby County were first up in the second round, and, although having a poor season they made the Clarets fight for a 3

– 2 victory. The third round appeared to be a different proposition as high-flying Bolton Wanderers were the visitors. However, the Clarets turned in an inspirational performance and soundly defeated their opponents 3 – 0. The draw for the next round was to provide what many Burnley fans thought to be an insurmountable obstacle – reigning league champions Sunderland at Roker Park. It was the tie of the round and a repeat of the previous season's semi-final clash. As before, the first game ended in a goalless draw but this time it was the battling Clarets who came out top in the replay, 2 – 1, after a superb team performance.

All four semi-finalists were First Division clubs. Three of them, Sheffield United, Burnley and Liverpool, were middle of the table clubs separated by only a few points. The team to avoid was Aston Villa, reigning Cup holders and second in the table. This they did, being paired against Sheffield United. And, if Burnley were to lift the Cup that season, they were going to have to defeat five First Division clubs in one FA Cup campaign, a feat never achieved before. Could the Clarets succeed where none before had? With the experience of the previous season's semi-final behind them, the Clarets went into the semi-final perhaps with a slight edge on their opponents who had done nothing in the Cup since 1902. A goalless draw at Old Trafford meant a Wednesday replay at Goodison Park. With only 17 minutes of the replay remaining, a glorious strike by Boyle broke the deadlock and sealed Burnley's first ever Cup Final appearance.

With everyone's Cup favourites Aston Villa surprisingly beaten in the other semi-final played at White Hart Lane, the Clarets faced Liverpool in the Final at Crystal Palace. Liverpool had experienced an undistinguished season and had been given kind Cup draws at home to non-league Gillingham and QPR and Second Division Barnsley, but Aston Villa was a formidable scalp in the semi-final. Burnley, too, had overcome indifferent league form to defeat illustrious opposition in the Cup. They had had by far the hardest series of games to reach the Final overcoming the challenge of four other First Division Clubs. They were also the club on the up, on the cusp of great and lasting achievements. The club had invested in new players and their directors had made their ambitions known to the town. Our predecessors on the terraces at Turf Moor discovered a new-found faith that their team would deliver.

At Long Last – The Semi-Final (*Burnley Express* Editorial May 4th, 1914)

Burnley have had a long, and to many football enthusiasts, a weary wait for their first appearance in an English Cup Final. In the last four years they have made the bravest attempts in that direction in all their history. Last year, they were only defeated by the odd goal in five at Birmingham by Sunderland, after a drawn game at Sheffield, in which the Turfites showed the better football. This season they have disposed of four First Division clubs, and the champions of the North-Eastern League; and if they do win the Cup eventually they will add another to the many records they have been establishing in late years – that of being the only Cup holders to defeat five First Division teams in the course of one season's competition. That their task has been a hard one all will readily admit, and those who witnessed the two games against Sheffield United will agree with the opinion that we expressed when the draw was first announced – that the men from Sheffield were just the men to throw the Turfites off their customary game. There were times both at Manchester and at Everton when it appeared likely that the Blades would prove victorious. Near the closing stage of the first half on Wednesday, indeed, it looked 'all Lombard Street to a hayseed' that Gillespie's magnificent drive would score. The shot, travelling at express speed, was going to Sewell's right-hand side while the custodian was at the left. Just when everyone felt certain it was going through, Sewell made a magnificent leap and dive, and diverted the ball round the posts. Even then it took the spectators a second or two to realise that a save had been effected. A less agile and resourceful keeper would have been defeated, and the crowd cheered lustily for several minutes in acknowledgement of a feat that has seldom been equalled or surpassed.

Sewell's superlative saves, indeed, were, next to Boyle's 'goal in a thousand,' the outstanding features of Wednesday's replay. The ex-Gainsborough man, by his dexterity, anticipation, judgement, coolness and effectiveness, more than repaid his club, in hard cash alone, for any transfer fee the directors paid when they 'nobbled' the whole of the Gainsborough Trinity defence last season. Even the disappointed Sheffield supporters could not help refrain from expressing admiration at his prowess, and it was difficult to make the general body of spectators believe that so brilliant a custodian was, after all, only Burnley's reserve goalkeeper. In the first half, two shots saved by him would have beaten any ordinary man. The first was the one already described, and the next was a particularly strong drive from the right at point-blank range, which was coolly driven for a corner though the ball was brought into play afterwards and put through the goal. However, Mr Taylor's whistle had already gone, and the flag kick was duly taken and the situation saved. In the second-half too, Sewell saved his charge finely – once from a dangerous dropping shot, which he seized under the bar, and once from a left-wing drive, which he coolly put over his head for a corner with three opponents on him. Thus Sewell's superlative saves were among the finest features of Wednesday's game, and as much as anything else enabled Burnley to qualify for the Final game at Crystal Palace three weeks hence. Well did Sewell deserve the admiration and applause he received on Wednesday, both after the save from Gillespie, on retiring to the dressing room at the interval, on taking up position for the second-half, on finally leaving the field, and when, along with Burnley's brilliant captain and strategist, he was chaired on leaving Bank Top station when the team returned to Burnley.

Tommy Boyle has done many good things for Burnley since he became its captain, but we think it will be generally acknowledged that his two outstanding feats have been the goals he scored at Ewood Park last year when Burnley disposed of Blackburn Rovers in the fourth round, and on Wednesday, when, seventeen minutes before the close, his cannon-like shot settled the fate of Sheffield United. Though it was apparent he had not fully recovered from the illness which affected his play at Manchester, Boyle played an immensely improved game at Everton, as indeed did all the other members of the Burnley team. He was here, there, everywhere, helping the attack or the defence as occasion demanded, and casting a critical eye on the movement and disposition of his men. We saw in him the astute general when he caused Mosscrop and Nesbitt to exchange places. English, the fine left-back of the United – one of the very best of the 22 players who have figured in these two games – was limping about, and yet kicking wonderfully well, despite his handicap. Boyle's penetrating eye saw a chance of Mosscrop's speed being utilised to the full advantage.

Thereafter, Burnley pressed to good purpose. Almost immediately Mosscrop had the hardest of hard lines in heading on to instead of just under the bar. Then, from a very bad foul by Cook, Watson sent in a glorious shot. This was headed out, and Mosscrop returned splendidly. Gough drove the ball down with his fists, and it got to the edge of the penalty line, with a direct open course. Boyle took three or four mighty strides then kicked with a force that even put his usual penalty shots in the shade. From the time the ball left the Burnley captain's trusty right toe there was no shadow of a doubt as to the result. It passed like lightning to the back of the net, which shivered and shook for several seconds as if it had been caught by a whirlwind. It was indeed a 'goal in a thousand' and thoroughly repaid the Burnley enthusiast for the trouble and anxiety – to say nothing of the expense – attending these two remarkable semi-finals.

The scene which followed was indescribable. If any doubt had previously existed as to which was the popular side, it was set completely at rest by Boyle's big and successful effort. All the Burnley players save and except Sewell, of course, rushed up to their captain and literally hugged him, while the crowd cheered with stentorian force. How some of the Burnley spectators recovered their hearts is a mystery, for at that moment none of them seemed to care what became of themselves or what Wemmings would have called their 'portable property.' From this point onwards, there was only one team in it. The United captain followed Boyle's example in exchanging his centre and extreme right winger, but it was only Utley himself who did anything dangerous, and one of his shots provided Sewell with another opportunity of displaying his superb custodianship. But it was Burnley who dominated the remainder of the game, and just before the close it looked odds on another score. Freeman had been badly kicked in the face, not only badly, but to all appearances, deliberately

– and after he had been attended by the trainer, Boyle sent a powerful and well-directed shot at the Sheffield goal. All that Gough could do was throw himself full-length and rush the ball back. Freeman dashed up and kicked with terrific force. The ball seemed to be through, but Gough was rising at the moment, and the ball, striking his shoulder, went behind for a corner. This was indeed a slice of luck for Sheffield. From this point onwards, Burnley had the game safely in hand and when the whistle blew for full time the players threw their hands in the air and darted off the field. Boyle and Sewell experienced the greatest difficulty in escaping the chairing which some of the enthusiasts in the concourse were bent on giving.

Burnley were undoubtedly the better team on Wednesday, though the players as a whole did not rise to the heights of their form against Bolton Wanderers or Sunderland. But this we attribute rather to the fact that the Sheffield halves, with their towering height and vigorous methods, prevented the forwards from settling to their proper game. Mr Taylor, the referee, spoke to more than one of the United players, and at one time appeared to be lecturing Utley upon the tactics his men were pursuing. Both on Saturday and on Wednesday the policy of the Sheffield players appeared to be to spoil the Burnley vanguard at all costs. Hence it was that in both games fouls were frequent and it is some satisfaction, from a Burnley point of view, that the only goal the three hours football produced came directly from the punishment awarded for foul play.

Mr Taylor and his linesmen deserve every credit for the firm and impartial way in which they controlled two exceedingly difficult games. Sheffield players would do well to take lesson of their defeat to heart. If the halves and rear-guard had played like English, all would have been well. The Sheffield left-back is a model man, kicking well and cleanly, and tackling with scrupulous fairness. He and Gough, the goalkeeper, have nothing to reproach themselves about. They played the game honestly and in sterling fashion. But the majority of the team resorted to other tactics and just retribution overtook the side. In our opinion, the two most unpleasant ties in this season's competition, so far as Burnley are concerned, have been with the Derby County and Sheffield clubs and we hope that the lessons of both contests will not be lost in either quarter. Burnley used to have a name for forcible play. That has, happily both for the game and club, now disappeared, and other organisations would do well to copy the example set by the Turf Moor directors, and insist upon the game being played with skill rather than brute force.

As a result of Burnley's hard-earned victory on Wednesday, there will be a Lancashire Final at Crystal Palace. It is exactly ten years since two clubs representing the County Palatine fought in the last round of the national trophy. The contestants in 1904 were Manchester City and Bolton Wanderers. That Liverpudlians desired Burnley rather than Sheffield United as their opponents was demonstrated by the all-round enthusiasm displayed when Boyle scored the only goal in Wednesday's match three weeks hence. Probably Liverpool people realise that Burnley play the same game as Aston Villa, and argue that, as they have already routed the famous Birmingham eleven, they can, with equal if not greater ease, account for the Turfites. That Liverpool are foes worthy of our steel no Burnley enthusiast will attempt to deny. They beat Newcastle at Tyneside only on Wednesday and, on their day, they appear to be invincible. But anyone who saw them at Turf Moor and witnessed the way in which Burnley, after permitting them to draw level, put on three more goals and eventually won 5 – 2, would regard them as equal to the Turfites at their best.

But Burnley will have to be at their very best to become what we all hope at the end of the season will find them – English Cup holders for the first time in the club's chequered history. Besides, they still have six league games to play, and it is essential that they should add to the points they have already secured if they want to avoid relegation. Including last Wednesday's match, their programme includes eight matches this month, and there is the possibility of a replay in the Final itself. This is a strenuous programme for a team already overworked, with not a few of its members suffering from injuries. In the circumstances, it can hardly be expected that they will reproduce their highest form; but we trust to them with confidence that they will make this the most memorable season in the club's history by bringing the English Cup back to the banks of the Brun.

Burnley Bring Home the English Cup

The first Cup Final ever honoured by the presence of the King was won at Crystal Palace on Saturday by Burnley by the only goal. The two finalists hailed from the County Palatine, from Burnley and from Liverpool. The Duke of Lancaster, as the King is now toasted in our country, witnessed the game, shook hands with the respective captains and presented the Cup and the medals; and the majority of the crowd had come up from this northern area. It was a memorable scene. The spacious ground in the huge park was lined with rows of people, estimated to number 90,000, and in the summer-like sunshine the sight was to live in the memory for its kaleidoscopic effect alone. But add to all this the scenes of enthusiasm when the military bands paraded the ground and then lined up in front of the pavilion to greet the King; the spontaneous outbursts of cheering as His Majesty arrived, greeted the rival captains, and, finally presented the trophy, followed by the hearty singing of the National Anthem by all present; and you have Burnley associated with a Final that, in all probability, will be unique in history.

It was a wonderful eye-picture – there is a spectacular suitability about the Crystal Palace ground that cannot be beaten, however many disadvantages the pitch possesses in other respects. As the brilliant sunshine flooded the arena, the scene was one of striking beauty. From the King's chair, in a little gilt-railed enclosure in the centre of the pavilion, the solid mass of humanity on the banks and stands was curiously fascinating as it roared itself hoarse in song or thundered its cheers. Behind and above the spring tints of the foliage of the fringe of trees (dotted here and there with daring climbers to their topmost boughs) added the necessary touch of natural beauty. The Royal Standard was in readiness to be broken from the flag staff over the pavilion when His Majesty arrived.

There was a round of cheering when, about half-past one, the drum and fife band of the 1st King's Liverpool regiment formed up and marched to a lively quickstep round the arena. Then the band of the regiment took up the tail while the band of the Irish Guards arranged their music stands. Then the first notes of 'Tunnhauser' were heard. All the bustle and murmur ceased as the guards played the great

John Haworth and the 1914 Cup Final

overture. It was a magnificent performance and the crowd expressed its approval in a storm of applause.

The visiting room set apart for the King was very plain, according to the wishes of His Majesty. Truth to tell, he had not a few moments to spend in it. His car was heralded by cheering outside the enclosure, where there were thousands of people, and the King and his suite arrived about five minutes before the scheduled time for the kick-off. The crowd were waiting. The bands were massed in front of the pavilion; the King was received by Lord Derby, Lord Kinnaird and the leading officials of the Football Association and at once proceeded through the gaily coloured entrance of the pavilion. A few moments later, His Majesty emerged to take his seat in front of the great multitude; the bands played the National Anthem, and a tremendous cheer burst from the huge mass in front. His Majesty was clearly delighted.

Prior to the kick-off, both teams with the referee in the centre lined up in front of the pavilion and cheered His Majesty. Both captains were called back from the line to be presented to the King by Mr F T Wall, the secretary of the Football Association. His Majesty took a keen interest in the game and, as had been hoped, was able to stay till the end, and present the Cup and medals. Thus, Boyle had the unique honour of receiving, for a Lancashire club, the national trophy at the hands of the Duke of Lancaster. The King spoke a few words of congratulation and then handed to each of the players the specially struck gold medal. There was tremendous enthusiasm when the great assembly cheered His Majesty and sang 'God Save the King', and again when he drove away.

Burnley added another record of their own. They are the first club in the history of the Cup which has defeated five First Division Clubs in the several rounds from the first tie to the last. And, as draws go this is likely to remain a unique feature of the competition for a long number of years. Afterwards, the Burnley players and officials left the precincts of the fateful ground in taxis amid the cheers of a waiting throng of supporters and, later, took the Cup to a celebration dinner at the invitation of the Member for the Borough and Lady Ottoline Morrell. Sunday was mostly spent in a drive, in two motor charabancs, in the lovely country around Kew, Virginia Water, Windsor and Hampton Court. On Monday they received such a welcome that even the most imaginative person could not have preconceived.

***

Up in London: The Lancashire Invasion

The following newspaper reports convey the enthusiasm and elation of the Burnley fans on the day of the Final:

Doing the Sights by Brunhilde

Once of a day, on a long distance trip, people were content to set off and land in London as 'luck leet' and return ditto. Nowadays, you can have everything pat, arranged in a proper programme, and a marvellous amount for your money. Gone are the days when you get on a train and never know when it arrives. For Saturday, for instance, you could leave Burnley about midnight, arrive in London at 6 o' clock, spend the morning in driving about, have three meals, be carried to and from Crystal Palace – and all for a guinea. It is wonderful. I spoke to one of the thousands who saw London this way, and his verdict was summed up in the all-embracing word 'champion.'

Large numbers of people made a weekend of it. They travelled comfortably in corridor trains and dining cars for a fare and a third, and I was told by one gentleman that he had, during the previous ten days, written to over half a dozen hotels of medium tariff and couldn't get a room. But the vast majority of London's invaders were not of this order. They went for the day, travelled through one night going and travelled through the next night returning. In spite of the tiring schedule of the journey they were most lively; and as early as six or seven o' clock, could be seen ferrying round the principal thoroughfares. After having witnessed all the chief sights, there was enough time for the exhibition of their party colours and some hearty cheering. There were all ages amidst the throng, though all were partisans – in claret and blue for Burnley and red and white for

Liverpool. They were conspicuous the whole way to the Crystal Palace ground, with claret and blue and red and white everywhere. Some had entire overcoats in their team's colours, while others had ribbons in hats and lapels. The Liverpudlians went mad beforehand – it was as well they got their shout in, for they never got one at the match. It was Burnley who had the last laugh, and the best laugh.

There had been nineteen Cup Finals at the Crystal Palace, and there has never been a wet day yet, I am told. Well there has never been a finer one than Saturday. The sun shone uninterruptedly all day, and the trippers, estimated at over a hundred thousand – a fair proportion never went to the match, but simply took advantage of the cheap facilities – had a perfect time. In the early hours, thousands of wearied, sleepy beings left the northern railway stations. In all the hubbub and babble of Euston Road, with its conglomerate population of provincials and foreigners, the Lancastrian was the predominating personality. Breakfast was something of the nature of a movable feast. Ham and eggs were purveyed around King's Cross and Euston as early as 2 a.m., and at 10 o' clock the typical meal of the provinces was still being consumed by ravenous excursionists. Long before London itself awoke for business, the invaders had moved far afield. They took possession of The Strand, Piccadilly, Holborn and Regent Street before London had aroused itself. Cumbersome four-in-hands, which return from obscurity once a year, moved slowly along, and impeded the scurrying, impatient motor buses of the 20th century. Busy Londoners hurrying towards the City, tried to dodge in and out between the crowds of rosetted holiday-makers. Street hawkers had a busy time.

In addition to hundreds of four-in-hand brakes which carried the excursionists through the principal streets, a fleet of motor omnibuses was chartered for the purpose of conveying parties on a round of sight-seeing. Westminster Abbey, St Paul's Cathedral, the Tower, and the hundred and one recognised haunts of the tourist were crowded out, almost as soon as they opened their doors. Though sight-seeing was so enthusiastically entered upon, time was limited. The vehicles met the excursion trains at the railway terminal, ran about London for some hours, and then conveyed their passengers to Sydenham. Those on top of the omnibuses were not slow to take advantage of their position, and they leant over the sides, cheering loudly and making raucous noises with rattles and other specialities. Those who walked about were chiefly to be found near the Embankment, Trafalgar Square and the Houses of Parliament. Those who were tired out were to be seen in hundreds sound asleep on the grass in Hyde Park.

Mr Morrell, MP, and Lady Ottoline Morrell had engaged to show visitors round the Houses of Parliament. About 300 to 400 people accepted their invitation, and they had the assistance of Mr F E Harvey, MP (Leeds), and Sir F Cawley, MP (Prestwich Division) as guides. As showing the enthusiasm of the day, Mr Morrell received a postcard as follows: 'Dear Mr Morrell, I shall be very pleased to accept your invitation for a visit through the Houses of Parliament. I have reached the age of 72 years, and I am coming to London for the first time, bringing my five sons with me. Hoping we shall have a good time and win the Cup.' Mr J Beaumont the writer, duly came with his five sons, and had the good time he desired.

What did they Expect?: Altogether there were from one part of the country or another close upon a hundred thousand trippers. These included over 15,000 from the Burnley district and about 20,000 from Liverpool. The first of the crowded trains reached London at eleven o' clock on Friday night, and from then onwards the five lines which dealt with the main part of the enormous traffic recorded the following arrivals: London and North Western, 45 trains, Great Northern, 41 trains; Great Western 40 trains; Great Central, 25 trains; and Midland, 20 trains. The great majority arrived during the early hours of the morning, of course, and Euston, St Pancras, King's Cross and Marylebone stations were choked from three o' clock in the morning. Many of the local trains had to be suspended or were delayed to get the trip trains and their loads away.

One does not know what London expected to see in the Lancashire visitors. Evidently, their impression stopped at dirty colliers or men in clogs and girls in shawls, which is the usual description of southern critics. They were rather startled therefore, to find that, except for their speech, Lancashire people were very much like themselves, as well-dressed, as decorous and as smart. In fact, says one, 'For anything less like the Londoner's conception of mill girls in clogs and shawls,

John Haworth and the 1914 Cup Final

and anything more like the pretty misses of his own suburbs it would be impossible to find than these smart, staid young ladies from the North.' Of course it was the dialect that did it, but the Lancastrians were no more curiosities to the Londoners in this respect than the Southerners were to the Northerners.

Feeding the Hungry: London has always so many mouths to feed that it has no difficulty in dealing with an influx of a hundred thousand folk either as to quantity, quality or price – all tastes and pockets were catered for. It is not a bad idea, on these occasions, to go early to the Palace and to lunch there. In the grounds and the great glass hall is a plethora of entertainment and amusement. Here are great dining halls, and the following arrangements for the feeding of the multitude were made: 75lbs of beef, 25 sirloins, 35 ribs of beef, 60 loins of mutton, 100 shins of mutton, 250 fowls, 150 hams, 30cwt of pressed beef, 400 lettuces, 3,000lbs of potatoes, 2,500 veal and ham pies, 25,000 pats of butter, 30,000 rolls, 75,000 slices of bread and butter, 25,000 buns and scones, 50,000 slices of cake, 6,000 pastries, 1,500 gallons of milk, 1,500 dozen bottles of beer, and 2,000 gallons of beer. London, too, is used to such traffic and people that, with the exception of the 'decorated' ones, the invasion made no appreciable difference, except where several vehicles congregated together. So far as can be ascertained, there was no serious accident in the streets. There was a railway mishap to the north of London, in which 26 people received bruises and scratches, some of the passengers hailing from Manchester. None came from Burnley.

Over 250 motor and other buses conveyed special parties to and from Crystal Palace, and as they averaged 30 to 40 passengers apiece, there were thus 7,000 spectators accounted for. Others went by ordinary buses, brakes and taxis, and one of the most remarkable things about the day was the number of ordinary working men who thought nothing of paying half a sovereign each way for a special taxi. Crystal Palace is a long way out – you have to take something on wheels and there was no stint about the cost of getting there. On the way, one noticed, nearing Sydenham, that the houses on the line of the Royal route were decorated with flags and bunting, and there were thousands of spectators all along watching the excursionists in the first instance, and waiting for the King to pass afterwards. Many were astonished to find, when they alighted, that they had a shilling to pay to get inside the Palace buildings, and that this was in addition to the ground admission or the price of their booked seats. Among the sights was a big dog, dressed up in coat and trousers, in Liverpool colours. Inside, the astonishing size of the Palace hall of glass was an eye-opener to many. Just as we passed through, the organist was playing Rachmaninov's 'Prelude' on the great organ, and great as this amphitheatre seemed, it was but a portion of the tremendous building. In contradistinction to the organ recital, the officials were booking seats for Bombardier Wells' boxing match in the evening.

'By gum!' said one Burnley visitor as he gazed back to look at the wonderful glass façade on his way through the grounds to the football enclosure. 'Aw wouldn't like to go and mend a broken pane up theer. Aw'm a plumber but aw'd jib at that.' And so would most of us. It is a marvellous structure, and yet it has stood since 1851, and today looks as solid as can be. Paint and varnish would make a big difference. Down the terraces went the thousands, to be astonished at the size of the oval and the puny stands in comparison. The spectators on half the enclosure were massed back into the trees and, like rooks in a colony, scores were perilously perched at a giddy altitude on the branches of the trees. It was a most impressive sight in the brilliant sunshine to see this huge crowd. The immensity of it all seemed to prohibit any display of cheering, for the voices of hundreds in concert are lost. That is why, with a neutral crowd, things fell so flat. But one gathered what a noise can be made by a hundred thousand people of one mind when the King appeared, and when the military band manoeuvres electrified them into vocal activity.

Side-Shows: The game was – well, 'nowt to talk abart.' We won, and that's all that need be said here. Sportsman and Brunbank are more in that line and you can read what they say. The arrival and departure of the King was witnessed by a good many Burnleyites – the rest cheered in unison. Still it was a great afternoon, and it passed with many comic interludes. One was when some youths brought 'Burnley and the Cup' in effigy; another consisted in the efforts – not bad either – of a company of seedy looking acrobats who had, whilst clever and strong, come down to the cadging stage; and the third was the good-honoured squashing of the man who would give a dissertation on 'Be sure your sins will find you out.' But the most comical expressions to be seen on human countenances were, when at our end, a Liverpool contingent thought Lacey had scored and he hadn't, and when they thought Freeman hadn't scored – and he had. We'd exhibited the same expressions in our time, so we sympathised.

There was not half the crush getting away that one imagined, and one of the most remarkable things about the home journey was the fact that half an hour after the Final, so many waysiders enquired the result. Most of the trippers did not leave London until midnight, and to their chagrin found that nearly every place of entertainment was full. Thus they were left to walk the streets, which the Burnleyites did with cheerfulness and the Liverpool contingent with gloomy feelings. Nor did the East Lancashire lads forget to rub it in, for the Merseysiders had done all the crowing beforehand. At night, as huge crowds wended their way to the three principal railway termini, there was unmistakable evidence of Burnley's followers, who were a sober, orderly, yet joyous lot. In several instances, members of both sexes indulged in dances to the music supplied by the piano organs, amid the interested gaze of the Londoners.

Vendors of toys etc. which could be construed into mementoes of the Cup Final did a roaring trade, with such things as miniature cups, squeaking dolls, chanters which remind me of the bagpipe, paper trumpets of various colours, rattles and paper confections for headgear. Burnley colours were predominant. The vast crowd cheered as they wended their way to the stations, and altogether made a jovial set, the gentler sex forming by no means an insignificant number. There was no horseplay, however, the crowd was a very orderly one, if boisterously buoyant. Those who stayed the weekend were chiefly to be found on Sunday at Kew, Windsor and Hampton Court, or at Hendon, where looping the loop was in progress. Hampton Court grounds were simply beautiful.

Capturing the Cup by Sportsman

My first word, so to speak, must be one of congratulations to Burnley and the players at the deservedly happy position in which they find themselves. They visited the Palace as finalists, and upset the one-time tradition that newcomers are not successful at the first time of asking; but then that was sure to happen, because Liverpool were there also for the first time. However, Boyle's men were the successful side, and, in my opinion, just deserved this victory. But it was a near thing except the all-important factor, the goal which was scored by Freeman fourteen minutes after the resumption. The game will be not only a memorable one from a Burnley football point of view, but also from a historical standpoint, for it was the first time that the reigning monarch has graced the proceedings and presented the Cup and medals. Under the circumstances, His Majesty's gracious act, seeing that he is the Duke of Lancaster, was peculiarly appropriate, for though the meeting of two Lancashire teams was not unique in the history of the competition, it is of rare occurrence. And it served to show the loyalty of the followers of football to the throne, and it is questionable whether any act of His Majesty has aroused such enthusiasm as prevailed. Though the game, on the whole, was not up to Burnley's best standard, for which a number of extenuating circumstances can be forwarded, and will be dealt with later, the sight at the Palace was worth all the cost and trouble of making the journey.

The outstanding features of the occasion, except Freeman's goal, of course, for I am writing of football, to my mind were the fine evolutions by the three bands – the Irish Guards, the Liverpool Regiment, and the Drum and Fife band of the same, and the singing of the National Anthem to the accompaniment of the combined bands, the strains of which were nearly drowned so loud was the volume of the sound emitted from the throats of 80,000 loyal subjects, which could not fail to make an impression on the King, and compensate him for any trouble he had been put to in arriving on the scene to honour the occasion. It was a spontaneous outburst of loyalty, and the sight of the many thousands of uncovered heads was a most impressive one and will long be remembered, while the National Anthem was never more heartily sung by an assemblage of Britishers, for there were other people there besides Lancashire folk.

If the game was not the best on record – although Londoners

freely expressed the opinion it was quite as good as any Final for years – and did not produce the greatest sum of money on record, it was nevertheless a unique occasion, and will probably be known as the 'Monarch's Match'. Burnley have made history many times, but on Saturday they put the coping stone on the magnificent name they have built for themselves in the football world. It was indeed a great occasion and thrilled more thousands than were present, for the news of the result was awaited in all corners of the globe.

There were about 80,000 people on the ground, which presented a fine spectacle, but I don't think the ground is the best in the country on which to play a Final, except, perhaps, for its holding capacity. The going, at any rate at this time of year, was anything but conducive to the best football, especially under such meteorological conditions as prevailed on Saturday, for the weather was summer-like and the surroundings of the Palace were in their richest garb. I have been in the country around many scores of times, though never so early in the year, except when Burnley played Crystal Palace and decoyed them to Turf Moor in order to annihilate them, but I never saw the foliage of the forest trees and the blossom of the fruit trees to such perfection as on Saturday. The weather was summer-like and quite unsuitable for such a struggle as that in which Burnley and Liverpool were engaged. And the ground was too hard, which combined with the wind and the lively ball to spoil the game from a football point of view.

There was an absentee on each side, Dawson from Burnley and Lowe from Liverpool, and on that score perhaps Liverpool were the harder hit. Dawson, to his credit, be it said, did not think he would be able to do himself full justice, and thus Sewell got his opportunity to distinguish himself, and did much towards achieving the objective of the side, the growing ambition being to bring the Cup to Burnley and make themselves possessors of the Cup medal. The teams, who wore their regular colours, lined up as follows:

Burnley: Sewell, Bamford, Taylor, Halley, Boyle, Watson, Nesbitt, Lindley, Freeman, Hodgson and Mosscrop.

Liverpool: Campbell, Longworth, Purcell, Fairfoul, McKinley, Ferguson, Sheldon, Metcalfe, Miller, Lacey and Nicholl.

Referee: Mr H S Bamlett (Gateshead); Linesmen: Messrs Talks (Lincoln) and Rogers (London).

Boyle won the toss and availed himself of the wind, and it is no exaggeration to say that the Turf Moor men had the better of the opening phases, they showed the nearer approach to good football, for, generally speaking, the play lacked the fire one would expect to see in a game of such vital importance, and the prevailing feeling was that the players at the start were troubled with nerves, and one can quite forgive them under the circumstances. But though Burnley showed the neater football, the Liverpool men were quite as dangerous. Inside ten minutes Taylor slipped on the treacherous, slippy turf and the Burnley goal was endangered as a consequence, and at the end of ten minutes he got in the way of a fast shot from Nicholl, which struck the Burnley back in the face. It appeared to stun Taylor, but the probability is, it saved the Burnley goal, though of course Sewell may have saved the shot. The ex-Gainsborough man was eagerness itself, and once ran out as the Liverpool centre came with the ball. If he had stayed at home he might have been beaten, but in all probability he disconcerted the oncoming forward, who shot just outside the post.

While Sewell was tested a few times, Campbell had the greater share of the goalkeeping, and one of his best efforts was in saving from Lindley at the expense of a corner. Burnley did the greater part of the pressing, but the best chance fell to Metcalf, but the defence stood the strain of a serious assault at that period. Every now and again the Burnley wing men got going. Mosscrop centring fairly well on occasions, but the ball was much too lively for the Burnley forwards to control with their usual degree of accuracy, with the result that on quite a number of times the ball went into touch. Offside also spoiled play at times. The result was that the exhibition was comparatively poor during the initial stage, but, even allowing for the heat, play did not descend to the level of the semi-final at Old Trafford. On the whole, the play of the first stage was even, and at the interval there was a blank sheet.

Freeman's Fine Finish: For the first ten minutes of the game, the play was such as to cause the feeling that extra-time would be required, but after a few minutes the game underwent a great change and the struggle was waged at a quicker pace, with the result that there were far more incidents which bordered on the thrilling than had characterised the opening portion of the game. As regards custodianship, Sewell was the first to be troubled, though the first corner, wrested by Lindley, fell to Burnley. Sewell cleared on the 'instalment' system two or three times, and the Burnley backs were found employment. But at the end of just inside fourteen minutes there was no doubt in the minds of Burnleyites as to the outcome of the fray, though in fairness it should be said that Liverpool played up well after the fatal blow, as the sequel showed it to be, inflicted by Freeman.

From a throw-in on the right, Nesbitt sent a cross to Hodgson, who cleverly headed the ball to Freeman who, in a twinkling first-time shot, without any pulse-beating preliminaries, shot the ball into the far corner of the net. Campbell had not the ghost of a chance. For a spell, nobody knew exactly what had happened, but there were a few Burnleyites behind the goal, and they first gave the welcome news to the onlookers at a distance, for they, like the Liverpool defenders, were completely bewildered by the rapidity with which the feat was performed. It was a fine goal and no doubt, and merited the enthusiastic shouts from the Turfites assembled and the admiration of others. For a time Burnley were, in familiar language, all over their opponents, and with a little steadiness would have scored at least on two occasions. At the same time, as the game progressed, Burnley did not get it all their own way. Two splendid chances of scoring were missed. From Mosscrop's fine centre from the line, Lindley was given the best chance of the match, but his final shot struck the corner of the post and crossbar, while on the other occasion Mosscrop got down on his own and when at close range shot over.

Towards the end, Liverpool caused great anxiety, for three or four long shots were directed at the Burnley goal, which Sewell saved in fine style. One was a long dropping shot from about halfway, which he secured after the fashion of an outfielder at cricket after watching the flight of the ball and patiently waiting for it. Another he saved on his knees, and a third he saved just under the crossbar, effecting a clearance from the rebound.

Burnley men had been in the wars. First Taylor was hurt, and then Boyle came out of a collision with Fairfoul badly damaged and fell, evidently suffering great agony, and was carried to the side of the field for attention. After a few minutes the skipper was able to resume. Then Hodgson received an accidental kick in the face, and received attention, resuming with a plaster on his face. These mishaps caused anxiety among the Burnley section, but happily the players were able to finish the game, and the defence being sound, Burnley won a memorable victory by 1 – 0.

Though Burnley, at any rate, did not reproduce their Bolton and Sunderland form. They did not descend to the Old Trafford display, but there were signs of similarity, if not to the same extent, for offside and out into touch, which often spoiled play – too frequently to make for the success of the game as an exhibition. While there was unmistakable evidence of spoiling play, it was never so marked as in the first encounter in the semi-final. For the going out on the touchline, the hardness of the ground, the lively ball and the wind had a good deal to do, for many times when the players were indulging in play which nearly, if not quite, approached their regular standard of excellence, the pace of the ball beat the man to whom it was passed. Then the ground was slippery, and in consequence the players had not the same confidence on the sward that they would have had if the ground had been well-degged by Jupiter Pluvius.

Two or three days rain would in my opinion have made the game nearly, if not quite, equal to the highest standards of a Final. Therefore I hold the conditions to blame for the play not reaching the standard of excellence one would have desired to see, and if the display was not the best on record for a Palace event, it was certainly not the worst by far, for there was an absence of events which marked the Final which produced the record attendance, and there was not a single incident to mar the sportsmanlike incidents of the game; in short, though there were regrettable incidents in the shape of injuries, especially to Burnley players, who, I am happy to say completely recovered, there were no incidents to mar the game which could by a wide stretch of imagination be described as tending to lower the tone of the game, which was fought out in purely clean and sportsmanlike fashion.

That Burnley deserved to win I have no doubt, and they would have been unlucky to have had to play extra-time. All the players were more or less affected by nerves, and under the tension and all the difficulties inseparable from a ground and the meteorological state of affairs, which did not conduce to the best of football, the game must be described as a good one, for, handicapped as the players were by the heat of the day and the ground and the ball conditions, it was almost impossible for them to reproduce the standard of football of which they are capable. Still, accustomed as we are to see football of the highest class – I am now only repeating the opinions expressed by leading expert critics of the game – the display was a rather disappointing description to many Burnley people, who had become so accustomed to Burnley's play that it rarely sent the Turfite followers into the same ecstasies of delight that was expressed when the critics have come to Turf Moor and marvelled at the excellence of the fare served up.

Dawson acted the part of the sportsman when he told the officials he was not fit, and if anything, he stands higher in the estimation of the Burnley followers than he ever did. Sewell did all that was expected of him, though he did nothing that approached the brilliance which marked his custodianship of the semi-final at Everton, and thoroughly deserved to share in the honours of the fray. While all the players did yeoman service, I hold Sewell and Freeman most in esteem for the satisfactory termination of the historic Final. The backs, while doing well, did not shine as resplendently as they have been known to do, but Taylor was handicapped by his early injury, and Bamford in the second stage especially, played a capital game. The intermediate line, while not touching their best form, all did well, and none better than Boyle, whose injury in the critical phases of the game caused a feeling akin to dismay. The forwards played an in-and-out sort of game at times up to their best standard, and at others they were the reverse, for while in their happiest moments they worked splendidly to the vicinity of the goal, they finished badly, and at least two golden opportunities slipped by which in a League game would, in all probability, have been snapped up. But there is no limit to praise for the manner in which the all-important goal was got, and in this Freeman was the hero, and while he has scored many brilliant goals for the club, he has never got one either so priceless from a monetary and an honour point of view as that which brought the Cup to Burnley without, at any rate, a replay.

Liverpool also failed at two almost equally good openings, but the Merseyside men one and all are to be commended for their sportsmanlike and spirited bid to obtain the equaliser, and which but for the safety of Sewell they might have obtained. They played up well and deserved all the commendations which have been lavished upon them. Campbell had rather more work than Sewell and the backs and half-backs did their duty well, and if the forwards did not approach the incisiveness of the Burnley quintet, who frequently worked to close quarters in their most approved fashion, to fail lamentably, they put in all they knew and shot whenever they got the opportunity, the majority of the attempts on goal being from long range. Some of these with a less capable custodian than Sewell, whom one of the London critics described as approaching international ability, while another declared he will go further, might easily have found the net to the discomfiture of the Burnley people, the vast majority of whom were confident of the ability of the team to pull through.

**

The Gentle Art of Football
Dawson's Great Sacrifice by Brunbank

'And it came to pass' that we went to Crystal Palace. There is something about that biblical way of introduction which is particularly applicable – and not irreverent – to the fatalism with which we have regarded cup-ties this season. For six seasons in general, and two in particular, we have been gradually working up to this consummation. It seemed as if it had to be this time. From the very beginning of the Cup rounds, there had been a wonderful confidence and complacency among Burnley's supporters. The Cup had to be ours. When necessary, our team, as witness the Derby, Bolton and Sunderland ties, played the game of their lives; at other times, our opponents played worse than the worst. I believe that in writing of the Sheffield United semi-final I used the good old Lancashire phrase 'nobbut just' when we got through. It was 'nobbut just' again on Saturday – but it was good enough, and we have the Cup at last. If anybody now wants to know where Burnley is, he need not consult a map or gazetteer. Burnley is where the English Cup is.

The 'After You' Game: I went 'up' to London. I was determined like others, to see Burnley through with it one way or the other. But after it all, I must confess that I couldn't fag with another Cup Final unless Burnley were in it again. I shall never forget, when coming away from the Everton ground when Burnley – or Boyle – won the semi-final, a man who seemed to know all about it (perhaps he was an old player), remarked that he had seen men so nervous before a Final that they were incapable of tying their boot laces. I don't suppose for a minute that our Burnley lads were as bad as that, but it must be frankly admitted that they were over-anxious. And so, more so, were Liverpool. There seemed to be a general tendency on the part of every man to let the responsibility of shooting rest with somebody else. Liverpool were worse than Burnley in that respect. And to me, it seemed as if it were this hesitation and nervousness which prevented the Merseysiders scoring in the first half. There were chances enough to both sides which, in an ordinary League game, would have been seized without any thought; but most of the men were obsessed with the occasion, and with fear of missing. Consequently they missed.

Freeman's Finish: On the Burnley side, the two most notable exceptions were Freeman and Sewell. The latter after two fumbles early on due to some misunderstanding with his backs more than anything else played that cat-like game which seemed to make him anticipate everything to a nicety. He was a tower in the defence. At the opposite end, Freeman, though he rambled a good deal, was a cool and methodical worker. The goal of his which settled the destination of the Cup was a masterpiece. So far as shooting went, up to that point nobody felt that a goal would ever be scored if the teams played all afternoon and night. But it was Freeman's unexpected that happened. He has a knack of doing just what nobody thinks possible.

Hodgson, who all through the game had trapped the ball perhaps better than any man on the field, leaped high in the air and headed the ball over the half-back. Before anybody realised what had happened, Freeman darted in like a flash of lightening, and taking the ball before it touched the ground hooked it with his instep into the left-hand corner of the net, halfway up the net upright, with Campbell and his two backs looking ruefully on. Bert Freeman is notably an opportunist. Never did he get a more unexpected yet bonnier goal. There was no doubt about his intention or accuracy. Yet it was all so sudden it was hard to realise it had happened at all. It was some seconds before the Burnley spectators could even yell their delight, and when they did their shouts were lost in the huge enclosure crowded with more or less neutral spectators. I never would have believed that a goal like that could have passed with such little demonstration.

Splendid Spectacle: It was a Royal Final too. For the first time in the history of the game the reigning Monarch was an attender and presented the Cup and medals. Boyle must have been a proud man on Saturday. Before the match he was called hurriedly back from the touchline to shake hands with King George. But as it was already time to kick off, and the Burnley skipper was so anxious to get to business, he forgot that little bit of etiquette that requires that a subject should back away from the presence of Royalty. However, the King knows that a man of heart and soul in his work knows no laws but those of getting to the scene of action. It was indeed a memorable sight. Probably it was the prettiest Final from a spectator point of view on record. It was the King's first patronage of the FA Cup Final and in his honour there was a military display which, in interest, exceeded the quality of football served up.

'What a dish to set before a King,' is one London scribe's trenchant description of the play. The King's Liverpool Regiment were there, and the Band of the Irish Guards. One was a drum and fife band, and the other a full regiment. Both gave selections while the crowd was assembling, and just before the King arrived they stood at attention before the Royal dais. Immediately the King came, with Lord Derby and Lord Kinnaird, the band played the National Anthem, and there was a demonstration of affectionate loyalty which must have touched the

King's heart. Thousands who could not see him joined in the chorus and swelled the cheering, and this was renewed when the men of both teams lined up to salute and cheer him on their own. But, the vast concourse of people found little to enthuse over in the first half, and was therefore all the more ready to admire and appreciate the pretty manoeuvring of the two regimental bands during the interval. One played the drum and fifes and bugles, and the other marched to the strains of 'Here's to the maiden of bashful fifteen.' They marched, turned and intertwined in exceedingly pretty fashion, and it was a treat to watch the drum-major.

Lack of Vivacity: The game itself fell far short of ordinary league football. In the presence of the King every man played an exceptionally keen game – and probably this over anxiety to avoid any transgression which would be a blot on the game and the over-scrupulousness shore the game of that vigour and excitement which would otherwise have been the case. There were other factors of course, not the least being that the ground was hard as concrete. It was just as if the men were on a foreign ground. They slid about and fell because there was no foothold, and as everybody knows, this is not the sort of ground which Burnley likes. The turf was baked and cracked, and consequently the ball bounced high and at unaccountable angles. Therefore, considering all the circumstances, the game cannot be said to be as poor as some of the London journalists would make out. The fact is that no London interest being at stake, these gentlemen have gone in for satire. The same game between the Villa and say, Tottenham, would have been described as good. I cannot help feeling that they never got over the fact that Liverpool and Burnley prevented a Villa and Sunderland Final again, and that they were obsessed by the impression that neither team had any business at Crystal Palace.

See-Saw: Of course, the forward play on both sides left much to be desired, but the issue was always in doubt. Lindley might have scored in the first minute if he had run in closer before shooting. Mosscrop kept Campbell on the *que vive* with some beautiful dropping crosses on the run. Taylor was laid out with a terrific smack on the head; and Sewell stopped a drive from Lacey when all the Liverpudlians behind the goal

The Best of Burnley

fondly imagined it was in the net. This was all in the first half, a poor one generally, but the second portion of the game became sometimes exciting. Burnley began to control the ball better with the sun at their backs, and when Freeman put the climax onto a determined raid, it looked odds on one or two more goals following. Indeed, Hodgson had the hardest lines of the match, after a superb effort, for he hit the upright, whilst Lindley, one of three ready to take Mosscrop's pretty centre, missed an open goal. During the last ten minutes, Liverpool, whose hash ought to have been settled long ago, tried determinedly to equalise. They didn't show much combination, but there was the one main objective to lunge the ball in the goalmouth and bundle it through. It might have happened too, for Boyle was laid out and rolled about in agony. He was carried to the side but refused to go off – I believe he would have to be killed first – and he was back to block Liverpool at all costs, well supported by Bamford's earnestness and Sewell's agility and Taylor's resourcefulness. If anybody expects perfect football at a Final, they had better stay at home; but to describe the game as being devoid of anxiety is to be unfair. The fact is, the rival patrons were so lost in the huge park-like enclosure that they never had a chance of concentrating their cheers and cries. The same game at Burnley, or Bolton, glad we haven't had to be there today, would have been productive of any amount of excitement. It felt like being the only one to laugh in a theatre filled with a chilly audience.

Dawson's Self-Sacrifice: Poor Jerry. Brave Jerry. It is often a nobler act to stay and watch a fight than to be in it, and in deliberately sacrificing his own ambitions for the good of the team Dawson not only showed the true mettle of the sportsman, but he fulfilled the noblest of all obligations – to subserve self to the general interest. He was not fully recovered from the nasty knock to his ribs the previous Sunday. As he himself said, he would be safe at high shots, but might be a little unsafe at low ones. More than that; another knock on the injured spot might have incapacitated him. Out of regard for his past glorious service to the club Dawson was given his choice. He commendably decided to forego his chance of a Cup medal. Such sacrifice is not without precedence of course, but it is nonetheless hard lines. But Jerry's name will go down in Burnley's history as that of a man who has performed great feats for his club and team, and who gave the noblest exhibition of loyalty in his career on Saturday. 'Greater love hath no man' than to give up a lifetime's ambition for the sake of his fellows and Dawson will have all the sympathy a sporting public can give him as well as all their admiration; poor Jerry, yet noble Jerry.

***

Phil Whalley continues:

April 1914 and there was jubilation in Burnley. After the Final, 40,000 people crowded into Turf Moor for the final league game to see the Cup being paraded and to cheer the players. Shortly afterwards they left for the first ever continental tour by a Burnley team. They played against Berlin Victoria, Ferencvaros and Rapid Vienna.

In June, however, the assassination of Archduke Ferdinand of Austria would result in catastrophic and lasting effects. Events moved swiftly in Europe as one by one the nations took sides and declared war on each other. Eventually Great Britain declared war on Germany and the scene was set for four years of the most horrendous fighting and the most horrific casualties as the cream of Europe's manhood was slaughtered. By the end of this ghastly war in 1918, Burnley's Cup Final win seemed not four but a hundred years earlier.

Season 1914/15 went ahead as normal but after that the Football League competition was suspended and organised regionally. Not until season 1919/20 did it resume properly again. By then Teddy Hodgson of the Cup Final team had died at the age of 33 of kidney trouble.

The only first team player to be killed in action, although he did not play in the Cup Final, was William Pickering aged 23 in Mesopotamia. He appeared in 14 League and Cup games scoring five goals. He played mainly in the reserves being a regular scorer.

John Haworth achieved greatness with Burnley. In the last full season before the War broke out, Burnley were fourth just three points away from the title. In 1919/20 after the war they were runners-up to West Brom. The triumph of the 1920/21 season is well documented. In the following season they were third.

John Haworth's premature death on December 4th, 1924 was

tragic. He was only 48 years old. Correspondence from his son, also called John, revealed the details of his untimely passing:

'We all know that Burnley was one of the founder members of the Football League. Of the very early history of the club I know little, but from hearsay I learned that Mr Whittaker who was manager around the 1910 era was killed in a fall from a train, and following this sad affair my father, John (Jack) Haworth, was appointed as secretary/manager. This was about the time I was born in Mizpah Street, Burnley, in January 1911. I naturally do not remember those early years especially the 1913/14 season when Burnley won the FA (then known as the English) Cup. I do know however that the final took place at Crystal Palace and Burnley beat Liverpool 1 – 0. This was the first time that the reigning monarch, King George V, presented the Cup and medals.

'In the early 20s I was sufficiently old enough to take an interest in the doings of the team, and together with a close friend, Alfred Boland, attended most of the home matches (free gratis and for nothing, as the saying goes). We used to sit in the Press Box. Older Burnley supporters will remember the excitement when the team won the League Division One Championship, and created the then record of 30 games without defeat. This was in the days of the 2 – 3 – 5 combination. Why ever did they change it?

'Then came the month of December 1924, a sad day for Burnley FC and for my invalid mother and myself. My dad had suffered from asthma for some years, and took a trip to Preston to secure the services of a young up and coming player, Roberts. As a boy of 13, I remember he made a mad dash to Preston to secure the necessary signatures. So urgent was the matter he took an open taxi to Preston in the pouring rain and as a result contracted a chill, followed by pneumonia, and he died on December 4th 1924 at 9.40 pm. His funeral was the following Tuesday and the route from Burnley to Accrington Cemetery was lined with mourners. The flowers took the hearse and an extra open carriage.'

How sad it is that the name John Haworth is so rarely mentioned today. Distant history is quickly forgotten. We remember the 'now' and the immediate past. Even for the older generations of Burnley supporters, knowledge of pre-1940 events is negligible. But John Haworth was a pioneer and there is no doubt he laid the foundations of Clarets history. The Cup win of 1914, the achievements of 1920/21 are still the yardsticks by which we judge and compare. The names, Halley, Boyle and Watson, Bob Kelly, Jerry Dawson and perhaps Bert Freeman are still well known even after all these years. Haworth's name really should be up there with those of Cliff Britton, Alan Brown, Harry Potts, Chairman Bob Lord, and Sean Dyche.

2

1932 Tommy Boyle is Taken Away

One of the best sports novels I have read is This Sporting Life *by David Storey. For sure it's no light-hearted bedroom romp. It is rugby based not football, all grit and northern darkness and gloom. You can taste the fog and smell the mud. Storey makes it work because the actual clubs are left to your imagination. They're never named. It's all about people, with such power in the writing. It's a stark and unhappy book with the weariness of the central character and the brutality of the game he plays, brought home time and again.*

So, with drama in mind I jotted down a few of the characters you could have in a football novel. What about one each of the following: a superb footballer, a gifted athlete, a strong leader of men, a tough Yorkshire miner, a war hero, a publican, a bereaved father, a deserted husband, a drunkard, a brawler, a vagrant, and finally a lunatic. If you put all these characters into the mix, set the story in a northern mill town in the depressed 20s and 30s, using the local football club, unemployment and poverty as the background then surely you'd have the basis of a convincing and highly saleable piece of fiction?

Next, think up a few scenes that are real tear jerkers: a doting father seeing his beloved daughter pass away, a husband returning home one day to find his wife has left him, a once famous hero pawning all his medals and trophies for just 50 quid. And then the final pièce de résistance: a shuffling, bewildered lunatic being undressed in the hospital by the orderlies when out of his grubby raincoat falls a torn and tattered envelope and inside it is a collection of faded cuttings, torn clippings and dog-eared photographs; poignant reminders and all that he had left of his once glittering career and glorious fame.

But then failing all that you could just write the story of Tommy Boyle and astonishingly you have all the above in one ultimately sad character who spends the last eight years of his life locked away in Whittingham Hospital, a place where society in those bygone days put not just those who really were insane but simply anyone who was deemed not capable of looking after themselves, or who were simply unwanted. There was no Care in the Community when Tommy Boyle needed it. It is arguable whether or not he really was insane or simply had what today would be deemed as treatable mental health problems. Asylums years ago were used to lock away those who were simply a nuisance to society, and/or, to their families.

Mike Smith begins the story with a stark and graphic chapter, written almost as a novel, except that it is real. It takes you straight into the degradation and fall from grace. It draws you into the story, sucks you in and has you glued to the pages. Succeeding pages take you through his youth, his life down the mines, then Barnsley FC and being a Cup Finalist. Then comes the story of the move to Burnley, the creation of a truly great team, a Cup winner's medal, the war years and military service; then the Championship side of 1920/21, a spell as a publican, an unsuccessful time at Wrexham, marriage, the death of his young daughter, coaching in Germany, and his wife's desertion. And following all that comes the sad, sad decline of a once great footballer; a true hero who becomes jobless, without any purpose, all self-esteem gone and the descent into drunken disorderliness and violence in and around Burnley. Eventually comes the final placement at Whittingham when doctors deemed him unfit to live in the world outside. It was an age of lock 'em away and throw away the key and, in truth, the word harrowing would not go amiss. How mentally unwell he really was will not come out until 2032 when the hospital records will become available. Mike will be 77 then but I fancy he will be waiting at the office door to find out more and write one more chapter of the story. His most difficult task was to find out what happened to his wife Annie after she left Tommy.

Students of Burnley FC history might say that the real history and tradition of the club began with this great, great captain and leader Tommy Boyle, along with Manager John Haworth. Boyle arrived in

The Best of Burnley

1911. Ten years later there had been a war, but also a promotion, a Cup Final triumph and a Division One title. John Haworth (whose name should be up there with Cliff Britton, Alan Brown and Harry Potts) assembled the players; skipper Tommy Boyle galvanised them, inspired them and made them tick. The names of Halley, Boyle and Watson were as revered then as the names of Adamson and McIlroy are now. Jerry Dawson was the iconic goalkeeper, Bob Kelly the magical, twinkle-toed ball artist who some said was even better than Jimmy Mac. And there was wee Billy Nesbitt who was so deaf he couldn't hear the whistle. Just how do you play football if you are deaf? Then there was Bert Freeman who scored the winning goal in the Cup Final.

In Mike Smith's book we hear their names time and again as they become real people, not just names from the distant past. We also see just what a brutal and tough game it was then. Here's something to try. Go out into the garden and shoulder-charge the biggest, thickest tree you can find; or if you have no trees your biggest, thickest neighbour. After that get your wife, or the same neighbour, to kick you on the shins a dozen times as hard as they can, wearing a pair of clogs or hob-nailed boots, and then endlessly hit you on the back of the head. Next, go and head-bang the garage door or the tree you shoulder-charged. And, do all these things whilst kicking a ball that is so heavy it feels like concrete; and eventually when you feel dizzy and ill, pour ice-cold water over yourself with a giant sponge. That, I suspect, was what football was like in Tommy Boyle's day, in all weathers and on mudbath pitches. In one game he played, he missed a simple heading chance because there was so much blood pouring down his face from a head wound that he couldn't see a thing. These players were as hard as nails and played on fearlessly in the most appalling conditions and carrying injuries on a regular basis. Vendettas were on-going. The word gentlemanly was virtually unknown.

These guys really were heroes and they brought pride and light into the lives of people who faced poverty, hunger, unemployment and mill closures. Bob Lord wrote about how he felt when, as a little boy, he saw Tommy Boyle lift up the Cup so that Burnley folk could see it and share in the achievement. Think how we felt when Caldwell and his team returned from Wembley in 2009 and toured the town. Multiply that by ten and that's what it was like winning the Cup in 1914.

All Tommy Boyle wanted to do was play football. When his skill declined he had little else to turn to. He hung on for as long as he could and, like an ageing fighter, wanted just one more fight. When Manager Haworth died it was thought by some that Boyle would replace him but it didn't happen. He had money at the end of his career but it was all frittered away on betting and drinking. He won good money in Bowls tournaments in Blackpool but that didn't last long. He worked as a labourer when he could but the jobs became fewer. The man who had shaken hands with the King was reduced to sleeping rough, cadging a roof for the night, or living in a crowded hostel. His public behaviour became more and more unacceptable.

He had suffered the hammer blows of shell-shock and serious injury in the war, the emotional trauma of losing his only daughter and the after effects of heading a heavy, sodden ball in game after game. All of these must have contributed to his mental depression and deterioration; and to add to all of that, he was alone.

In terms of Burnley history, this book sits nicely alongside The Jimmy Hogan Story in terms of painting a picture of a different football and social world. With its detail and lengthy stories of the FA Cup success and 1920/21 title win, along with the 30-game unbeaten run in that season, it fleshes out the Clarets Chronicles. But above all, it brings into the spotlight one man who was an absolute hero and one of the foundation stones of the club's history. Alas when Boyle died in Whittingham on 2 January 1940 he was a forgotten man. Now, he can be properly remembered.

***

Mike Smith was born and brought up in Burnley and as a five-year old saw the 1959/60 Burnley team touring the town after winning the Championship. He has been a Burnley supporter ever since and still lives in the area. He now works at the University of Manchester and teaches for the Open University. Broken Hero, *the harrowing story of*

Tommy Boyle, is his first published work and since then he has written The Road to Glory, *the story of the 1914 Burnley FA Cup win.*

***

Tommy Boyle: Broken Hero by Mike Smith (Grosvenor House Publishing) From Chapter 1: Primrose Bank Infirmary

The black Humber Pullman with its four occupants slowed to a halt on the gravel driveway outside the rear entrance of the Infirmary. The driver left the engine running and the wipers going as the heavy rain continued to pour down from black-grey skies. It was blowing a gale outside where, in the rain, stood two men wearing white hospital-issue jackets with matching trousers. Both held on to an umbrella in an attempt to keep dry. They were waiting for him.

In the back of the Humber sat a man flanked by two police officers. 'Where's the rest of the welcoming committee? Where's the papers and the bloody mayor?' asked the man. The two officers sitting on either side of him glanced at each other but made no reply. There would be no welcoming committee today, no press and no mayoral welcome. No fuss, that's what the chief had instructed.

The rear doors of the Humber opened and the two officers and their prisoner, handcuffed to one of them, stepped out. At six foot, the two officers towered over the man in their custody by a good six inches. The prisoner looked pale and undernourished. He wore a long, shabby gabardine overcoat with no belt, a shirt buttoned at the neck with no tie and trousers that had not seen creases for some months. Unshaven and reeking of last night's booze, he sported a week-old black eye and looked like he'd slept in his clothes for the last month.

Through bloodshot eyes the man looked upwards through the rain and it suddenly clicked where he was.

'Bloody hell, back 'ere,' he grinned to himself.

He knew where this place was; he'd been here before lots of times. They'd fix him up good-style so he could play again, no problem. But right now he could do with something to cure the pounding in his head that felt like it was about to split open.

The two officers and their prisoner went inside and were followed by the two white coats. One of them closed and locked the heavy outer door, then locked the inner iron gate behind it with a loud, *clang.* The door secured, the five men shook off the rain and climbed the stone staircase to the first floor, their footsteps echoing in the damp hallway. The white coats followed the three visitors up the stairs and whispered to each other. They couldn't believe who it was.

Tommy Boyle arrived on the male mental wing of Primrose Bank Infirmary in Burnley on Wednesday 24 February 1932 for what was officially deemed *'a period of observation.'* It was said he had been 'unwell' for a number of weeks and had arrived at the Infirmary in a police car following a night in Burnley police station cells. No charges had been made about the incident that took place on the Tuesday evening and no record was kept of it. Tommy Boyle was a well-known character in the town and had been for well over twenty years. He knew the police and the Chief Inspector well enough from his football days and his previous charity work in the town. He knew them for another reason, the charges that they had made against him nine years before. He'd not forgotten that.

In recent weeks he'd been in trouble again. He had allegedly been barred entry from a number of town centre pubs for causing trouble, so the previous evening when the landlord of one pub refused him a drink, he had gone berserk and swiped all the glasses off the bar. That was one story. The police were called and they carted him off to the station. It wasn't the first time and when the Chief Inspector found out, it was the last straw.

On the day of his admittance to Primrose Bank, Tommy Boyle was forty six years old. The booze had added another ten years to his appearance. Only a decade before, he'd had it all: worshipped by his adoring fans, a local celebrity with a glittering career behind him and idolised in the press; Tommy Boyle, leader of the legendary 'Boyle's Brigade', England international, FA Cup winner and league champion. He'd even met the King. With money in his pocket, his own pub in the centre of the town, he was the main man, Mr Burnley and drinks all round. Ten years down the road, he was Tommy Boyle of no fixed abode, on the dole and sleeping rough in the local doss-house. The good times were long gone; in fact everything had gone: the pub, the house, the money and Annie *(his wife)* had left him. If the last eighteen months had seen a decline in Tommy's personal and financial affairs, more worrying was his disturbed mental state and his temper, which after the previous night's performance in the pub, had been brought to the full attention of the Burnley authorities.

Primrose Bank Infirmary was located on a ten-acre site on the outskirts of town. Opened in 1876 as the Burnley Union Workhouse it had been converted into an infirmary twenty years later. As a workhouse it had employed a strict regime in which inmates faced harsh working conditions in repayment for food and lodgings. Even after its conversion, the place still wasn't exactly The Savoy. The infirmary was large enough to accommodate male and female patients, the chronic sick and elderly patients and sick children. It had two secure mental wings that could accommodate up to seventy four male and the same number of female patients. The mental wings were located on the ground floor, which also contained the guardians' boardroom, master's offices and a store room for the inmates' clothes. The master's and matron's bedrooms were located on the first floor at the rear along with the resident medical officer's office. Male patients were accommodated in the west wing and females in the east. To enable segregation of the sexes, the corridors were barred with locked iron gates. The facilities for mental patients at Primrose Bank supported mainly short-stay patients until more permanent accommodation could be found.

The procedure of having someone committed under the 1930 Mental Health Act was a quite straightforward one. A family member – a father, mother, husband or wife – could inform the authorities that their relative had, in their opinion, gone insane. On their say-so, committal forms would be completed and signed, sanctioning that the person be taken into care initially for a period of observation. The police would usually be called, as Peter Barham describes in this example from *Lunatics of the Great War:*

'John H. remembers the day when his father was taken away.

He watched the Black Maria arrive with two policemen to take his father away, he recalls. His mother signed the form afraid he might do something violent. John recalls his father chopping up all the furniture into little pieces and putting them on the fire until there was nothing left.'

Two independent doctors were required to assess the patient and provide separate opinions. If they agreed then a simple form was completed and the person in question would then be taken in by the Infirmary staff.

The five men reached the first floor landing. 'You'll be OK in here Tommy,' said the officer who was handcuffed to him, 'they'll feed you up and look after you.' Tommy stared at him, thinking, *after all I've done for you 'an all*. He made no reply to the officer who he knew and looked down at the stone floor. *There were people waiting in there, in that room, clever people who would fix things so I can go out and play again.*

In his oak-panelled office on the first-floor landing, William Alexander Mair, the resident medical officer at the Infirmary, sat at his desk preparing the admission paperwork. Outside in the small waiting room were Primrose Bank's master, Mr Ray; the matron, Miss Bennett; superintendent of the male mental ward, Robert Kirby; and chairman of the Infirmary Committee Board of Guardians, Hezekiah Proctor JP. Miss Bennett knocked and notified Mair that the patient had arrived and the group went through to Mair's office. One of the officers handed over a folder to Mair who took it and checked its contents. The other officer released Tommy's handcuffs and Mair thanked them for their service and they were both dismissed. Tommy sat down in a chair in the middle of the floor facing the window rubbing life back into his hand. The rain continued to bucket down outside. In front of Tommy was a long bench table and behind it five chairs. In the corner of the room the warmth from a coal-fire was welcoming. *Just like home* Tommy thought as he rubbed his hands in the warm glow of the fire.

Across the table from him, the welcoming committee sat down and prepared themselves; Proctor, Kirby, Mair, Ray and Bennett. Laid out in front of them was an array of files, books, forms and folders, notes and ink pens. Behind Tommy, the two white-coats sat quietly on each side of Mair's door. Tommy maintained a fixed gaze at the pattern on Mair's carpet. He coughed, his chest playing up again and holding his forehead asked for something to fix his splitting headache. Mair indicated to one of the white-coats to bring some aspirin and a glass of water, which Tommy thanked them for.

The formal admission procedure began with a welcome from Bill Mair followed by the staff introducing themselves and their roles. Through the blurred fuzz of the headache, Tommy was told why he was here and the reasons behind his admission. *They all look so bloody miserable, not even a smile for the cat,* he thought. He was to stay in Primrose Bank, Mair explained, for a period of up to 14 days while they assessed his health and his state of mind. Under the Mental Health Act, 14 days was the maximum period the hospital could detain a patient under the reception order. After that, the patient could be released back into the community or an extension order from a court was required. If the patient escaped and was not recaptured within the 14-day period, the whole admission procedure had to begin again. Mair went on to explain that a thorough medical examination would be carried out to assess Tommy's physical condition and over the following days there would be physical and mental tests, meetings with doctors and checks on his health, all to show that he was getting better and responding to treatment. Only when the medical staff agreed he was fine would he be released.

Tommy shifted in his seat. He wasn't listening though the headache was subsiding. Since his childhood he had hated small rooms, tunnels or being cooped up anywhere. He had to be outside: *Ever since that day, the day that Jimmy died.* The only thing on his mind right now was for this meeting to end and to get out of this place. He could feel the oak-panelled walls of Mair's office closing in, like the walls of the pit and the bars of the tiny cell he'd just spent the night in.

Mair went on, explaining that they wanted to look after him, sort him out and fix him up – the whole hospital line. Finally he asked Tommy if he had any questions. The five committee members looked at him and waited for a response but none was forthcoming. Tommy simply shook his head and at that, Mair stood up signalling the end of the meeting. Mair wished Tommy an enjoyable stay and confirmed that they all expected him to get well quickly.

The formalities over, Mair handed over to Robert Kirby and the two white-coats walked Tommy downstairs to the bathhouse where the Infirmary barber, Mr Fothergill, would give Tommy a shave, a haircut and a bath. Fothergill was a busy man. He knew all the male patients personally as they were not allowed to shave themselves. He certainly knew the man now sat in front of him, having seen him many times over the years, both in the newspapers and in the flesh in a claret and blue jersey at Turf Moor. Fothergill couldn't believe his eyes as he ran the cut-throat razor up and down the leather strop. Tommy was asked his collar size and other measurements and a white-coat went off to the stores to get a set of male-issue clothes while Tommy's were sent to the laundry. After a shave, Fothergill ran a hot bath that was taken with a white-coat present. There was little privacy here. Patients were not allowed to visit the bathroom unaccompanied, not for the first 48 hours.

Two months prior to Tommy's arrival at Primrose Bank, an occupancy audit of the mental wings was carried out by the Chief Medical Officer who recorded that 60 men were occupying 74 of the available beds in the male mental ward, 57 of them being long-stay patients; with 57 women in the female ward. So Tommy was not a lonely man on the ward. He was allocated a bed in the long male dormitory and then taken down to the canteen for a meal. Peter Barham describes that one of the Infirmary's first objectives was to feed the patient up: 'The inmate would be put on a high protein diet of eggs, milk pudding and beef tea and, depending on the patient, a dose of bromide or paraldehyde.' Following his meal Tommy was given a tour of the ward facilities and shown the day room. As with all patients, the days in the Infirmary were a common routine of sleeping and eating meals, with very few social activities. Essential in the daily regime were the tests to check whether patients were fit to be released and could be trusted not to harm themselves or others.

After only two days in this environment, Tommy was restless. He hated rules, routines, confinements and the bars on the windows drove him mad: *Hospital, more like a bloody prison camp.* He was unhappy and wanted out. There was nothing to do and there was nothing to interest him: no football, no racing, no papers, no beer and no women. *It was the match Saturday ... there was nothing wrong with me anyway. Two weeks in here in a bloody loony bin.* He paced the floor like a caged tiger. He stood out like a sore thumb and the other patients pointed and stared at him. He shouted and swore back at them.

First chance and I'm bloody out of here ... he planned his escape *... what am I doing here anyway with a load of bloody idiots. Bugger all wrong; and what the hell was that in the food.*

He dragged a chair over to the day room window, stepped on it and climbed on the window sill where he sat and looked out through the bars. In the distance he could see farms, hills and green fields *just like home.* He closed his eyes and his mind wandered back to the game, down the years to the start of a new season.

He breathed in the sweet smell of the football field, the scent of freshly cut grass, the dressing room odours of tobacco smoke, hot sugared tea, sweat and liniment. The anthem of boot studs stamping on the stone dressing room floor as he picked up the ball bounced it twice and shouted his war cry, 'C'maaan then,' before marching his boys out to do battle one more time; the increased roar from the crowd as they emerged from the darkness into the light; Boyle, Dawson, Taylor, Bamford, Halley, Watson, Mosscrop, Lindley, Freeman, Hodgson and Nesbitt always at the back. Seeing the faces of the pretty girls waving and blowing kisses from the enclosure and winking at the ones he fancied; the huge swaying crowd all around the arena, squeezed tightly together, cheering him and his boys on, their faces as far back as the eye could see.

Then he was back where it all began, the cold winter harshness of Platts Common, its grey, snow covered coal heaps under a heavy sky. Saturday afternoon and a sleet covered pitch at Hoyland; hitting the opposing centre-forward hard and taking the ball off him. Easy. Away and up the field with it; out to the winger. Carry on running, the cross coming in; leaping into the air and connecting with the frozen ball with his temple. BANG and watching the missile fly straight through the goalkeeper's outstretched hands. The cheers from the soaking wet spectators as the ball filled the back of the net. Wiping the blood, the mud and the slush from his forehead with the back of his hand, laughing, soaked to the skin; home afterwards and a hot bath in front of the fire. He'd loved every second of it. Then there was the time he'd played against …

He was abruptly wakened from his dream, a hand on his shoulder pulling him down from the window-sill.

'Come on Tommy, time to see the Doc,' said the white-coat.

'Piss off, I'm not goin'.'

He put his fist up and started swinging. He was being awkward again so one white-coat dragged him down from the window while the other pinned his arms by his side and fastened the waist belt round him, locking his wrists down by his sides. Then they frogmarched him downstairs.

'More bloody stupid questions? I'm saying nothing. There's bugger all wrong with me I tell thi!' he exclaimed.

The night-time was worst. *Horrible things happened to people in the dark.* In the dim light of the groaning, coughing dormitory, the haunting nightmares returned. The same terrible visions, over and over. He was miles underground in the bowels of the pit, in the dark, his lamp out. The unforgettable sound of splintering timber roof-props; the crushing, rumbling sound as the roof caved in. The smoke and the dust clearing, his best friend Jimmy Leach, a boy just like him, only his arms and head visible, reaching out, crying for him to help, the rest of his body trapped and crushed beneath huge boulders of stone.

'Help me, get me out Tommy,' the boy gasped.

He clawed at the rock with bare hands, his fingers bleeding, but with no shovel or help it was futile. He watched, helpless, for perhaps seconds as the roof crushed down harder and harder and Jimmy Leach choked to death on his own blood. He'd tried but there was nothing he could do. Nothing. He'd tried, again. He'd shouted for help. He heard them coming. But not men. They could smell the blood and fear; the army of huge pit rats coming for him and Jimmy Leach. They ran over him to get at their prey. Hungry, slithering, gnawing, he kicked at them with his feet …

Another scene: a smashed landscape that had once been a beautiful city. Ypres and its broken buildings ... trees that should have been in leaf turned to matchwood ... shells tearing across the night sky and exploding all around. Looking down and seeing his boot oozing blood through the lace holes. His pants in shreds, covered in blood, all his kit gone and the fear of gangrene setting in. They were here again, the scavenging rats, grown fat on the bodies of his dead mates, coming again, a whole army of them, coming for him ...

The final reel: he was standing in the doorway of a small bedroom lit only by candlelight. A child, his little girl, lifeless and cold ... the most beautiful and precious thing in his whole world was gone. His heart ripped out.

He was wide awake, sweating and gasping for breath. Throat dry as a bone. Screaming pains in his head again. The bars at the windows ... no way out. The horrible visions gone for now, replaced by a rage and a desperate need to get out of this place. He had tried escaping the night before but another inmate had shouted for the white-coats, so after they'd done he'd gone over and thumped the daft sod. They'd heard his screams and came running back. He'd been returned to bed, restrained, sedated with a white-coat posted at his bedside until the calming peace from the morphine eventually came.

Tommy Boyle's stay at Primrose Bank wasn't long. Five days after his arrival he was back in front of Bill Mair and the welcoming committee. There was nothing more they could do for him here. The institution wasn't equipped for violent cases though it did possess its own 'treatment' rooms that had been refitted in late 1931. Mair completed his report and wrote that Tommy had been 'striking other patients and staff.' Mair's mind was made up. It was clear to him that the patient was not fit to be released and wanted him off the books. He wasn't alone. The Chief Constable also wanted him removed, as far out of town as possible. The press had been sniffing around the past day or two and asking questions.

'We don't have the facilities you need here, Tommy; you need special care. We're transferring you to another unit,' said Mair.

Transfer ...

Along with Bill Mair and Robert Kirby, there were three new faces in the room that had not been present five days before. Patients who were to be admitted to a mental institution had to be certified as insane by two independent doctors and a Justice of the Peace. James Alfred Sampson JP was present and had already co-signed the order made out by Bill Mair that was addressed to the superintendent of the forwarding institution. Mair was putting the finishing touches to his report.

From across the room, Tommy looked on to see them in their huddle, gathered around Mair's long table. They all looked serious, asking questions, their voices low and difficult to make out. Finally, they nodded in agreement and looked up. Forms and pieces of paper were signed, contracts exchanged.

Looks like a deal ... They said he was being transferred, but to which club?

'Whittingham,' was all he heard them say.

'Who the soddin' hell are Whittingham and what bloody league do they play in?'

But they were not joking.

And so on Monday 29 February, five days after arriving at Primrose Bank Infirmary, Thomas William Boyle, 46 and of no fixed abode, Burnley Football Club's most successful captain in its history, made the final transfer of his career. He was bound for Whittingham Mental Hospital, the former Lancashire County Lunatic Asylum, near Preston, where he became patient number 24281, a number he would become for the rest of his life.

***

From Chapter 15: Whittingham

The journey to Whittingham from Burnley took just under an hour. The ambulance travelled via the quiet back roads of the Ribble Valley, avoiding the towns and arriving at Whittingham mid-afternoon. In the rear of the ambulance Tommy was accompanied by two Primrose Bank white-coats. The ambulance turned into Whittingham's main gate from which led a mile-long, tree-lined driveway. On one side through the trees stood a cricket pavilion and next to it was a football pitch. On the other, broad lawns led to other hospital buildings and wards, and in the distance a train with three carriages was pulling out of Whittingham railway station. Straight ahead, at the end of the driveway, was the main hospital building at Whittingham, St Luke's. The ambulance drew to a halt in front of the administration block. A three-storey, pillar-fronted, red-brick building with Georgian windows, the frontage of St Luke's ran for hundreds of yards to the left and right from the central admission and reception block. From above, St Luke's was shaped like a giant outspread hand, its patient wards stretching out like long fingers, two long male wards to the left and two female to the right.

On arrival Tommy and the two white-coats were brought into reception by a porter and offered a cup of tea. The patient's file, fastened with string around the middle like a legal document, was brought up to Dr Jason Gemmel's office by one of the staff. Gemmel untied it to find the medical certificate just completed by Bill Mair, which gave the account of what had gone on at Primrose Bank and any important points that had been noted by the staff there. Five days wasn't a long time to have assessed a patient fully, but that's all Gemmel had to go on. To have sent him here after only five days told Gemmel that Primrose Bank couldn't handle him and this was probably going to be a long stay patient.

(The certificate contained Mair's details and outlined his conclusions: that Boyle was delusional claiming that he owned 27 race horses and that he raced them in Germany and that one of the winner's trophies took two men to carry. He had struck other patients and staff and had hidden himself in the building. He had been restless and violent, exhibited threatening behaviour, had refused food, was oblivious to his surroundings and was always trying to escape through the windows.

From the file of documents handed to Gemmel, an old envelope fell to the floor. When he opened it he found newspaper clippings, postcards and photographs ranging from 1902 to 1928. There was the death certificate of a young child and pictures of Tommy at the peak of his fame and fitness. One of the postcards showed the King presenting the Cup to a football team. On the back were a few words Tommy had written to his sister saying that he was sorry she couldn't make it to the Final.

Gemmel's main concern was Tommy's violent behaviour but for this there were padded cells, harnesses, straitjackets, waist belts and electric shock facilities along with medicines and opiates, morphine, and bromide along with various drug mixtures. If these failed there was an operating theatre.)

The first asylum at Whittingham, designed to accommodate 1,000 patients, opened on a 60-acre site in Grimsargh near Preston in 1873. By the time Tommy arrived the patient population had grown to 3,000 and the site, now the size of a village, spread over 150 acres. The hospital buildings at Whittingham included St Luke's, the biggest block, the annexes of St Margaret's and St John's and a newly built block, Cameron House. The hospital had a staff of around 450. Its medical facilities also offered specialised treatment for infectious diseases and the hospital had also pioneered the use of electroencephalograms with mental patients.

Whittingham had its own branch-line and railway station for transporting supplies, staff and visitors to and from Preston a few miles away. There was a gas works, two churches (Anglican and Catholic), a post office, a bakery, a laundry, a butcher and farms for the patients to work on. Ken Ashton, editor of the Whittingham website 'The Asylum', says that the institution was run along military lines.

Monday to Friday, the day's routine at Whittingham would have been exactly the same. Woken between six and half-six, the patients would be dressed, washed and breakfasted. By eight they would be at work either indoors in the laundry, upholstery shop or printing shop, or outdoors working on the farms and vegetable gardens. Break times would be fixed. Lunch followed by more work and then home for supper. The patients would be washed and in bed by 9pm. At weekends there would be visiting times although patients received visitors around once a month and only then if they behaved. On Sunday mornings there would be a church service and more visiting time in the afternoon. On Saturday afternoons Whittingham offered a number of sports. The institution was famed for its women's hockey team and also its cricket and bowls teams that took part in the Preston District Leagues. According to Ken Ashton there was at least one football team at Whittingham.

The male and female wings in St Luke's were divided into 20 smaller dormitories, ten male and ten female, each dorm containing 25 iron-framed beds, packed so close the patients could almost touch each other. The dorms were staffed day and night by two attendants. Downstairs the male wing had a full-size billiard table and in the day-room set out with chairs there was a piano. For the men the hospital band was a popular pastime as was painting, and at the weekends, amateur dramatics or ballroom dancing took place when the gentlemen patients could meet the ladies. Whittingham even worked its own brewery and the patients were allowed a glass of home-brewed beer or cider every day.

(If this sounds to be an almost pleasant existence, the reality was much different with shortages of many personal items so that conditions of personal care and hygiene were far from satisfactory. Patients shivered through the winters without adequate clothing, suffered punishments for the slightest misbehaviour, and were tyrannised by the cruelty and abuse of staff bullies. Washing and toileting facilities without any privacy were totally inadequate. Still accepting patients in the 1960s, an enquiry that was the result of student nurses' complaints eventually resulted in a report that made horrific reading. A holiday camp, this was not.

And yet, despite many hardships, the abuse and being squeezed into the dormitories like sardines, it was all too easy for many of the inmates to succumb to the institutionalisation process, whereby if you hand over your independence and willpower, life becomes very simple and unstressed, indeed quite comfortable with three meals a day and no thinking of your own to do or taxing decisions to make. As the routine takes over the patient simply sinks into it.

With medication and more enlightened attitudes, it is unlikely that today Tommy Boyle would have been incarcerated in a mental institution for the final years of his life. It is reasonable to assume that back in the '30s many people were hospitalised who were borderline cases, and it is more than likely that many people were locked away, not because there was anything seriously wrong, but simply because they were unwanted by their families. Some of the inmates were soldiers suffering from traumatic stress. Basically, anyone deemed incapable of managing their own affairs could be institutionalised. The police in Burnley were certainly happy to see Boyle locked away. Records that give any indication of his time there are as yet unavailable to the public. One can only hope that he found some measure of peace through the work and sporting activities that were available to him there and the freedom within the grounds that one presumes he made use of.

The bundle of clippings and pictures in the faded envelope were all that he had left of his former prowess and achievements. Tommy Boyle's final years are a story filled with tragedy and pathos.)

2 January 1940

The cold spell that had set in over the Christmas period worsened as the New Year began. As people returned to work the day after the New Year's Day holiday, a blanket of snow covered much of England. Later that month the whole country froze when an ice-storm arrived. It became so cold that the Thames iced over and small birds froze to the tree branches. The winter had even delayed Hitler's expansion plans. The morning newspapers told stories of the war from across Europe. Soldiers of the British Expeditionary Force were on standby, ready to leave for France to give Jerry what for again. The only direct engagement for the British with the enemy was at sea with the sinking of allied shipping by German U-boats. That morning's *Daily Mirror* held a full-page advert from the Ministry of Food reminding householders to sign up for meat rationing. With league football cancelled the previous August because of the war, Burnley and Barnsley played each other in friendlies over the Christmas period with Burnley losing both games. On New Year's Day Barnsley had thrashed their rivals Sheffield Wednesday 5 – 0 at Oakwell.

It was pitch black at Whittingham as another working day was about to begin. At first light the grounds surrounding St Luke's were covered in a thick white frost, while the coloured Christmas tree lights still glowed brightly outside the main entrance. Male nurse John

Blackburn had risen in the nurse's block at 5.15am to begin his six until 2 o'clock shift. Blackburn hung up his coat in the ward office and began his rounds of the first dormitory on the male wing, gently shaking each patient awake to get him up for washing, dressing and breakfast. Blackburn had got a third of the way round when he shook Tommy's shoulder. He got no response. Checking further, he found the patient to be stone cold.

Blackburn shouted for assistance and the bed was screened off. One attendant ran down to The Lawns, the superintendent's house located at the back of St Luke's, to bring the doctor. Assistant Medical Officer, Dr Helen Murray and her superior, Dr R Gordon-McLaren, in charge of the male wing arrived not long after. McLaren checked for all vital signs but it was clearly too late. Thomas William Boyle, patient number 24281, was dead. The two doctors agreed that the patient had passed away quietly in the night and there were no untoward circumstances regarding the cause of death. Steps were taken to contact Tommy's next of kin to inform the family and to arrange for a formal identification of the body as a post-mortem would be necessary ...

... the post-mortem was carried out the same day; the single cause of death was given by Dr Gordon-McLaren as 'General Paralysis of the Insane'. GPI accounted for up to 20% of patients in mental institutions that occurred through tertiary syphilis, which with penicillin and other treatments has now been almost eradicated ...

(A week after his death, Tommy's body was brought back to Yorkshire by his family and he was buried in the family grave along with his mother and father in St Helen's churchyard in Hoyland. There was no headstone to mark the last resting place until in 2010 Burnley and Barnsley Football Clubs combined to fund a headstone that was unveiled and commemorated on Sunday 11 April. Members of Tommy's family were present, along with representatives from both football clubs. His contribution to both clubs had been immense.)

3

Burnley V West Ham, FA Cup 1964

It was a time of transition, said Manager Harry Potts and Chairman Bob Lord. Just over a year earlier, the incomparable Jimmy Mac had been sold and 1963/64 was the first full season without him. Most of the great title team were still at the club and, other than Jimmy Adamson, were still only in their late twenties. Blacklaw, Angus, Elder, Miller, Adamson, Connelly, Pointer, Harris, Robson were all still there. But, appearances by Robson and Pointer were intermittent and Elder was absent for the first half of the season. Adamson was almost totally absent and in came Brian O' Neil. Lochhead too was now in the team. Willie Morgan would emerge in the second half of the season. But all was not well; the team was inconsistent, players were asking for transfers, the season was plagued by injuries, gates were falling, and there was restlessness and uncertainty about the future. The city clubs were pulling ahead and swathes of fans still could not relate to a Burnley without McIlroy. The team was likened to an orchestra without a conductor. The end of season summary in the local Press was: 'A grand season of mediocrity.' Nevertheless in the FA Cup, the further they got, the more hope there was that the club was going to do well again and in the quarter-final they met West Ham. They were expected to win but the game ended in a controversial defeat. This chapter looks at season '63/64 and makes use of Brian Belton's West Ham book: The Men of 64 *as well as the editor's own book:* Harry Potts: Margaret's Story *chapter 7, 'Be Patient'.*

Harry Potts was in a positive mood at the beginning of 1963/64;

he was always in a positive mood. It was one of the reasons why so many players never had a bad word to say about him. 'Last season we finished third in the First Division and the reserves won the Central League Championship. I can see no good reason why we should not do as well this time. The injuries to Elder and Pointer are both big blows but these things happen in football and it is a challenge for us to get over them. We will give a good account of ourselves. My guess is that we will win more matches than we will lose.' He rejected any suggestion by discontented supporters that the club needed to break their policy and sign a big name to capture the local peoples' imagination. 'You can take it from me that we will continue our youth policy. It has been successful so far, why should it fail us now?'

Meanwhile, Jimmy Adamson announced he would like to continue playing for another two or three seasons, but recurring back problems bedevilled him. He believed that another top-six place was possible but was also aware that the big city clubs were beginning to dominate the game and that small-town Burnley would find it increasingly difficult to maintain any success.

'But,' said Bob Lord, 'We have the finest potential that the club has ever had; we have experience, there is no better defence in the country, and the number of forwards the manager has to choose from is an embarrassment. If some formation can click, there is no reason why we should not be successful.' Maybe his words –'if some formation can click' summed up the season by the time it ended; very little clicked. Potts had already warned that it would be a season of transition but team shuffles were too frequent as injuries hit selections regularly. Finding the formation that might click proved impossible. Bob Lord might have been publicly bombastic and confident, but privately he was worried. The same line-up for more than two or three games was a rare occasion, and when John Connelly was sold at the end of the season supporters found it a depressing finale, even though Spurs were thumped 7 – 2 in the very last game with the young 'uns shining – Lochhead, Morgan, O'Neil, Irvine and an 18 years old Sammy Todd. Potts was delighted of course with the 7 – 2 win and used it as a propaganda exercise. 'Quite honestly it didn't surprise me. I have said all along that our team is as good as any other if things are equal.

What we didn't know was that we would have such a tremendous number of injuries. They have caused us to finish lower down the league than usual. We have taken a few brickbats. We have to take the rough with the smooth.'

The rough might well have included the controversial Cup result at West Ham in the sixth round that Burnley lost. Bob Lord described the third goal as being one that should have been disallowed for an obvious foul. 'Robbed', he announced. 'We were robbed of a semi-final trip.'

Potts paid particular tribute to the younger players who had taken part in the season and the way all players had rallied against the injury jinx. Without that spirit, he added, Burnley would have been in relegation trouble. Early in the season John Connelly needed an appendix operation. The influential Adamson only played ten games. By the end of the season they did not have a single fit full-back.

An occasional game stood out. They went to Everton and won 4 – 3. It was Everton's first home defeat in 44 games. Arthur Bellamy was the star scoring a hat-trick. Bellamy was a Harry Potts disciple and was one of several players beginning to sense that Jimmy Adamson was exerting more influence at the club at team level. As a senior player, with Jimmy McIlroy, he had always been influential but the seeds of ambition were growing. He was a thinker and a tactician. Harry was not. Harry was old school; send the players out, gee them up and let them get on with it.

Other stand-out games were the 4 – 1 win over Fulham, Blackburn were beaten twice, 3 – 0 and 2 – 1. There was an amazing 6 – 1 win over Manchester United at Christmas at Turf Moor. Andy Lochhead scored four times. Willie Morgan was unplayable. United were run dizzy and Paddy Crerand was sent off for thumping Ian Towers. Amazingly, just 24 hours later, the scores were almost reversed as Manchester United beat Burnley 5 – 1. George Best, in only his second appearance for United, ran John Angus ragged. The game that everyone was waiting for took place in November and it marked the visit of Burnley to Stoke City and Jimmy Mac against Burnley in a Stoke City shirt. He was still an idol. Two coachloads of Burnley supporters went simply to see Jimmy Mac. Perhaps Bob Lord had been right all along however; perhaps his star was faded. It certainly seemed so by the time the game ended with a score of 4 – 4. Stoke had raced into a 3 – 0 lead and McIlroy smiled wryly at the directors box as he left the field at halftime. But if he was outstanding in the first half he was invisible in the second. It would be the same at Turf Moor later in the season with him hardly in the game.

In November of '63, Potts grabbed the headlines when he announced it was time that soccer was sorted out. Burnley had lost 3 – 2 at Tottenham but two of the goals were controversial coming after fouls that went unpunished. If there was one thing guaranteed to incense him it was unfair decisions and rough play. At Elland Road against Leeds all 22 players had to be called together by the referee and told to cut out the rough stuff. Harry Potts could not tolerate Don Revie and what he stood for – gamesmanship, cynicism, win at all costs – and came to detest him. At Birmingham, Burnley had four goals disallowed during a 0 – 0 draw. He stormed off the pitch and had angry words with the referee resulting in him being reported to the FA and Football League.

During the season speculation grew about Jimmy Adamson's future. With Bob Lord and Jimmy Adamson unavailable to shed light on the situation, it is reasonable to speculate that Lord was already planning for Adamson to take over one day. There were already rumours in one newspaper that someone would move over to make room for Adamson – though whether this referred to Potts or Billy Dougal was never clear. Lord and Adamson denied any such move. Lord did say that with regard to the future he already had something in mind but it hadn't been implemented yet. 'Jimmy Adamson goes with the wallpaper at Turf Moor,' announced Lord. One day Potts and Adamson might well form a team at the head of the dressing room, he added. It was not until a year later that Adamson officially became coach.

Willie Morgan had certainly come to the fore. He was Burnley's first glamour player with a Beatle haircut, eventually one of the first ever fan clubs, and a clothes boutique in the town. He was an entertainer and people came to watch him in the same way they used to come specially to see Jimmy McIlroy. He was described as 'the Johnny

Staccato of dribbling.' He was a self-confessed individual but Potts gave him room to breathe and a licence to be himself. Once Connelly was sold, his place in the side was secure. It could be said that Connelly was the first of the players to be sold still at the height of their powers. Until then the players sold had been considered expendable, or past their best. The Connelly sale set a new precedent. 'Who will be next?' asked supporters. It also confirmed that the great side of the early sixties was done; well and truly in the shadows. Players had been sold, Adamson was crocked; other players would never re-capture their best form. Potts had hoped that with just one or two gradual changes it could have gone on and enjoyed more success. It was not to be. The drawing board beckoned. The formation that would 'click' had not been found and for the first time in many years there would be no summer tour or a luxury cruise.

Only the FA Cup had provided any real hope of silverware as the competition progressed. One by one Rotherham, Newport County and Huddersfield were taken care of.

In Round Three, little Rotherham, in their first ever trip to Turf Moor, were no pushover. If Burnley expected a routine win they received rather a jolt. John Connelly returned to the team after an absence of several weeks and, apart from Adamson being missing, this was a full-strength team. For Rotherham, 18 years old Frank Casper made his debut. Everything looked set for a win when Lochhead put Burnley 1 – 0 ahead. Casper put Rotherham level just 18 minutes later. He was one of six teenagers in the side.

The newspapers were less than kind to the Clarets. Blacklaw was generally seen as the saviour making several critical saves; the man of the match, reported Keith McNee. Rotherham's shooting was tremendous and Blacklaw four times brilliantly foiled the Rotherham forwards. At the other end Rotherham survived a string of misses and a second half onslaught. Several chances went begging and O'Neil hit the post. Local reporter Granville Shackleton made Lochhead the best of the forwards. 'A spine-tingling game,' said John Leonard, with Rotherham deserving their draw after they refused to yield to Burnley's barrage that would have flattened lesser teams. All in all it was a game that both sides could have claimed they should have won – Burnley on account of the chances missed, and Rotherham on account of their shoot on sight policy forcing Blacklaw to have an outstanding game. The replay was no foregone conclusion and Burnley on the night won only by the skin of their teeth. Frank Clough described the game that was watched by a full house of 22,000:

'I was right – but these are the saddest words I shall write for a long time. On Saturday I tipped Burnley to beat Rotherham at Turf Moor, and boobed. I stuck my neck out again yesterday and once more tipped Burnley to win the replay. They did – but only after 90 bitter minutes when the raw courage and fight of the Second Division side had frightened Burnley to within an inch of their glossy, glamorous lives. The winner that made Burnley the luckiest team yet to go through to the fourth round came just four minutes from the end after Rotherham had played the last half hour with only ten men. They'd thrown aside the colossal handicap of losing left-back star 19 years old Colin Clish with a fractured left leg and still swarmed all over Burnley. Barry Lyons only 18 but yet another brilliant discovery from Manager Danny Williams' endless teenage stable had put Rotherham within a finger-snap of a great against the odds victory with two rip-snorting goals that knocked Burnley sideways. Then came the bitter moment of tragedy, when fight, fire and iron will, crumbled to cold, comfortless ashes.'

It was Burnley who took the lead through Connelly and they led 1 – 0 until half-time. After half-time, however, came Lyons' two super-strikes. 2 – 1 up it looked odds on that Rotherham would increase their score but then Clish was carried off. Lochhead equalised and then Ian Towers, restored to the side, grabbed the winner 13 minutes from the end leaving Rotherham and the majority of the crowd heartbroken. Without a shadow of doubt, Burnley had been lucky to win.

Within days there was conjecture that Connelly would be moving on. Spurs joined a host of clubs watching and following the Lancashire club with a view to making an offer for Connelly. The hope was that Burnley would be knocked out of the Cup by Rotherham and that Lord would then listen to offers. Interested clubs remembered his words from early in the season that Burnley had to sell to survive. With a place in the fourth round secured Connelly stayed. At the end of the *season, however, he would go to Manchester United.*

It was the minnows of Newport County next at Turf Moor. Yet again though Burnley struggled and County provided anything but fourth-rate opposition. At half-time they were unlucky not to be ahead after they recovered well from a Willie Morgan goal. It was pretty much Willie Morgan who dominated the game with a superb performance, scoring one and making the other for Connelly in the second half. Morgan's goal was lucky though. He shot from inside the area and though the goalkeeper seemed to have it covered it squirmed under his body and rolled home. The goal he made for Connelly came after a dazzling run, he beat the full-back, crossed the ball, and there was Connelly to head into the net, a headed goal being something of a collector's piece from the number seven. All in all this was a game where 'Cup luck' was on Burnley's side. Their fans chanted 'easy, easy' before the game. It was anything but. Their first half performance was poor but they bucked up in the second. Few players, in front of 23,000 fans, came out with any credit other than Morgan and Blacklaw. The legendary Bob Kelly – Bob Lord's favourite player of the 1920s – was a spectator at the game. 'A great prospect,' he said of Willie Morgan. . .

The two Cup games had been typical of the season so far. This was an inconsistent, stop-start, stuttering team, certainly not firing on all cylinders. Nor on the occasions that they had played well did they get the result they deserved. Just such a game was at Birmingham when four disallowed goals kept the score to 0 – 0, even though they had played superbly well. The atmosphere after the game and in the following days was acrimonious with accusations of slanging matches with referee Aldous. 'A load of baloney,' said Lord. 'If one can't speak to one's colleagues and not have anything made of it, then they're going to have to put sealing wax to our lips.' Lord insisted his ranting after the match was with Director Bill Pickard. The referee said it was at him. 'I will stand up for my rights,' announced Lord. 'Mr Aldous can please himself.'

A home defeat to Arsenal preceded the next cup-tie against Huddersfield Town. Jimmy Adamson returned to the side. A comfortable Cup win came from a flying start when Ray Pointer scored after just two minutes. The ease of the win did not disguise, however, the fact that all three goals were given away by Huddersfield.

'Huddersfield blunders put Burnley through,' wrote Ivan Sharpe. 'Surely the score in this match was an FA Cup record. Surely a team has not knocked itself out of the competition by giving away all three goals. And if that is not unique, there is the further sorrowful circumstance that in the crisis of the game, the losers failed with a penalty kick. That is how Burnley reached the last eight Cup fighters and that is why there will be no change for another 12 months in the photograph in Mr Harold Wilson's wallet, where Huddersfield Town's Cup-winning team of 1922 has resided for 42 years.'

The first goal came when goalkeeper Ray Wood dropped the ball at the feet of Ray Pointer after an Alex Elder cross. Pointer, another surprise recall, gratefully accepted the gift. In the 17th minute Huddersfield were awarded a penalty when Lewis was brought down by Angus. Lewis blazed the ball four feet wide. Burnley's second goal was another gift when centre-half Dinsdale clumsily fumbled with the ball when trying to control it. In came Lochhead, collected the ball and scored. The third goal too was the classic gift to the opposition – an own goal. In the 89th minute the Town defence got itself into all kinds of tangles under pressure from Lochhead, following a save from Harris; and Atkins the right back turned the ball into his own net.

With a shock appearance from Jimmy Adamson much to the surprise of supporters, it was a good display from Burnley despite the three gifted goals. Alan Dunn reported: 'In a first half of superb football Burnley gave notice that they are warming up for Wembley. The half brought them only one goal, but their mastery was so complete, that the second half was a formality. And feeding their sleek machine with the rich measured doses was the delightful Adamson, gracing the first team with his cool elegance for the first time since early October.'

There was disappointment that the next Cup game would be away at West Ham. But in truth it was only the third away tie out of the last ten for the Clarets. It was an away ground considered to be a lucky one for Burnley and the first Cup game between the two sides. Their manager, Ron Greenwood, was a Burnley boy, born and bred in Worsthorne. There was concern that Adamson would not be fit with a recurrence of his back problems. He admitted that he had always had back trouble and it could have put him out of the game for good. 'But I've been lucky.'

4,000 fans followed them down. 'ROBBED,' said Bob Lord after the game, cheated he felt of a semi-final appearance and maybe even Wembley again.

'Burnley shattered by lone star' wrote Denis Compton. 'Burnley yield the initiative' wrote John Arlott. 'A brilliant goal inspires West Ham' ... 'Unlucky Clarets' ... 'Burnley dispute winner' ... 'Robbed' said Bob Lord. 'That third goal of West Ham's should never have been allowed. Byrne was not only offside but he fouled John Talbut as he got the goal. As far as I'm concerned we got robbed of a semi-final trip.' Frank Taylor agreed that Byrne had pushed Talbut over before scoring. Other reports however suggested it was Brian Miller he pushed over.

Was this the only time that Burnley were ever watched and reported on by two cricket luminaries – John Arlott and Denis Compton? Most reporters agreed with Lord, that West Ham's third goal should not have stood. At the same time they were all agreed that the star of the match was the scorer, Johnny Byrne. In the first half Burnley had him under control and were the better side taking the lead through John Connelly. Sissons scored the equaliser and Byrne then scored twice. With ten minutes to go, Pointer scored a second for Burnley to set up a grandstand finish. West Ham held on whilst Lord and Potts fumed. The one goal they had scored in the muddy conditions in the first half could have been more and therein lay the seeds of their defeat. John Arlott as articulate on paper as he was on radio summed up the game: 'A match rare in its blend of skill, savagery, suspense and shifting emphasis went to West Ham ... the first half was Burnley's, the middle third went to West Ham, and then the last quarter of an hour belonged to Burnley.' Denis Compton enthused about Byrne's wonderful display at centre-forward: 'One of the most brilliant displays I have ever seen.'

With one of those football ironies that happen so often, Burnley's next game was at home to – West Ham. They beat them comfortably 3 – 1 and in truth the only incident of any real note was when Gordon Harris repeated his bad behaviour of the first game when he swung a punch and knocked out John Bond. 34,000 spectators saw it and many more on TV. One man did not – referee Jennings who found Bond inert on the ground amidst a bunch of players jostling and arguing. At Turf Moor, however, it was Bobby Moore he laid out, this time with a kick not a punch. Again the referee did not see the incident and to everyone's great surprise Harris was not sent off but only booked after the referee consulted the linesman. 'If I had seen him I would have sent him off,' he said the next day. It added a sour taste to the two games. With Harris notorious for his short fuse and Bob Lord notorious for his grumbling and outspokenness, it was no wonder that Burnley, despite the good football they could play, were beginning to lose quite a few friends and admirers. On top of that, many fans who had sworn never to return to Turf Moor after McIlroy was sold, had kept their word. Whilst they had remained in the Cup there was hope of some success. With the exit at West Ham, the unrest and dissatisfaction amongst supporters increased. And, on top of all that, the sale of more players was not far away, as newspaper speculation increased.

***

The Men of 64 by Brian Belton (Tempus)
From Chapter 4: The Sixth Round

Two days before the quarter-finals of the 1964 FA Cup, on 27 February, the Ronettes stood at number 11 in the British charts with *Baby I Love You*. Just behind the Ronettes, Cliff Richard lurked with *I'm the Lonely One* and one place ahead of the New York girls was *I'm the One* by Scousers Gerry and the Pacemakers. It was the eighth consecutive week that the Ronettes had been in the top 40 and they would remain there for another month. The charts had been very much dominated by Liverpool. Apart from Gerry Marsden and his 'Fab Four' lookalikes, at that point Cilla Black was at number 1 with her version of *Anyone Who Had a Heart,* The Merseybeats were at 5 with *I think of You* and Freddie and the Dreamers' *Over You* had just come in at number 20, whilst the Beatles had found what seemed like a permanent place in the record charts, having been hanging around for thirteen weeks with *I Want To Hold Your hand* and in the top 30 with *She Loves You* for the better part of seven months.

The Ronettes had first entered the British best-selling list on 17 October the previous year with *Be My Baby*, reaching a high point of number 4 on 21 November that year. That record was to stay in the charts for ten weeks, which meant that the Ronettes were not among the best-selling artistes in the British market for just two weeks during a six-month period and had become very much the ultra-sexy darlings of both Preston's and West Ham's Cup runs. Indeed their music had been a theme tune of the clubs' respective paths to Wembley. I was waiting with 36,550 others at the Boleyn Ground for the last-eight game with Burnley, having entered a good hour before kick-off and I recall singing along with the North Bank chorus: *West Ham, we love you, West Ham we love you, West Ham we love only you … Woh-ol. Woh-ol. Woh-ol …*

The Ronettes produced some very good, maybe even great rock and roll songs and are remembered as one of the premier girl groups of the 1960s. They changed the way female rock and roll looked and how it was performed. In a way, a bit like West Ham in football.

What Can You Say About Harry Potts?

You never knew what to expect from West Ham. But there's a limit to how much you should look at the other side to sort out what you are going to do, and we always fancied our chances if we could get them back to Turf Moor. (Harry Potts)

Burnley, Ron Greenwood's home-town club, came to Upton Park as West Ham's seventh opponent of February 1964. At that time there was not much to choose between the 'Cotton Town Kings' and the pride of East London in terms of league form. The Lancastrians were in eleventh place in Division One whilst West Ham were just a few points behind in fourteenth position. But the Irons faced a team with a proud tradition. Burnley had last won the Cup in 1913/14 but had been finalists in 1946/47 and as recently as 1961/62. They had been League Champions in 1920/21 and 1959/60 and finished as runners-up in 1919/20 and 1961/62 (a good but 'nearly' season for Burnley).

The Clarets had been winners of Division Two in 1897/98 and took second place in 1912/13 and 1946/47.

Burnley had finished just one point behind 111-goal League runners-up Tottenham Hotspur in the 1962/63 season and were greeted at Upton Park by an all-ticket crowd of 36,651 (including England Manager Alf Ramsey) a club record at the time. After needing two games to beat Rotherham in the Third Round, the Clarets had disposed of Newport from the Fourth Division and Huddersfield from the Second Division to make the last eight.

The Burnley manager had brought a distinguished side to East London. Harry Potts himself had been a product of Turf Moor's enlightened and ground-breaking youth policy. Born in Hetton le Hole in 1920, Potts had joined the Clarets as a professional in 1937. After breaking into the reserve side, the young Potts didn't get the opportunity to push his way into Second Division football before war broke out in 1939. Like many other promising players of the era, Harry's career stagnated during the first half of the 1940s, the world conflict robbing him of nearly seven of his peak playing years. However, he made his Football League debut along with more than half the Burnley team on the opening day of the 1946/47 season. He was 25 years old and was one of the inspirations behind the Burnley side of that term. The defensive-minded Potts was the engine room of the Clarets' midfield. For four years Harry was hardly out of the starting line-up, working to establish Burnley as a First Division outfit. However, the Turf Moor crowd probably never saw the best of him. He became unsettled and slapped in a transfer request in the summer of 1950 and he moved to Everton for a record fee in October of that year. He had scored fifty goals in 181 games for the Clarets.

At the end of Potts' first season with the Toffees, the Merseysiders went tumbling into Division Two and after that Harry was never able to command a regular first-team place at Goodison Park. Eventually, in 1956, he joined Wolves as chief coach. After his spell at Molineux he became manager at Shrewsbury Town and took charge of Burnley in January 1958. He inherited expert backroom staff including Billy Dougall and Ray Bennion, two of the people he classed as having a huge influence on his own playing career and the nucleus of the team that would become the most successful Burnley side in modern times.

At the end of his second full season as Burnley manager, Potts took Burnley to the First Division title. During his first years as manager, Harry gave Gordon Harris and Alex Elder their debuts, spotted the potential of John Connelly and nurtured Brian Miller's move through the ranks. Those players blended with established professionals like Ray Pointer and Burnley clinched the title in the very last game of 1959/60. That meant that Potts would lead Burnley into their inaugural European campaign whilst taking them to the FA Cup Final for the first time in 15 years.

The Clarets at Upton Park

After losing Colin McDonald when he broke his ankle at Chelsea in December 1956, Adam Blacklaw played eight matches in Burnley's first team as a nineteen year old, but it wasn't until March 1959, when McDonald's career came to an end that Blacklaw made the goalkeeper's shirt his own. His contribution to the League Championship campaign led to his first representative honours (two Scotland Under-23 caps). As the Clarets stormed to the title, Blacklaw missed just one match and his consistency over the following three years was exemplary. He won the first of his three full Scottish caps against Norway in Bergen in June 1963.

Perhaps the most famous picture of Adam Blacklaw is one of him being sent the wrong way by Danny Blanchflower from the penalty spot in the 1962 Cup Final. Another undoubted low point was a last-minute incident at Anfield in February 1963 in the FA Cup fourth round replay. With the seconds ticking away at the end of extra time, and the score 1 – 1, Blacklaw unaccountably kicked the ball against Ian St John and then had to pull the Scot down to prevent him scoring. Ronnie Moran stroked in the spot-kick. Liverpool were through and Burnley were out. Blacklaw's father had been critically ill before the match at Upton Park. Around 12.30 on the Sunday morning after arriving back in East Lancashire from east London he drove to Aberdeen knowing that his father was declining rapidly. He reached the 'Granite City' just in time to see his father before he passed away.

John Angus was a polished right-back. He signed for Burnley

on amateur terms from the Amble Boys Club in 1954 and became a professional on his 17th birthday the following year. Angus was an England Youth International and had represented the Football League. John was regarded as one of the very finest right-backs of his era. Many a Burnley fan expressed the feeling that he should have had more than his one full cap. Walter Winterbottom described his single England game against Austria on May 27, 1961, as the best international debut he had ever seen even though England lost 1 – 3. Angus was often seen as a better player than England's usual right-back of the time, Jimmy Armfield. He hardly ever seemed to get ruffled; it was not unknown for John to trap the ball on his own goal-line and dribble it out of his own area. He won a League Championship medal and an FA Cup runners-up medal with the Clarets.

Alex Elder was the only player to become established in the Championship winning side of 1959/60 who made his debut during that memorable campaign. He arrived from Glentoran in January 1959 and soon impressed with his hard-tackling style and mastery of the long ball out of defence. He made his first Division One appearance in September 1959 in a difficult game at Preston. The young Elder was detailed to mark the legendary Tom Finney and, although the Clarets lost the game 1 – 0, Elder had done enough to make the left-back position his own for the foreseeable future. Still only eighteen, he made his full Northern Ireland debut against Wales in April 1960, going on to win 34 caps in his time at Turf Moor. Oddly, he won his only Under-23 cap in 1964, four years after making his first senior international appearance. A broken ankle kept Elder out of the side for more than half of the 1963/64 season.

Brian O'Neil was a hard tackling, no-nonsense, never-say-die midfielder. The 'Bedlington Terrier' first arrived at Turf Moor as a junior in 1960 and made his first team debut in April 1963, taking over the number four shirt from Jimmy Adamson. The contrast between the two players could not have been starker; Adamson was a silky mover and a great thinker; O'Neil was a non-stop player who concentrated on moving the ball from 'A' to 'B' as quickly as possible.

England schoolboy international centre-half, Oxford born John Talbut, signed for Burnley in 1957 aged 17, and made his initial appearance in league football in two games against Leicester City over Christmas 1958. The competition for places in the middle of Burnley's defence was fierce at the time. Tommy Cummings and Brian Miller were always going to be difficult to supplant, and Talbut played in only seven League games in four years. But he displaced Cummings as first-choice centre-half in 1962 and for three seasons his name was synonymous with the position, his dependable performances winning him seven England Under-23 caps in 1964.

One of a small number of locally born players to make the grade with Burnley, Brian Miller was born in Hapton in 1937 and joined the Clarets as a junior in February 1954. He made his first-team debut, deputising for Les Shannon during the FA Cup marathon with Chelsea in 1956. Up against a formidable trio like Adamson, Seith and Shannon, and with the injured Tommy Cummings waiting to come back, Miller did well to force himself into the reckoning over the next few years with his solid, hard tackling style. He was ever-present in the League Championship season and won three England Under-23 caps in 1960. His consistency over the following seasons was a major factor in Burnley's success and should perhaps have earned him more than his solitary full England cap in Vienna in May 1961, the same match in which his team-mate John Angus also made his only appearance for his country. Both men played out of position during that game, Angus at left-back and Miller at right-half.

Reputed to be the first British footballer to have his own fan club, Willie Morgan was the idol of many Burnley followers in the 1960s. A right-winger of the highest order, Morgan was snapped up by Burnley scouts after being spotted in Glasgow (his place of birth). Willie became a seventeen-year old apprentice at Turf Moor in October 1961. On the last day of the following season he made his first-team debut as a replacement for the legendary John Connelly. He ousted the club stalwart from the right-wing position the following campaign, when Connelly switched to the left flank.

Boasting a strike rate of more than one goal in every two games, Ray Pointer had one of the best goals-per-game ratios in the honourable history of Burnley Football Club. The 'Blonde Bombshell' failed a trial at Blackpool and returned to his native Northeast. It was from Dudley Welfare that the Cramlington born goal scorer joined the Clarets in 1957. England Under-23 honours and three full caps followed as Pointer became a vital component in the Burnley team that won the First Division title in 1959/60 and reached the FA Cup Final two years later.

Andy Lochhead was born in Milngavie in 1941 and signed for Burnley in December 1958 from the Renfrew club Paisley. He was amongst the goals when he deputised for Ray Pointer in 1960/61, but it was not until 1962/63 that he made the number 9 shirt his own, Pointer moving to inside-right. Following the departure of both Pointer and Jimmy Robson, Lochhead was to form a very effective partnership with Willie Irvine. His power in the air and his skill both on and off the ball had already won him a Scottish Under-23 cap in 1962, but the Scottish selectors chose to ignore him for full honours.

Gordon 'Bomber' Harris was a stocky, powerfully built 'engine-room' type of player who was deceptively quick. He was renowned for the cannon-ball drives that regularly detonated from his left foot, possessing arguably the hardest shot of any Burnley player. He was born in Worksop in 1940 and was playing for a colliery team at nearby Firbeck when Burnley spotted his talents and brought him to Turf Moor in January 1958. In his first two years he played only occasionally but established himself in 1961 when Brian Pilkington had left for Bolton Wanderers.

John Connelly was born in St Helens, in the heart of Rugby League country, in 1938. He was serving his apprenticeship as a joiner whilst playing for St Helens Town when he joined the Clarets in November 1956. Connelly did not make an immediate impact in the first team (Billy Gray and Doug Newlands were vying for the right-wing position) and played only spasmodically in his first two seasons. He staked his claim to the number 7 shirt during the 1958/59 season and finished his first campaign as a regular and second-highest scorer behind Ray Pointer. He went one better during the Championship season as Connelly, Pointer and Robson hit 57 of the team's 85 goals. Injury forced John to miss the run-in to the title, his replacement, Trevor Meredith, scored the goal that clinched the Championship in the final match. Of all the goals that John Connelly scored in his Burnley career, none was more memorable than his solo effort in the away leg of the European cup-tie against Reims. Picking the ball up in his own half, he rode a number of wild tackles, and letting fly from 25 yards, surprised the French keeper by sending the ball dipping into the net. The goal effectively won the tie for Burnley and set up an epic struggle against Hamburg in the next round. Connelly won 10 England caps in his time at Turf Moor, his first as early as 1959. He scored four goals for his country before his exciting wing play inevitably attracted the big clubs.

Claret and Blue V Claret and Blue

After hearing the draw for the quarter-final, Harry Potts was asked what was going to be done about the clash of colours, both West Ham and Burnley traditionally wearing claret and blue strips. He replied: 'West Ham will wear claret with blue stripes and we will wear blue with claret stripes.'

He recalled the game at Upton Park (in a later year): 'It's a game that sticks in my mind because it was one of those we should have won. We did well in the first half, one of the best of that season. I think it is fair to say we outplayed West Ham. John Connelly got a great individual goal to give us the lead at half-time. It was a bit like the goal he scored against Reims in Paris when we played in the European Cup. He ran through three or four tackles and scored from about 35 yards out. He was a great player. We could have gone further ahead. Andy Lochhead and Gordon Harris had near misses with the West Ham goalkeeper beaten.'

It was soon after coming out for the second half that Lochhead got a clear run, but was 'zealously curtailed' by Bovington. It was the twelfth minute after the break that West Ham struck back. Harry Potts recalled: 'Their outside-left Sissons pulled the ball along the by-line and, from a very sharp angle, sent it towards our goal. It rolled just over the line. Elder got it out but not before it was in.'

The West Ham equaliser seemed to rock Burnley and the Hammers took advantage. Three minutes later Brabrook's centre was picked up by Byrne on the volley and went over Blacklaw to put the home side into the lead for the first time. Byrne had achieved a new post-war scoring record of 28 goals in a season. Less than 50 seconds later the

Irons seemed to secure the tie. Harry Potts saw it thus: 'I think Byrne was offside, but apart from that he pushed Brian Miller over before he scored. But that's the way it goes sometimes.'

As soon as Worcestershire referee Mr Jennings awarded the goal the Burnley players went into a frenzy that included Harris striking John Bond. For all this, Budgie's effort had been impressive, having overcome Miller and dribbled round Blacklaw. The Burnley players rallied at what they saw as an injustice and were rewarded with hope. With just ten minutes of the match to go Pointer scored with a juicy shot. This provoked the visitors into a tremendous last effort to force a replay. Potts remembered: 'Connelly was brought down in the box but we didn't get the penalty. I think if that had gone in and we had got them back to Turf Moor we could have beaten them. We had the better of them for a lot of the time on their own ground.'

But that was not to be. West Ham joined Preston, Manchester United and Swansea in the semi-finals. The Hammers had reached the last four of the FA Cup for the third time in the club's history (excluding the War Cup victory in 1940) and their first semi-final appearance (in peacetime) since 1933.

The League win at Ewood Park had been the season's turning point for West Ham, but the match against Burnley marked the moment when the Hammers came of age. The side demonstrated a ruthless determination that had often been lacking in their make-up. Byrne played wonderfully and his performance dominated the headlines of the morning papers after the match. He was, probably quite correctly, given the credit for taking West Ham into the last four. His alacrity and control on a problematical surface had indeed been the difference between the two sides.

Burnley got some recompense a few days later when in early March at Turf Moor they went in at the break two up and made it three just after half-time. A Byrne special came too late to save the Irons from defeat and Hurst's two strikes against the woodwork were consigned to the world of 'what might have been'.

4

1977 Brian Laws Joins Burnley

There was a most unlikely promotion for Burnley at the end of the 1981/82 season. It was John Jackson who had taken up the chairmanship of the club, now in Division Three. Bob Lord had passed away after more than 25 years as club chairman, leaving the club in a very poor state. In truth it was more or less insolvent but a last harvest of home grown players teamed with tried and trusted experienced professionals combined to achieve a most unexpected triumph.

Brian Laws was one of that group of home grown players along with Vince Overson, Trevor Steven, Andy Wharton, Derek Scott, Kevin Young and Mike Phelan. It was the last harvest of nurtured talent. After it, very little would be produced at Gawthorpe. Along with the vast experience of Martin Dobson and goalkeeper Alan Stevenson and the power of centre-forward Billy Hamilton, it became a potent and ultimately successful team.

They were turbulent times when Laws joined in 1977. Adamson had been sacked in 1976 and Joe Brown had come in to replace him. Relegation followed. Brown was replaced by Harry Potts. Potts steadied the ship for a while but then came relegation into Division Three and he too was replaced in 1979 by Brian Miller. The financial state of the club was perilous. Bob Lord was hanging on and refusing to give up the chairmanship but was not in the best of health.

Brian Miller after a poor start to the 1981/82 season decided that one answer to the troubles might be to employ Martin Dobson in a sweeper role. Results picked up and the wins and draws accumulated. At one stage early on the club had actually been bottom of the division and that was before there were defeats against Millwall and

Carlisle. Even as late as December they were in 20th position. But from December onwards Burnley moved upwards relentlessly and promotion was assured with a win away at Southend.

Brian Laws' contribution was immense. His defensive play allied to storming forward runs marked him as a crowd favourite. From the full-back position he crashed home six goals, a massive contribution bearing in mind that top scorer Billy Hamilton netted just 11 goals.

It was in 1979 that Laws turned pro at Burnley, eventually leaving for Huddersfield Town in August 1983. After leaving Huddersfield in March 1985 he moved to Middlesbrough, and then in July 1988 joined Brian Clough at Nottingham Forest. In November 1994 he joined Grimsby as player-manager thereby beginning his long career as a manager taking in Scunthorpe United, Sheffield Wednesday and Burnley from where he eventually returned to Scunthorpe.

After playing for Northumberland Schoolboys he joined the pathway to Turf Moor and the training fields of Gawthorpe. His progress was swift and, without making too many reserve team appearances, he made his first-team debut in the last match of relegation season 1978/79. He spent the next three seasons as Burnley's first-choice right-back. In 1981/82 he was voted 'Young Player of the Year' but the following season Burnley were relegation bound, despite two superb cup runs.

It was when John Bond arrived in 1983 that Laws' days were numbered. Bond told him he didn't like his defensive qualities and he was sold for a cut price £50,000 to Huddersfield. It wasn't that much earlier that West Ham had offered around £170,000 for him! According to Brian's book, it was Frank Casper who phoned him and asked what on earth was he doing? But, when his face didn't fit any more, what else could he do? He had made 162 appearances in total, scoring 15 goals.

After Huddersfield, there was a relegation and two promotions at Middlesbrough and then came probably the best time of his career when, at Nottingham Forest with the legend that was Brian Clough, he won a Littlewoods Cup medal, appeared in FA Cup semi-finals, won a second Littlewoods Cup medal in 1990 and then there was an FA Cup Final in 1991, albeit on the losing side.

In the north-east in his boyhood days his team was Newcastle United and his great hero was Malcolm 'Supermac' Macdonald. As his school-days neared their end, a letter arrived for his parents inviting Brian to a trial at Newcastle. He was thrilled but less so by the actual trial and training when he got there. It was on a car park and when one lad broke an ankle he was just packed off home without any treatment. 'Not for me,' Laws thought. In the meantime Burnley had shown an interest so that's where he headed pleased to find they already had a contingent of Geordies and a fine reputation for developing players – and selling them.

***

Laws of the Jungle: Surviving Football's Monkey Business by Brian Laws and Alan Biggs (Vertical Editions)
From Chapter 2: Hello Burnley, Bye-Bye Supermac

I finished my exams at Burnside School on one day and went straight to Turf Moor the next. I was so excited I just threw my school uniform in the bin. And I never bothered to check my results; I've no idea of them even now. All I was interested in was one small bit of geography – finding my way from the heavy industrial heartland of the north-east to the mill areas of East Lancashire. It was July 1977 and I was signing as an apprentice for Burnley at the age of 16. They were a club with a proud history – Football League champions in 1960, runners-up two years later when they were also FA Cup finalists, and competitors in European competitions. They also had an unbroken spell in the old First Division from 1947 to 1971 but were in the Second Division when I arrived. The manager was Harry Potts who had returned to the club after being the inspiration for some of their most successful years.

For all the excitement I quickly became homesick. It was all very emotional, leaving home for the first time and saying goodbye to all my mates as they all went off in different directions. It was heart-wrenching to be away. Every weekend I wanted to go home to my family and friends. But it's a fact of life that when you are chasing your dreams you have to travel. And, I think that makes you more respectful of people and instils a greater desire to achieve. Once I had made the decision to join Burnley, I was determined to stick with it. This has been a trait I have followed wherever I have been as a player or manager. Call me stubborn I suppose. Once my mind is made up, you can try to drag me any way you like, but I will always follow the direction I thought was right in the first place.

I believed Burnley was the right place to be, going there as a young striker. Let's not forget though, that it was a different world for young kids trying to carve out a football career in those days. Life as an apprentice was so, so hard. The hours that a junior had to put in far exceeded the demands on senior players. Besides their own training, the youngsters had loads of chores to do. I had come from doing very little other than being at school and playing for kicks. So, I quickly became the most tired I have ever felt. It took me months to get used to this schedule. All I ever wanted to do when I got back to my digs was to go to bed and rest.

There were about ten of us apprentices at Burnley and often our first job on a Monday morning was to sweep the terraces after the previous Saturday's game. The amount of stuff dropped on the floor and left behind by the fans was amazing. We used to find wallets and sometimes the odd fiver that had dropped out of someone's pocket. So the work had its compensations. Your head was always down, wondering what you were going to find next. But we hated it if it was a windy day because then we would often have to start all over again, brushing the terraces from top to bottom. On days like that the job seemed to take forever.

Away from the ground I was living in digs. In fact, I must have stayed in eight different places during my early days at Burnley. That's a lot, and a lot too many for a young player trying to settle away from home for the first time. Acclimatising to a new life is one of the hardest challenges facing a youngster in football. The suitability of digs is vital for anyone who has uprooted his life at an early age. For me, circumstances made it a very difficult transition. The first place I stayed in was near the training ground and it was like a hostel more than anything with young police cadets living there, too. I couldn't settle and eventually went to see the manager. I was miserable as the only player there and felt it was important to say something about not being in a football environment. It proved to be the first of several moves as I struggled to find somewhere permanent. I landed in some fairly peculiar places with some oddball characters and it was a while before I felt comfortable anywhere.

One day in particular I will never forget. Suddenly I heard a loud crack from above where I was working. I looked up to see that a large hole had appeared in the roofing on top of the stand. And, to my horror, falling through it was a workman who had been carrying out some repairs. He wasn't wearing a safety harness and he plunged down like some rag doll. His body crashed from one giant roof girder to another before smacking onto the concrete terracing below. It was a huge drop and he landed very close to us. Somehow he was still alive but there was blood everywhere and a huge gap in his forehead. He even tried to getup but couldn't. Everybody was in shock but one of the lads ran to get the club physio while the rest of us did our best to comfort the man. He was still breathing but really he had 'gone' and despite all the best work of the paramedics, he died in the ambulance on the way to hospital.

By the time I was a second-year apprentice at Burnley, I was getting fed up of having to wait for trains whenever I had the chance to go home to Newcastle. But it took me three attempts to pass my driving test. At the end of the first, I sat smugly at the wheel expecting the examiner to tell me I had passed. But I was rudely awakened.

'I am failing you for driving too wide when overtaking a parked car,' he said.

I went: 'What is that it?' I couldn't believe I'd done anything wrong.

But he said: 'Mr Laws, you have failed will you please leave the vehicle.' I could have strangled him. My instructor told me to put in for a second test straightaway. It came six weeks later – with the same examiner who had failed me! My heart sank, but he assured me everything would be alright, just to remember what I had done wrong the first time. So off we went and once more I thought I had done really well. Just a few questions about the Highway Code and that would be it.

Then came the verdict: 'I'm sorry Mr Laws, you've failed.'

'What for this time?' I demanded.

He replied: 'You went over the line and cut it too sharp when taking a right hand turn.'

I was gobsmacked. My brother came up with the answer. He suggested I should take the test somewhere else and got me booked in close to home at Bedlington where he used to live. First, I had to have a couple of lessons and I showed my instructor the documents stating why I had failed the first two tests.

'You'd never have failed for that up here,' he said. Sure enough, I passed. It was that easy.

Buying a car was the next struggle. On £17 a week, it was a problem. Once again, brother John came to the rescue, taking out a £400 loan under his name on condition that I paid him back a tenner each week. That left me only £7 to live on, but I was so excited at the prospect of owning a car that I jumped at the offer. And I never let John down with the payments. I bought a K registered green Avenger – not really my choice of colour but at a price I could now afford. I thought it was mint, just fantastic. And besides enabling me to get home every weekend, I found a way of balancing the books. We had a lot of young guys from the north-east at Burnley. I'd offer to drop them off wherever – but it was really going to cost them! A bit of the manager in me coming out early, because I even made a small profit. Then as I moved up the car market, I sold the Avenger to best mate Jimmy for £250. And it collapsed on him a few weeks later, needing a new gearbox, clutch, engine, the works. The moral of the story is ... never sell a car to a friend.

Meanwhile I was about to become a reconditioned footballer. In my second season as a Burnley apprentice I suffered an injury that changed the course of my career. It happened on the training ground playing in my usual position up front. I was never scared of the physical side and would always be brave enough to rough the defenders up a bit. I went up for a header with the centre-half and with both our eyes firmly fixed on the ball, we ended up heading each other. My head split open and I needed 20-odd stitches in a wound across my forehead where there is still a scar. I was so groggy that the youth coach, Frank Casper, wanted to put me out of harm's way while the injury healed. He suggested playing right-back because I could always stick my foot in and tackle. I did that for a couple of games and then came the time when I wanted to go back up front. Frank wouldn't have it. 'No,' he said. 'I think you can be a better right-back.'

I was distraught. I liked the glory of scoring goals. Being a defender was alien to me. I tried to fight Frank and demanded to see the manager. But they held firm and a few weeks later I had a great game playing right-back in the FA Youth Cup against Liverpool. The local paper gave me a good write-up and I thought: 'I could get to like that.' By accident I had found a new position that was going to take me to the top level in English football. Who knows, if I had won the battle to stay up front and try to become the new Malcolm Macdonald, I might never have had a professional career.

Another regular job for the apprentices was to clean the boots of certain senior pros after training. I copped for Steve Kindon, Brian Flynn and Leighton James. Now Brian was a real gentleman, but the other two were totally the opposite. They made my life hell – hammered me, absolutely murdered me. 'Taffy' James, a Welsh international winger, had only just returned to Burnley in a then club record £165,000 move from Queens Park Rangers. He was a great footballer who went on to play 54 times for his country – but he was also an arrogant git. I had to call him 'sir' and knock on the dressing room door to see if I could take his boots to be cleaned. It was the same with Kindon. He was about six feet three and just as wide. I would polish the boots until I could almost see my face in them.

Kindon would always warn me never to get boot polish on the laces. One morning he bawled out: 'Lawsy, what's this?' He had some boot polish on his fingers, grabbed me in a headlock and rubbed it all over my face. Then he banged me into the dressing room wall. Life as an apprentice was tough but at least it taught you discipline and teamwork – even though we would often try to set each other up to get into trouble with the seniors. It's very different for the trainees of today. When they join a club most of them think they have already got it made. But only a small percentage will be kept on. Rightly, there is more emphasis on coaching and also on education with trainees expected to spend much time each week on studies. They are not asked to do too much donkey work round the ground. On the negative side, though, this has changed the discipline of young players and the way they talk to you. In my day you always had to be polite and never answer back. Compare that with an experience I had as manager at Scunthorpe when I overheard one of my pros ask a young trainee to clean his boots. The response: 'Sorry I can't, I'm just off for my massage.' Can you imagine how Kindon and James would have reacted to that?

I've now seen both sides of youngsters being told they haven't made the grade and are not being retained. It's the hardest job in the world for a manager. In my time at Burnley, Manager Brian Miller had us in his office one by one. The three lads in front of me each came out with tears in their eyes having been told their fate. I thought I would be the next because nobody had given me any indication I would be one of the lucky ones. My heart was pounding and my hands were soaked in sweat. I was so worked up that I was shaking when I entered the manager's office. He sat me down and I just stared at an object on his desk, a pencil, waiting for the news I dreaded. Miller was glancing at some paperwork and then began to talk. 'You've seen some of the lads leave my office today disappointed,' he said. 'But I am not going to disappoint you. I am going to offer you a professional contract.'

I was stunned and speechless. When I finally stood up to leave, I wanted to shout and skip and scream. But I knew there were boys out there in tears. Proud as I was for myself and my family, my thoughts were for the other lads at that time. They were my friends and we had gone through so much in two years together. I didn't want to rub their noses in it. Only two of us had been kept on, myself and Dean Walker, who was also from Newcastle. It was only later when I rang my family that I could let rip with my emotions – and I burst into tears.

My first season as a professional saw Burnley relegated to the Third Division, but it became a high spot for me personally. Despite a run of seven games without defeat, we were already down with Fulham and Charlton when we travelled to Watford for the final game of the

1979/80 season. I was included in the squad for the first time. It did not come as a big surprise because a lot of younger players had been in the squad just for the experience of being part of things. I assumed it was my turn just to taste travelling with the team and learning from them. At Vicarage Road I helped unload the kit from the bus and lay it out in the dressing room where, to my great shock, my name was on the teamsheet. I had been picked to play at right-back instead of Ian Wood who had joined the club the previous summer after 500 games with Oldham. Discovering this, only an hour or so before kick-off, gave me little time to get nervous, but the tension boiled inside me as three o'clock approached. It was my first experience of playing in front of a proper-sized crowd. This was the day I had dreamed of since those distant times with Battle Hill in the Newcastle Junior League. But we lost 4 – 0 to Watford and, to make matters worse, their number 11, Keith Pritchett, my opposite number, scored twice. He only managed nine goals in his entire 133-game career with the Hornets and two of them were against me.

I thought I had a nightmare, my worst game ever. I felt nervous, didn't know what to do and when I came off I thought that was me finished where the first team was concerned; my career over before it had even started. If it was sink or swim, I had drowned.

Come the summer break back home and it was the first time I had felt depressed about football. The man who helped pick me up was Stewart Barrowclough, who had played for Newcastle. Stewart, who knew my uncle, had a landscaping business and he invited me to go and work for him that summer to take my mind off things. It was all labouring, putting up fences, laying driveways and generally getting my fingers dirty. More than making me forget what had happened at Watford, I found some muscles that summer. And when I went back to Turf Moor for pre-season training, I felt good, really strong. I got my opportunity again when Woody had a stinker and the manager threw me back in. This time I never looked back and played nearly every game that season as we finished eighth without ever getting into contention for a play-off place. The following season, 1981/82, proved to be memorable with Burnley finishing as Third Division champions above Carlisle and Fulham who were also promoted. It was my first taste of success and I loved it. Not all of it though: after clinching promotion with a 4 – 1 win at Southend we nearly drank our hotel dry. I had so much red wine it put me off the stuff for years.

The chairman was Bob Lord – and what a scary man he was. (*Although in season 1981/82 the chairman was John Jackson. DT*) He ruled Burnley Football Club with a rod of iron and did the same at the FA. Everyone was wary of him, a massive man with big ears. When you walked down the corridor you had a job getting past him – and those ears of his. He never spoke to me, apart from the day I made my home debut. The corridors at Turf Moor were so narrow that two people couldn't pass without facing each other. I saw Bob Lord coming towards me and thought: 'Oh shit, do I pull off into another room and hide or do I just keep walking?' In the end, I kept walking and we both had to stop so he could get his big belly round me. I was trying not to make eye contact in case I found myself in trouble. We had almost got past each other when he grabbed my arm and said: 'Well done today.' That was it and he walked on past.

I was lucky. We had a great team at Turf Moor in those days with players like former England man Martin Dobson, future international Trevor Steven, Mickey Phelan and Northern Ireland's Billy Hamilton. I had massive respect for Martin Dobson as a great old pro and he took me under his wing a bit. I'll always remember the advice he gave me. The social temptations for a young footballer are massive, even more so today. Martin would tell me: 'Always look after number one. Keep focused on what you are aiming to be and don't let other people distract you. Then you can do very well.' It was my great fortune to be in a dressing room with Martin. It's where players can talk, let off steam at times, and express their feelings. That is what players do now, and as a manager I have to respect that. That is why it is important to have someone like Martin who the others can look up to and respect.

Mind you, all that help he gave me came at a cost. He said one day: 'Lawsy, is it right that you are something of a handyman as a builder? Well, you owe me. I have some work I need doing in the garden.' I thought it was only going to be a five-minute job. But I had to build a wall and dig out trenches. And he let me do it all by myself. So yes, I do think I paid him back.

As a young player I would often get asked to go for a drink. Remembering Martin's advice, I would say 'no.' Probably some of the others thought I was a bit of a miserable bugger. Yet all I was bothered about was being a professional footballer and I wasn't going to let anything else get in the way. Nowadays, with all the money in the game, I see good young players and think that with two or three years of real hard graft and application there is a chance for them to become a millionaire. I always ask them the sort of question instilled into me by Martin Dobson: 'Could you have given more? Could you have done better? Could you have been more professional?' If the answer is yes to any of those questions then they have not given it their best shot. They have let themselves down and that is why they have failed.

Brian Miller, the manager who gave me my first chance, was also a hard taskmaster. He was Burnley through and through, the only club he ever played for as a tough-tackling wing-half who was capped by England in 1961, the season after he helped the Clarets win the title. He was a big sergeant-major figure with closely cropped hair. Miller could be a bit loopy at times but we all had a lot of respect for him. He always said what he thought and wanted us to give our all for the club. You knew when he was not happy because his head would go completely red. That was a time to stay out of his way. At half-time in one game he was having a go at our centre-half for not heading the ball.

'I'm trying boss,' the lad protested.

'Well you're not trying hard enough,' fumed Miller. 'It's easy, I'll show you. Just imagine the ball is there.' And he headed the door with such force that he headed a massive hole in it. We all held our breath and went quiet. 'Hey look, it doesn't hurt does it?' said Miller. But then he walked out of the room and I reckon he must have had some real pain.

I loved it at Burnley and had a real good rapport with the fans who voted me the player of the season when we went up. They were fanatical. Although they caned you for playing badly, the euphoria they whipped up in the good times was unbelievable. On the downside, Burnley were always a selling club. They always had to let their best players go. And the season after promotion we went straight back down again despite doing well in both cups. We got to the quarter-finals of the FA Cup and the semis in the League Cup with the club banking about £600,000. Unbeknown to me, this was to be my last season at Turf Moor. Brian Miller was sacked after our relegation in May 1983 and John Bond replaced him. His arrival was the beginning of the end for me.

We all knew about Bond's flamboyant past at Manchester City and sure enough he swaggered into Turf Moor, big cigar, big ego and plenty of jewellery. He was big and brash and he seemed to have little respect for anyone in the dressing room. We went to the Isle of Man as part of our pre-season preparations and he was bothered most about stocking up with his cigars. Once, on the way to training, he stopped the bus to go into a tobacconist shop to get his beloved cigars.

All Bond was interested in was big, big, big. He brought in all his old cronies on big wages and didn't want anything to do with those who were already there. It was his big spending that was to be the demise of the club. Bond showed total disrespect for Martin Dobson. That hurt Martin, and it hurt me. Bond had never seen me play and he never spoke to me. The only time he did he had a real smug smile on his face and sneered: 'You're not good enough. You're not wanted here.' I was stunned. I'd hardly missed a game for four seasons. It was all so sad. I did not want to leave Burnley having been so happy there. But after Bond's arrival, I could not wait to get out and just took the first opportunity that came along. I was 21 years of age and had made 152 league appearances for the Clarets, scoring 12 goals.

But I had many cherished memories, once taking over in goal during a big derby against Blackpool. We were reduced to ten men when Alan Stevenson was sent off for kicking someone up the backside after a challenge he didn't like. For some reason I'd always fancied myself as a keeper and was first to volunteer to pick up the gloves. There I was, all five feet nine inches of me, trying to fill the goal against a Blackpool side which had Alan Ball pulling the strings. I'm sure Bally must have fancied his chances but luckily I managed to pull off a couple of good saves, and we beat them. I got a lot of mickey-taking from the lads but was praised in the papers – maybe I missed my real vocation.

On the other side of the coin, I have always been blessed with a powerful shot. Once with the Clarets, I let fly from 25 yards with an effort that I swear was flying into the top corner until it hit the referee on the head and knocked him out cold. I don't remember what they called him, but I do know he had the name 'Mitre' printed on his forehead. It was one of the funniest things I have ever seen. He keeled over completely.

Another time at Burnley I was 'fortunate' enough to get an award for the best televised goal of the season. If only there had been Sky cameras present in those days, you would still be seeing it over and over again. Unfortunately it was an own goal, from all of 45 yards. We were at Gillingham. Steve Bruce, who had been at the same Wallsend Boys Club as me, was playing for them and he didn't half take the piss out of me afterwards. There was a ball coming across the field at me from one direction and a player coming to put me under pressure from the other. I thought I would play it back to Alan Stevenson who was standing on the edge of his box. Somehow I hit it so sweetly that Alan was left vainly trying to grasp the ball out of the air as it flew over him and, without bouncing, hit the back of the net. Everybody in the ground burst out laughing – apart from me. What quality: it got goal of the season on Gillingham's local TV. I've hit some good ones at the right end over the years – but none better than that one.

It was at Burnley that I met and married my first wife Margaret – and where our daughter Danielle was born. Danielle became the 'little miss' who arrived after my 'big miss' of the night before. We were playing away at Crystal Palace in the fifth round of the FA Cup. With a quarter-final place at stake it was a big match for both clubs and a tight one as well. Defences were very much on top. Then we got a penalty and that was my job. It's a role I always used to relish and I had a good record. But this time I missed and the game finished goalless. Anyway, the drama of it must have sent Margaret into labour and the very next day Danielle was born prompting the headline 'Big miss becomes Little Miss.' It was a happy moment for us and I was even happier when Burnley won the replay at Turf Moor before falling to

Sheffield Wednesday at the next hurdle.

But my Burnley chapter would not be complete without mentioning Dora Whitefield, the dear old landlady who took me in after my unhappy experiences living in digs. I was the last of about six Burnley players, including Brian Flynn, who stayed with her over the years. Dora worked at the club and everybody loved her. She had lost her husband many years earlier and, with no family, lived on her own in a little terraced house near the ground. Dora would stand no nonsense, mind you. She would bollock me good and proper if I did something wrong and would be there waiting, tapping her feet if I was back late. And, she would threaten to tell the manager. But she taught me a lot and I loved her to bits.

I kept in touch with Dora through my various moves and I would sometimes visit her at weekends, by which time she was too old to take in players. She was on her own and yet I felt she was part of my family. I would fetch her across for weekends at my home occasionally as her health began to deteriorate. One night I got a phone call from the hospital in Burnley telling me Dora had fallen over wandering the streets. They said the only person she could turn to was me. Immediately I drove over to the hospital and said I would keep an eye on her as best I could. When she returned home I kept in touch with a neighbour to make sure she was OK. But it quickly became clear that, although her body was sound enough, her mind was going. Her doctors carried out tests which showed it was no longer safe for her to live on her own. Dora had to go into an old people's home, which was really hard for me as well because I had to take her out of the house where she had lived most of her life.

With no-one else around, I had to be the executor for Dora's estate and looked for a home for her. I didn't have a clue really, but knew the cost of the home would have to be offset by the sale of her house. How sad is that considering how hard she had worked all her life – and her husband too, when he was alive, delivering milk around the streets of Burnley by horse and cart. Eventually we found a suitable home for Dora and the house was sold for little more than peanuts – £12,000 I think, was the price.

Dora would keep telling me she didn't like her new place and wanted to go back to her own home. She seemed so upset; it made me wonder about the care she was getting. I was always supposed to arrange visits in advance, but one day I decided to turn up unannounced and what I found turned my stomach. Dora was sitting there in a soaking wet armchair. Her clothes were sodden and she had obviously urinated. Worse, she had evidently been left like that for a while. No-one had gone to clean her up.

I knew immediately that this was not the right place for her. After all she had done in her life and all her help for others, she deserved better than that. I couldn't find anywhere in the Burnley district. By this time I was playing for Forest and a thought struck me: 'Why don't I bring her over to the Nottingham area and find a home there so she can be near me?' I found somewhere suitable in the village where I lived. Dora still recognised me and I would try to see her every other day. Sadly, she had a fall and had to be transferred to hospital.

By now her mind had completely gone, but one day she made me laugh when suddenly she blurted: 'Brian, you know I can't give you any children any more. I want you to go and find somebody else.' I did my best to pacify her saying it didn't matter and that I only wanted to be with her. But she was insistent and began shouting. Everyone in the room looked over at us and I'm sure they must have wondered just what was going on.

Eventually Dora was well enough to return home where she passed away a few months later. My family were the only ones at the funeral. We arranged her final wish, which was to have her ashes spread near her husband's grave. To me, Dora was much, much more than an old landlady. I just hoped that what I was able to do for her made her final years as pleasant as possible. What made losing Dora doubly painful was that it came not long after I had seen my own mother die.

***

The Owen Coyle departure from Burnley is well documented and the club chose Brian Laws to be his replacement. As a manager he'd had success at Scunthorpe United working on a shoestring. At Sheffield Wednesday there was no success and he was asked to leave. At the time of Owen Coyle's appointment, he had, in fact, been fancied by the directors to take over at Burnley but the Sheffield Wednesday chairman refused Burnley permission to talk to him. Thus it was Owen Coyle who arrived replacing Steve Cotterill.

Much has been made since Laws' departure of the choice the directors' made in selecting Laws when Coyle walked out. (Entertainment Heroes and Villains *published by Vertical Editions*)

It was an appointment that left just about every supporter mystified. He had just been dismissed by Sheffield Wednesday with them in the relegation places. Time has done nothing to make supporters feel any differently. If the supporters were underwhelmed, the players were simply staggered. It was against this background that he arrived at Turf Moor and his first game was at Old Trafford. Despite the scepticism and the questions being asked, he received the warmest of welcomes onto the pitch.

***

From Chapter 15: Parachuted Into the Premiership

Who could have predicted that within a month of leaving Sheffield Wednesday I would be back in work? Certainly not me, or that I would be managing in the Premier League for the first time. But I had strong links with Burnley and so the events that saw me take charge at Turf Moor, dramatic though they were, could not have been more far-fetched. Burnley had closely examined my record at Sheffield Wednesday. They had figures to show that I had over-achieved with limited resources. I had a high return in points for pounds spent. Besides, life is full of surprises … more so in football that in most other walks of life.

Take, for instance, the circumstances that saw me undertake a parachute jump during my time at Hillsborough. I still can't believe I've written that sentence. It was all in a very good cause, mind you, but the result of a rather rash promise. Not that I regret it one bit. The story unfolded after I took a call from a charity organiser from Sheffield Children's Hospital. At Sheffield Wednesday, we had close links with the hospital and the fundraiser told me about the plight of an 11-year old boy from Scunthorpe called Daniel Grice. Daniel was in the hospital suffering from terminal leukaemia. Could I pay him a visit to give him a lift?

We are lucky in football to be in a position where we are asked to do this sort of thing. It's a pleasure and a privilege and I've always been one to take such a responsibility seriously. So, as an ex-manager of Daniel's hometown club I went along to see him. In the ward I picked him out straightaway. His pillow case and duvet cover had Scunthorpe United emblazoned all over. Daniel gave me a big smile when I walked in and we hit it off right away. For all the problems he had – he had a really bright personality. I discovered that his illness had come to light after he'd played football and there was this bruise on his leg which wouldn't go. It turned the family's life upside down but they would always be at his bedside.

Daniel's big concern was to raise awareness of the disease in order to help others. He'd done a walk for the hospital charity and was trying to think of other ways of fundraising. Daniel and his dad came up with parachuting – and dared me to do a jump. Flippantly, I said yes. What else could I say? But it was tongue in cheek and I didn't think I'd hear any more about it. Then, a few weeks later, I received through the post an information pack for a jump at Hibaldstow airfield in Lincolnshire.

One word popped out of my mouth. I just went 'fuck!' I couldn't not do it, could I? So I rang the parachute club to ask what was involved. They said I would be jumping from 15,000 feet – and not to worry. I didn't need to practice! 'It'll be all right on the day,' they said. I was totally out of my comfort zone. But, they advertised the jump on the children's hospital website and raised over £10,000 – another reason why I had to go ahead.

All too quickly came the morning of the jump, which was in July, 2008. I've never been so nervous in my life. Puts even the prospect of playing in front of 100,000 people at Wembley or standing on the touchline in front of a baying mob in the shade. But it was only when I was going through the basics with an instructor that the reality hit me. I was to be flown to a great height and then jump out of a perfectly serviceable aircraft. I hadn't taken in the reality of a 15,000 feet leap until a few weeks earlier when, after the jump had been arranged, I was flying on holiday. There was a digital display of the flight details and when we got to 15,000 feet I looked out of the window. We were above the clouds and I could barely see the ground, bloody high, bloody hell!

It was to be a tandem jump and I was strapped to one of these parachute guys. There were just four hooks securing us together. I'd have preferred to have been behind him and let him hit the ground first. But, oh no, I was the front man. Up we went in a small plane which was very noisy. My partner tapped me on the shoulder and pointed at the altimeter in front of me. At 7,000 feet we were at cloud level. He indicated the reading again when we reached 12,000 feet and just said 'get ready.' But how do you prepare yourself for something like this? I was sweating profusely and my heart was thumping as we levelled off and the door was opened. Together, we shuffled to the opening. He said: 'Right, lift your feet and cross your arms.' He was still inside the plane and I was outside it. We seem to be an age suspended in that position. I'm thinking: 'Go! Let's bloody do it!'

Then we lean forward and hurtle down at 100 miles per hour.

Panic: I can't feel the guy behind me. Is he still there? I think I'll scream but we're hurtling so fast that the only screaming is in my head. There's nothing coming out of my mouth because of the air rushing into my face. We were a minute in free-fall and the only time I knew the other guy was still there was when the parachute opened. It had been the most frightening minute of my life. Talk about an adrenalin rush. When we landed safely I swear I could have lifted a car with my bare hands. I suppose it's why those adrenalin-junkie skydivers do it over and over again. But for me it was my first jump and my last.

The rewards were tremendous, though. Not least the fact that Daniel was there. Tragically, he died the following month. I'm just glad that he was able to see the fundraising idea in action. Sky was among the television crews at the airfield and the jump can still be viewed on the internet. I've got nothing but admiration for Daniel. I'm in awe of people like him. He never thought about himself, only about his mum and dad. His attitude was so uplifting. I spoke at Daniel's funeral and still keep in touch with his family.

Only a month or so later I met up with another young kid from Scunthorpe facing a similar plight – James Neal, aged 13. I wasn't prepared to do another sky jump but I did try to change James' allegiance to Sheffield Wednesday and he came with us to a game. I didn't succeed as he stayed loyal to Scunthorpe. James died the following year and I did what I could to support his family. It's so important for players and managers to help where possible. We are looked up to as heroes and the effect we can have on people's lives is priceless.

And so to my Premiership adventure. Trouble is, there wasn't a parachute in sight. The timing wasn't the best, either, even though it was an exciting opportunity. I was drained physically and mentally at the end of my time at Sheffield Wednesday. I loved my time there but felt I had exhausted the players too. I had wrung them dry with the squad we had; got as much out of them as I possibly could. We went nine games in which we managed a few draws but no wins. I still felt there were more than enough games for us to stay up. Yet my replacement, Alan Irvine, went on to have the same problem I had, no money. Anyway I felt my time was up after a defeat at Leicester. If you can't change the players then it's easier to change the manager. I thought the feeling was mutual. I had a great rapport with the fans and wanted the club to stay in the Championship. I felt a new voice might help and there was enough time to get the team safe. It was a disappointment to me when they didn't stay up.

There was a positive for me in leaving. I was drained and could take my first break from the game in many years. I knew there was no easy route back but at least I could enjoy the rarity of spending Christmas with the family, thinking it would be no bad thing if I didn't return until the following season. Then again, you can never choose your opportunities in football; certainly not the timing. And a chance came up that would have been impossible to refuse. Remember at this point that it had always been my belief that I would have to take a team up to the top flight in order to operate at the highest level. Here I was, losing my job at a club fighting relegation from the

Championship and suddenly in the sights of a Premier League outfit … albeit one also fighting against the drop. But while I accept that the move will have surprised people, the job is the same at whatever level you operate. It's about managing people and I had a lot of experience in this regard. I'd been a manager for 16 years up to that point and nobody could say that I hadn't served my apprenticeship. Not only that, but I'd played at the top level.

What triggered my change of fortune was Owen Coyle's decision to leave Burnley for Bolton. Owen had taken Burnley to the Premiership in the first place and I completely understood his reasons for leaving. Beyond looking to advance his career, perhaps he'd taken the Clarets as far as it was possible to go at that time. But the fans didn't see it Owen's way. They felt he should have been 100% loyal and they let him know that. I looked on, wondering if Burnley's previous interest in me might be re-ignited. On the other hand, they were now in a higher league and my circumstances had changed as well. So, I didn't think I was in with much of a shout.

That is, until I spoke with Brendan Flood, the Burnley director who was the club's main backer. Meeting Brendan changed my thoughts. He and the chairman, Barry Kilby, knew that it would be a tough job for anybody to keep Burnley up, especially after they had lost their hero manager. The club had the lowest budget in the Premier League by a mile but they knew I could work within limited resources, as I had done at Hillsborough and elsewhere. Also fresh in their mind was that my Wednesday team had beaten Burnley twice during their promotion season, scoring eight goals in the process. They knew the kind of football I played, which was very much in line with Turf Moor traditions. It was an unusual one from the outside looking in, but considering my affinity with the club there was a natural fit. Brendan asked for my CV and then I got a call about taking the job. I had a great belief that I could do it and it wasn't just about staying up. If we dropped we had to be in a position to go up again. And we did – only for me to lose my job at Burnley just over a year later. It still rankles with me as the most hurtful parting of my career.

∗ ∗ ∗

From Chapter 16: In at Old Trafford … Out to a Bolted Boardroom Door

Looking back, the reasons why it was an unequal battle trying to keep Burnley in the Premier League are pretty obvious. Even at the time I went there, in mid-January 2010, the omens were stacking up against us. The team was competitively placed at third from bottom but hadn't won in the league for 10 games. Not that this could possibly be in my head when I took charge of my first game – at Old Trafford of all places. I had gone from one of the lowest feelings of my career in leaving Wednesday to an incredible high. Manchester United gave our club a refreshing reception and the Burnley supporters were superb that day. OK, we lost 3 – 0; no surprise there, a respectable scoreline even. And I recall we played really well. We could even have taken the lead only for David Nugent, through on goal, to miss the target. That only served to wake up United who went straight on down the other end and Wayne Rooney scored.

The Old Trafford experience apart, my eyes were wide open. It's become almost a routine for promoted teams to have a good start, as Burnley had done. They were used to winning games and all the enthusiasm, the momentum they had built up, carried them forward. But the adrenalin surge only lasts for so long. These were not necessarily Premier League players. They were Championship players who had risen above their expectations. Eventually, there comes a stage when they are mentally drained and get demoralised. That's what happened to Burnley. There was also the shock to the players of losing Owen Coyle. They were close to him, as you would expect. I had no quick fix, but I did need to reorganise things behind the scenes. This proved the hardest part of the job. Owen had taken all his staff with him; there was no back-up and I also met with a certain resistance from the players. In a short time we had to bring in six new staff all the way down to a chief scout and a physio. And on top of that, the transfer window was shut. It was incredibly difficult, as you can imagine.

As is the way of the world, the media began to put my two winless runs together, the nine games at Wednesday and the first four at

The Best of Burnley

Burnley, which were all defeats. It certainly wasn't a losing streak. There had been some draws in my closing sequence at Hillsborough and some very narrow defeats in games that could have gone either way. For instance in my penultimate game at Sheffield Wednesday we had the better of a close game at Doncaster only for Billy Sharpe to pop up with a headed winner near the end. That was a cruel blow and the sort of thing that happens when you're having a difficult time. Another reason why I felt it was below the belt to put the Wednesday and Burnley stats together is that winning in the Premier League is especially hard at the best of times. But it was a great feeling to get my first victory for Burnley in the next game, 2 – 1 at home to West Ham on February 6th. I had almost forgotten how it felt to win. Beyond that it was a case of winning over Owen's players and getting three points goes a long way towards that. Then they start to believe in your methods and your ethos. I felt it was important to keep a similar style and it remained pretty free-flowing. But it was also kamikaze stuff at times and I had to curtail that tendency. The team's desire to go forward was great, but their enthusiasm to get back and defend wasn't.

All things considered, it was a very tall order and our records of three wins at the back end of the season was better than that of other relegated clubs like Hull and Blackpool in similar circumstances. We were actually very close to surviving. The decider was away at Wigan. Had we won there, Wigan would have gone down. It's a very fine line. As for the reaction of the supporters, I wasn't their favoured choice when I took the job. Burnley's promotion to the Premier League had attracted a new breed of supporter and I was up against those. But they were willing to give me an opportunity, albeit a brief one. Their anger at Coyle's departure was bound to be channelled somewhere and it was me who copped for it. I didn't take it as personal, at least not at first. Beating Manchester United at Turf Moor early in the season had also changed expectancy levels. A team like Burnley might do that once in 100 meetings. Probably it was the worst thing that could have happened. The only way we were ever going to win was when every player on the park played to the absolute maximum. If one of them is off-key, it's difficult. If it's two, you lose. So the task was almost impossible.

But we finished on a high with a 4 – 2 home win over Spurs in the last game. Harry Redknapp's side were looking for a top-four place and took an early two-goal lead. The response of our players in overturning it gave me great heart. It showed the fans that the players were with me. And the great lift from that result carried over into a board meeting on the way ahead. It was felt that if we could keep the squad together and add a couple with Championship experience we could bounce straight back. Everyone agreed that the minimum we should be looking at was a place in the play-offs. Finishing in the top six was effectively my remit. I thought the supporters would go with me on that. Still, the mood was brittle enough for me to think: 'God forbid if we lose two games on the bounce.' But, in truth, we never did. And yet I was fired. Had we won what proved to be my last game – a defeat at home to Scunthorpe – we would have gone fourth in the table.

My future had become the subject of intense speculation ahead of the previous game at Barnsley. Those rumours were at the back of my mind. On top of that, Burnley had not won at Oakwell for 79 years. Talk about pressure; but I never showed it to the players. It turned into one of our best performances. Barnsley took the lead and people must have thought 'here we go'. The geography at Oakwell is not great for visiting managers. Their fans are at the end that houses the dressing-rooms. It was a long walk at half-time with us trailing 1 – 0 and I got a lot of stick. This shocked me because we were actually playing well. I concentrated on working with the players who listened and we stepped up a gear to win deservedly 2 – 1. At the final whistle, instead of cheers, all I heard from our supporters was jeers. That was heart-breaking. It was almost as if they were disappointed we'd won. What true supporter goes to a game with that attitude? The whole situation beggared belief. It was surreal. That's when I thought: 'We've got a problem here.' The players got the same vibes. They were stunned. One of them said: 'That's disgraceful. What's going on here?'

It was against that bizarre background that I got a message from the board – a reassuring one – after the game. I received a text from Chairman Kilby congratulating me on the win and saying it was a great achievement. He also said the board were right behind me.

And so the scene shifts to Turf Moor for the visit of Scunthorpe two days later. The atmosphere was very poor and I could sense something wasn't right. I named the same team and prepared them as normal. But right from the first whistle, any mistake by a player was seized on by supporters as an opportunity to have a go at me. Let me tell you that any fan who thinks that booing will make a player better is having a laugh. In that climate, it's almost impossible to relax, enjoy the game and play your best.

Not surprisingly, we failed to get the win or even a draw. Although we were sixth and still in a play-off spot, the Barnsley game told me I had to watch out for my next defeat. Having lost 2 – 0, I knew the writing was on the wall but I followed my normal routine, which was always to go into the boardroom after a game. I got there only to find the door shut and locked. There was no-one there, they had all left. That certainly told me something even if I didn't know it already. The only people left were my family sitting in a corner waiting. We were all looking at each other, thinking 'something's going on here.'

All I could do was get in the car and drive home. I knew that Kilby was away in America, so I tried to make contact with Brendan Flood on the journey back. He didn't answer his phone or return my call; another massive alarm bell. Other than the ringing inside my head, I heard nothing more that night.

It was the following day that I received a phone call, THE phone call. The man on the other end was Kilby, which surprised me considering he was away and not at the game. It was the shortest conversation you can imagine. If I said it only lasted a minute that would not be overstating the case. Kilby came straight to the point. 'Look,' he said. 'There's no point beating about the bush. We'd like you to stand down.'

I said: 'I totally disagree. However, you've made your mind up. We'll talk when you get back.'

We never spoke again. About an hour later, Burnley put out an announcement that I was leaving. I was disappointed both with the decision and the manner of it. I thought I had a better working relationship and understanding with the club than that. For all my love for the club over the years, this wasn't a pleasant experience. I can't dress it up any other way. The supporters upset me and I was dismayed at the way it ended from the club's point of view.

I did speak afterwards to Flood. I said we hadn't lost two games on the bounce all season. He replied that he hadn't known that. Brendan's reasoning was that if we lost again, the supporters would turn on the board. I thought they would have been stronger than that. Not many managers lose their job in that kind of position. We were on target for the play-offs.

Burnley then decided to bring in a very young manager in Eddie Howe of Bournemouth, where he had made a promising start in the job. No disrespect to Eddie, the youngest manager in the Football League, but when he was appointed by Burnley at age 31 in 2009, the change didn't really have the desired effect. Burnley finished well short of the play-offs. Change doesn't necessarily equal progress and what was so galling for me was that the board could have been more supportive, especially as I was on target for our objective.

Brian Laws' book and the Burnley chapters leave so many questions unanswered. His time at Burnley was really quite turbulent and controversial. We'd all still like to know details of the problems he had to overcome when faced by the Premiership squad; was it real antipathy, a lack of respect, a loss of any real interest in playing for Burnley once the Coyle spirit had vanished? He mentions 'resistance' but doesn't expand on that which he could have done without actually naming players if that was what he wanted to avoid.

Certain games stood out as being real let-downs – the home games against Blackburn, Wolves and Portsmouth were absolute no-shows by the Burnley players. To this day I'll wager that at least one of those games would have been won had Coyle still been at Burnley. And for sure, I'd love to know what really happened at half-time in the infamous home game against Manchester City when there are stories that there were clashes with players and Kevin MacDonald simply walked out and went to meet friends and family in a local drinking club. It was a game that seemed to sum up the debacle that was developing at the club.

There were certainly moves to dismiss Laws before the end of the

Premiership season but it was decided to stick with him. Because of the victories at the end of the season, it was decided to stay with him through the summer and allow him to continue in the Championship.

If Owen Coyle was the right man at the right time then there is no question that Brian Laws was the wrong man at the wrong time. The directors will always ask, when criticised by supporters, well who would you have appointed? If we knew the precise details of exactly who had thrown their hat into the ring and expressed interest (Villas-Boas was certainly one, along with Sven Goran Ericsson of all people, Iain Dowie was another), who was approached, who was interviewed, which of them wanted too much money; then perhaps we could answer the question.

One thing that astonished us all, just as much as the appointment itself, was the length of the contract and the generous salary. It cost a lot to dismiss him and his staff. The job cried out for a short term appointment and the carrot of a large bonus if the new man was successful at the end of the season.

5

1982 And So to Doncaster

From *Something to Write Home About*, the Magazine of the London Clarets. Article by Dave Thomas

9 February 1982 is a date imprinted in my head. I hadn't got much longer as Deputy Head at St Margaret's School in Horsforth, Leeds. At Easter I'd be gone, heading for Thorpe, a small ex-mining village in South Leeds. The idea of being the Head of a little village school had always appealed. Except this was no leafy lane little village nestling in the greenery of the Dales or the mellowness of the Cotswolds; this was an ex-industrial village with closed down railway yards, an old quarry and derelict pits. It was a tiny place of terraced rows and a council estate and, given where it was, didn't know whether it belonged to Leeds or Wakefield. This was a school and a part of Leeds that was quite the opposite of the one I would leave behind.

Both Thorpe village and the school were shabby and run down with a staff that had been there in residence for many years. If you'd said 'boo' to them they wouldn't so much jump but just slowly turn round and yawn. It didn't bode well that one of them was draped in cobwebs when I first found her in a cupboard. Another year and she'd have been a Miss Faversham lookalike in a Dickens novel. Another one, the ageing deputy, had a smiley face with one of those comb overs that Bobby Charlton and Ralphie Coates used to sport; when they ran their long strands of hair would float behind them. Nothing fazed mild-mannered Derek, a lovely man but he'd been there since Mafeking.

The Best of Burnley

Prior to the interview I'd visited the school and spent a worrying couple of hours there. I'd have my work cut out, I realised. For the interview I polished my shoes, something I hadn't done since I'd got married. I noticed one of the interviewing panel staring at them as I sat before a long table at which they all sat. I like to think it was the shoes that got me the job. It was either that, or bad luck.

However that was all to come but for the time being, life had a nice comfort-zone feel to it and a settled routine in affluent Horsforth; a nice suburb, nice shops, nice children, nice grateful parents who all sent nice presents at Christmas and on my nice birthday. You get the picture. In the meantime there was a toddler daughter to bring up, half a dozen hens in a shed at the bottom of our garden, and a football team at Burnley to follow whenever we got the chance.

Keeping hens was rather nice. We had a huge garden and the hens had an enclosed area, a nice warm dry shed and they hopped into it every night and then one of us would go down and shut the pop-hole in case the foxes got in. The first time an egg was laid Mrs T actually phoned me at school to give me the good news. For most folks it was a telegram in those days to announce the first baby. We celebrated the arrival of an egg. When they really got going, going down the garden every morning, first thing, to collect the eggs was something of which we never got tired. They cost a fortune in straw and feed but nevertheless collecting those eggs was akin to getting something for nothing. And boy did they taste good with yokes the colour of the sun. We grew potatoes and so on the occasion we had egg and chips we thought, 'boy this really is *The Good Life*.'

All this was well and good until two disasters happened. One night the fox did get in and we hadn't fastened the pop-hole. The feathers and corpses the next morning made a sorry sight. Undeterred, we got a new batch and settled them in although we didn't go as far as giving them names. Disaster number two was the intruder who then started sneaking in and, one by one over a few nights, removed the hens equating them with free food. Whoever it was wasn't the sharpest tool in the box. The nearby houses were mostly flats inhabited by social service cases, students and dropouts. A trail of feathers one morning led to one house in particular and there in the dustbin was a carcase. The police of course thought it was a huge joke, did bugger all and sadly that was the end of our hen-keeping.

The toddler on Saturdays was deposited with grandparents in Todmorden near Burnley so we could go to the match. We would return to meat and 'tatie pie with mashed carrots. It never varied. Todmorden at this time was famed for its UFO sightings. In fact the valley was known as UFO alley there were so many. The most famous story was that of PC Alan Godfrey in late 1980. Todmorden rarely got in the news unless it flooded, but the PC Godfrey story really hit the headlines.

PC Godfrey had been on patrol during the night of 28 November 1980. He was looking for stray cows that were apparently roaming around on the edge of the town. Unable to locate them he was about to sign off and return to base and was driving along Burnley Road about 5 in the morning. Then, in front of him he saw an oval shaped object rotating at high speed on the deserted road ahead. Trees and bushes were shaking in its slipstream. The officer stopped and sketched the object on a pad that was in the front of the car. Suddenly there was a burst of light and the next thing he knew he was driving the car again but a hundred yards further down the road. There was no sign of the object. He stopped the car and turned round and getting out of the vehicle he examined the spot where he had seen the mysterious phenomenon. In the road was a dried circular patch marked with swirl patterns. The rest of the road was wet as it had rained earlier. Back at the station he then realised that in the timeline of events he tried to figure out, there were 15 minutes or so that he could not account for. Another motorist who had been three miles further along the road reported strange lights. Another police patrol engaged in a look-out for stolen motor vehicles up on the moors high above Todmorden also reported a brilliant light descending into the valley at the same time that PC Godfrey had his encounter.

When PC Godfrey was later subjected to hypnosis, he described being transported into the alien craft, a metallic dome with a row of windows, by a beam of light. Inside, he met a human-like being named Josef whose clothing resembled those of Biblical times. Once aboard, he was examined and questioned. In all the years since the

The Best of Burnley

event happened, he has never once changed his story.

It wasn't the first time that PC Godfrey had been involved in something unexplained. Six months earlier the body of a bloke from miles away was found on top of a coal heap at a depot almost in the centre of Todmorden by the railway lines. On 6 June Jan Adamski had set out from his home in Tingley near Leeds to do some shopping. The next day he was to attend a family wedding. His body was found five days later by Trevor Parker, the son of the coal yard owner. On examination it was found he had died of a heart attack but had peculiar burn marks on his neck and shoulders. Forensic scientists could not identify the mysterious cream that had been applied to the burns. The case has not been solved to this day and there are strong suspicions that this was a classic alien abduction. Why, was it asked, if this was a murder, the result of family quarrels as was suggested later, should the body have been dumped at the very top of a large coal heap in the middle of a town many miles away from Tingley? What caused the mystery burns? What was the mysterious unidentified cream? The coroner stated it was the most puzzling case in his whole career describing it as a most bizarre place to leave a body.

More explicable were the horrendous floods of 1982 in the town. There were no complications about this, just the river, much of which flowed through culverts under the town. These were underneath the streets and houses in the valley, overflowing after torrential rain. A thunderstorm started in the late afternoon and within 30 minutes the roads had become rivers. Buses were marooned in the deep water. Cars and dustbins floated down the waterways. People went swimming in the waters of the flooded cricket field. It took months to clean up the town with many people unable to use their homes for several weeks.

Our Saturdays were especially good because this was a season when things were on the up. There was what we might today call the Last Harvest. A good group of Burnley young 'uns had miraculously come through, led by the wily and experienced Martin Dobson, with the great Billy Hamilton at centre-forward, and with the still agile Alan Stevenson in goal. But it was a season that started slowly with no sign at all that Manager Miller would find the formula that would see the season end so successfully.

The new chairman was John Jackson. Bob Lord had passed away leaving the club in a financial disaster zone. Derek Gill's report on the state of the club was damning. Jackson and Derek Gill got on famously – as long as there was a winning team. When things went pear-shaped in the next season the fracture lines would grow and deepen. When John Bond arrived after that, the divisions were as deep as the Grand Canyon.

My little school football team continued on Saturday mornings in the few months before I left St Margaret's. A couple of the lads went on to join the famed Pudsey Juniors set-up. There was a cracking young goalkeeper called Adrian Scott. I was certain he would go on to great things in professional football. But no, he didn't. But boy what a prospect he was at the age of 11. A guy I knew called Alan Cowley ran Pudsey Juniors. Years later the name would crop up again when Burnley hero Roger Eli and I worked on a book. Roger played for Alan at Pudsey Juniors around the same time that I was doing junior football. Without us knowing, our paths had already sort of crossed.

Leeds had recovered from the infamous Yorkshire Ripper, or at least the city streets were safer places. In May of '81 he was convicted and we all breathed a sigh of relief and got back to normal. At its worst the situation was dreadful and no woman went out alone. Every woman looked over her shoulder. Two of the attacks were within walking distance of where we lived in Headingley. Whenever I drove home at night once dark had descended I peered into every other car wondering, 'Is that him?' Everyone did. Drivers probably looked at me wondering the same.

Whilst Jimmy Adamson was manager of Leeds for his short spell at the same time as the Ripper murders, he was none too popular. When police went round the pubs playing the infamous Geordie accent tape, and asked, 'Does anyone recognise this voice?' The reply was inevitably, 'It's Jimmy bloody Adamson.' Jimmy Adamson at Leeds United was a strange one. If ever a man seemed out of place at a club it was Jimmy. I could never quite figure out how he fitted in. He had slammed Leeds and Don Revie often enough. When he was appointed I was quite taken aback. What became abundantly clear was that

The Best of Burnley

he was past his best. Appearances on the training ground dwindled. Drink took its toll. He was undermined by at least one senior player there. The directors were split over him. He confided he could never trust them. He had been such an integral part of my teenage years when he was a player at Burnley and then in the '70s when he very nearly produced his 'Team of the Seventies' at Turf Moor. At Leeds he seemed such a fish out of water until he called it a day and retired from football completely.

1982: Princess Diana was still married to Charles and gave birth to William, we had the Greenham Common demonstrations, the IRA bombing of Horse Guards parade, the collapse of Freddie Laker's airline, riots in Poland and Lech Walesa, the first 20p coins, Channel Four, the go-ahead for satellite television, and the death of Soviet leader Brezhnev. The Falkland's war began in April, Margaret Thatcher at the height of her powers, the Queen fended off a bedroom intruder and it wasn't Prince Philip, Pope John Paul was the first Pope to visit Britain.

We followed the Falklands War on TV and it felt like watching a cinema film, except it wasn't, it was real. You watched ships sink, aircraft crash and missiles hit home. You saw men killed and burned and maimed while you ate your tea. It was almost the first TV reality show. It was all manner of things: surreal, harrowing but compelling. It was the first time TV had graphically covered a war up close and personal. You sat and thought this is awful, I shouldn't be watching this – but you did.

Italy won the World Cup, Aston Villa won the European Cup and Tottenham won the FA Cup with Liverpool winning Division One, whilst Burnley went on to win Division Three. Jimmy Connors won Wimbledon, Larry Holmes was heavyweight boxing champion and Graham Gooch took his 'rebel' cricket team to South Africa. At Doncaster, Touching Wood won the St Leger.

On TV we watched *Dallas, Dukes of Hazard, Fantasy Island, The Love Boat, Dynasty, Magnum, Hill Street Blues, Knight Rider, The Fall Guy* and for the last time we watched *Tiswas*. Top films were *ET, Tootsie, An Officer and a Gentleman, Star Trek 2, Rocky 3, Blade Runner* and *Poltergeist. Ghandi* won best picture at the Academy Awards.

We listened to Human League, Bucks Fizz, Shakin' Stevens, Tight Fit, Madness, Adam Ant, Kraftwerk, Dexy's Midnight Runners, Culture Club, The Jam, Toto, Hall and Oates, Olivia Newton-John, Earth Wind and Fire, Paul McCartney, Orchestral Manoeuvres in the Dark, and even Chas and Dave.

By '82 I was well into the swing of keeping a personal diary at home when I'd sit down in the evening and scribble down the day's events. I found the entry that described the experience of watching Burnley 0 Runcorn 0 in the early November rounds of the FA Cup. It says it was one of the most excruciating experiences imaginable. Thank goodness there was the pie to look forward to back in Todmorden on the way home.

I used to cut things out of newspapers that caught my eye and stick them in the diary with the thought that one day I could look back at them. In September '81 there was one about people's pay. A council cleaner was on £48 a week. A crematorium attendant was on £66 a week. A newly qualified teacher got £72 a week. A Deputy Head – me – was on around £100 a week. The average fireman earned £118 a week and a police constable around £142. When I leapt to the heady heights of being a headmaster I started at £150 a week. God, the things I used to do. Many a time I cleaned out the boys' filthy urinal if the caretaker hadn't come in, got the gas boiler going down in the cellar when it went out, mopped flooded floors, cleaned out blocked drains, stood by the trolleys every dinnertime for 14 years to make sure these kids got a decent meal down them, shovelled snow off the drive and the steps every winter; and frequently acted as unpaid taxi driver ferrying sick kids home or accident-prone kids to the nearest hospital in Wakefield. If the secretary was away ill I did her job as well as a matter of course. I still have nightmares about doing the dinner books on Monday morning. By the time I finished there in '96 I was on £650 a week and earned every penny of it, especially with the added pleasure of trying to make sense of the new National Curriculum that landed on the mat in 12 great ring binders with things called attainment targets. I used to look at a dustbin lorry driver's wage with all the overtime and wondered why I bothered being a headteacher. Meanwhile the Archbishop of Canterbury was on £12,500 a year.

1982: and the football club was on the way to recovering from the sad final years of Bob Lord's chairmanship when he must have known he was hanging on to a sinking ship. The club was insolvent, cheques bounced as high as the ceiling and the safe was empty. People used to knock at the door to ask for payment of unpaid bills. Bob would shout to Albert Maddox, 'tell them I'm not in.' One wonders what he thought as he sat in his seat on a matchday and what he saw through his ageing, misted eyes, as he looked across to the deserted Longside on the opposite side of the ground with gates dwindling by the week. From where we lived in Leeds the club's plight was distant and never seemed real. We viewed it from afar. The glory days were gone and they were sad days for him and supporters alike. But he clung on as defiant and bullish as ever. His business empire of butchers shops and wholesale meat supply was a thing of the past.

The report that John Jackson commissioned Derek Gill to produce was damning. Throughout the club there had been a significant lack of communication and coordination with too many staff taking their instructions direct from Bob Lord. People were afraid to make decisions. Two crucial positions: general secretary and commercial manager, functioned poorly. These incumbents needed replacing. The secretary's office was an untidy shambles and administration over-manned and badly run. The secretarial disorganisation resulted in organisation by panic. One typist frequently sat around with little to do because most matters were considered too confidential for her to see. There was no systematic accounting. The activities of the maintenance man were a mystery. The secretary's office lacked organisation and the workload was determined by the latest crisis telephone call. One example: 30 copies of an FA letter for the players were still lying in the secretary's office three weeks later. Basic record keeping was inadequate. Crucial information was stored on loose-leaf papers that soon became buried by the mass of documents that were piled up following years of malfunction. Methods of administrative operation had not changed in many years; preparation of wages was by outdated methods with the entire staff paid weekly and mostly in cash. There was overdue work that staff seemed unaware of. Books of cheques signed by two directors were left lying around so that the

1982 And So to Doncaster

secretary was effectively the sole signatory. A computerised service and its introduction was needed badly. There was little attempt to seek sponsorships from the local community. Lotteries provided the only real income. Key staff members showed little imagination.

Perhaps the most damning part of the report referred to Bob Lord: 'Travelling and incidental expenses of directors must be seen to be beyond reproach and this has not been the case in the past. So far I have avoided going back very far or creating a sort of witch-hunt, but I regret to state that I do not believe that the regular 'Cash Expenses' claimed by Mr Lord have been adequately detailed nor have they been substantiated by receipts. The secretary has been placed in the invidious position of being required to pass over cash on the authority of trivial note-paper requests of the then chairman. Supply of proper receipts would at least have enabled the club to reclaim VAT on the numerous meals claimed. Petrol receipts are superior evidence to 'X' miles at 20p per mile. No receipts for meals have been provided. The amounts involved last year are probably around £6,000 and the costs are submerged in the charges for travelling and hotel expenses.'

Too ill to attend a board meeting (Bob Lord had not long to live), John Jackson took the chair and went on to overlook a season of triumph. Martin Dobson was moved to a sweeper's role, the young lads blossomed, Trevor Steven was a diamond, the team began to win and the coffers began to fill. By the end of the season with Derek Gill taking care of the accounts and bringing in new sponsors, the club was well and truly solvent again. The turnaround was remarkable but if only someone there had possessed a crystal ball that might have warned them of what was to come.

'We thought we were such clever buggers,' says Derek Gill 30 years on.

1982: We went to a fair few games that season, and the one that sticks in the mind is the away game at Doncaster. We were eighth in the table, eight points behind the leaders Chesterfield when we went there to the ground called Belle View. In truth there was little that was belle about it. It was Tuesday 9 February on a night that was so cold that if you'd been a penguin you'd have thought twice about stepping outside. It was a 1-0 win and the goal was scored by a raiding full-back called Andy Wharton. I remember it well because we stood out in the open uncovered end and we shivered and froze all night. The ladies toilet was a little brick hut with an earthen floor. In the corner was a red bucket. I know that because Mrs T told me to stick my head round the door and take a look. I'm glad I did. Even in primitive Doncaster I would never have thought there would be something as basic as this. It is one of my treasured football memories, along with my Jimmy McIlroy autographs and a condom in a special packet with a picture of Adam Blacklaw on the front.

Jimmy signed all his autographs in clear, bold, legible handwriting. This is unlike the modern footballer whose scribble is an insult to the people who pay their wages and the kids who look up to them with real hero-worship. I was once told a lot of them think it's a joke and they have competitions to see who can produce the most indecipherable scrawl. As a token they might add the number from their shirt as a clue to who they are. It's the kind of doodling that kids do at the age of 3 in their nursery schools when they have a pencil in their hands for the first time. Nursery teachers call it mark-making. I don't bother with autographs any more. Condoms are far more interesting.

Anyway, the 1-0 win at Doncaster on that shivering night was another step in '82 to the away game at Southend that Burnley won 4-1 to seal the title. Doncaster was a hotchpotch of a ground, built on ash carted from the coalfields that filled the area and still provided work and power. One of the wooden stands had been jacked up and wheeled down the road to Belle View from where it once stood at Bennetthorpe, a former home of Doncaster Rovers. It was an impressive piece of re-cycling.

Doncaster Rovers had no great claims to fame. Perhaps the nearest is that the great Peter Doherty once played for them and steered them to promotion. Comedian Charlie Williams was once a centre-half there. He was one of the first black footballers. One of his jokes on the club circuit was that there were so many coalmines in the area that everybody in Doncaster was black, and so no-one noticed him. Racism was rampant, so when he was heckled he'd tell the audience, 'If you don't stop I'll come and live next door to you.' His catchphrase was 'Right me owld flower' and he came to prominence on two TV shows, *The Comedians* and *The Golden Shot*. As a footballer he once memorably said, 'I was never a fancy player but I could always stop them buggers that were.'

Alick Jeffrey is the other notable name associated with Doncaster Rovers and his is a tragic story. But for breaking his leg in an U23 international game he would have been signed by Manchester United. He had everything: power, ability, could shoot with either foot, head a ball magnificently, and when passing could land the ball on a sixpence. Matt Busby said that had he signed him, it is unlikely that Bobby Charlton would have got into his first team. Jeffrey was an original boy wonder. He signed for Doncaster as a youth because Peter Doherty beat Matt Busby to him. Busby was far from pleased and told Jeffrey he would one day come back for him. But, his broken leg ended any chance he had of a top-flight career. He was out of the game for a considerable length of time but made a come-back at Doncaster and played another 191 games scoring 95 goals.

Doncaster is hardly the tourist centre of the north but it is a place steeped in history. It goes back to Roman times. It is the home of the St Leger. The area once teemed with coalmines. It was once a thriving railway centre and its workshops built the Flying Scotsman and Mallard. It was an important location on the A1, the main route from London to Scotland, once known as the Great North Road. If history is your thing, in the surrounding areas are Conisborough Castle, Cusworth Hall and Brodsworth Hall. All are must-see places.

I've still got the programme from the Doncaster game. When we moved from the big old Victorian house we had in Headingley to a smaller one in the suburbs of Leeds, I threw away hundreds of old programmes. Today I can't believe what I did. At least I had the sense to keep some of them and picked the ones that had covers I liked. The Doncaster programme was one of them. Billy Bremner was their manager back then and Terry Cooper was at full-back. They were seventh from bottom and it cost just 30p. I like these little snapshots of yesteryear with their quaint adverts and the feel of a time gone by. Today's programmes are like glossy magazines and cost a fortune. For all their glitzy content, photographs and presentation they lack the 'feel' of the thin flimsy issues of the past with their handful of pages

The Best of Burnley

and brief pen pictures of players. The place to eat was Le Bistro (the players' choice). Yankees had the original and best Burgers. Cameron's beers were head and shoulders above the rest. Whelmar Homes built Doncaster's outstanding developments from just £12,000.

In his notes, Manager Bremner thought they'd played brilliantly at Norwich in a cup-tie in front of 3,000 of their own supporters. But they lost. He saw the Burnley game as a chance to get back to winning ways having already won 1-0 at Turf Moor earlier in the season.

It was only the second time I'd been anywhere near Doncaster. The first had been years earlier when I was a college student and a pal and I did a memorable trip from Todmorden down to Norfolk on his scooter. We stopped in Doncaster for a breakfast in a truckers' café. My backside was numb even at that early stage and when hours later this scooter reached Norfolk I got off and walked with bowed legs for a fortnight.

I'd like to say we came back from Doncaster on that February night on a high and well pleased with the win. But in fact the drive home in the car driven by the headmaster of the school where I worked was a nightmare and reduced us all to nervous wrecks. In my diary of the time I noted: 'God what a cold place it was. We stood at the open end with the Burnley mob and I can't remember feeling cold like it anywhere else, not even Oldham Athletic. Anyway Burnley won 1-0 and that was 16 games without defeat. It made up for the bitter cold and the lunatic driving of the headmaster. He doesn't drive; he just points the car at the space in front and puts his foot down, be it through red lights, straight across roundabouts, up the back ends of big Lorries, two inches behind little minis and we exited the car park at the ground playing dodgems with the other cars around him. For his pièce de résistance when at last we got to our back door in Headingley and he dropped us off, he roared away, or at least began to, before Mrs T had even got both feet out the door. We had to yell at him to stop. I'd seen adverts for cars that do 0 to 60 in nine seconds. I reckon his target was to do Doncaster to Leeds in nine minutes. We left the car park at 9.25 and astonishingly were in Leeds by 10. On this terrifying journey home we had oncoming vehicles flashing us, honking horns at us and other drivers shielding their eyes from his undipped headlights.'

'I'm not driving too fast for you am I?' he enquired once or twice as we cowered in our seats most of the time with our eyes closed. He and I parted company at Easter '82 when I moved to the headship at Thorpe.

He passed away in 2013. He will be remembered by me for his incredible driving.

***

26 years passed by and Doncaster was just a name I saw on Motorway signs as we sped down the M1 to Kent or Sussex. A helluva lot happened in those 26 years at Burnley and in my own life. I stayed at Thorpe School until 1996, watching fewer and fewer Burnley games. By 2008 we'd been through a procession of managers including Frank Casper, John Bond, Jimmy Mullen, Chris Waddle, Stan Ternent, Steve Cotterill and then Owen Coyle. Until 2000 there were more ups and downs than a fiddler's elbow until Stan got the club into the Championship. Having got the club as far as he could on an economy budget he was replaced by the dour Steve Cotterill, and when he too could get the players no further, and by the sound of things 'had lost the dressing room,' he was replaced by the bubbling energy and brightness of Owen Coyle.

After a shaky start to the 2008/09 season Coyle's team had been doing well and were well up near the top end of the table. There had been wonderful Carling Cup games against Chelsea and Arsenal. But then there was a slump and five league defeats on the bounce.

On Boxing Day, filled with turkey and stuffing and mince pies, we'd see them lose 1-2 at home to Barnsley and even after the defeat Burnley were still fourth. It was one of those games when the home side has all the shots, Jensen the goalkeeper only touched the ball three times, but twice it was to collect it from the back of the net. 16,500 were there and, with a new enthusiasm and spirit kindled by Coyle and his team, we had no thoughts of a defeat. The extra 5,000 spectators who had come largely because it was a Christmas game and a sort of traditional thing to do, must have wondered why they came. Next was the away game at Doncaster on 28 December and surely, we thought, there would be a recovery.

28 December 2008: Doncaster Rovers 2 Burnley 1

Driving to the Doncaster game I couldn't help thinking back 26 years to the last visit. My God, 26 years and I was now in my 60s. It had been 20 years since I'd last seen the headmaster who thought he was Juan Fangio. 26 years earlier it had been that ramshackle stadium where they used buckets for the ladies loos and the team was in the Third Division. You can't help being nostalgic.

Now it was a new ground – The Keepmoat Stadium – and when Doncaster had been to Turf Moor earlier in the season they had played Burnley off the park and we were lucky to take a point. In 26 years Doncaster had been right down to the bottom and out of the league. In 2003 they were in the Conference and it is perhaps here we should tell the story of Ken Richardson.

During the early 1990s, Ken Richardson, who was later described by detectives as 'the type that would trample over a two-year-old to pick up a 2p bit,' took over as the majority shareholder of the club. He ploughed a lot of money into Doncaster Rovers with one thing in mind, a new stadium. When he was refused a new stadium by the council he soon lost interest. So, Richardson hired three men to torch the Belle View ground and planned to sell the site to developers. By all accounts the guys he hired weren't the sharpest tools in the box and the attempt failed and all came to light so that Richardson was jailed for four years. Belle View was ruined with Rovers also edging closer to relegation. In 1998 Rovers dropped right out of the league with a minus 83 goal difference. With all Richardson's financial backing withdrawn the club was then subject to an administration order.

At this point the story becomes quite surreal because years later the guy who sorted out the Doncaster insolvency mess, Walter Green, got in touch with me to order some Burnley FC books. He, a Burnley supporter, emailed me from his ranch in Texas, the Double D Ranch in Driftwood, somewhere between Dallas and Houston, where he was living in retirement. I still haven't taken him up on his invitation to visit the ranch where he rides around on his horse, wearing a Stetson and his Burnley shirt.

Penniless, Doncaster then lost most of their better players and the ones left behind were nowhere near good enough to save Rovers from their exit out of the Football League. The fans, quite naturally, blamed Richardson for the mess and even held a mock funeral at the last game of season 1997/98 when a coffin was carried along Carr House Road. Just weeks after Rovers were relegated, fans felt some measure of satisfaction when Richardson was jailed, guilty of trying to set fire to the ground, apparently hoping to pay off all the club debts with the insurance money according to reports of the time.

2008: and as we drove over there once more I thought of the old headmaster, and said a silent prayer of thanks that it was me driving us this time. And I wondered too if the old red bucket in the corner of the ladies loo was perhaps in a glass cabinet on display as a treasured piece of memorabilia. Now, both clubs were in comparable situations, both were small clubs, money too tight to mention and currently striving for better things.

Having messed things up two days earlier against Barnsley, a point at least at Doncaster was imperative. The bad news was that Doncaster had come good at Nottingham Forest and clattered them 4 – 2. Against Barnsley, Owen Coyle had played both Eagles and Elliot in the same team. It didn't work. With both of them in the side it made a weak midfield. To the astonishment of all of us who saw them flounder against Barnsley, it was the same team that emerged. Predictable Burnley in a let-down of a game lost 2 – 1.

To compound matters Steve Caldwell was sent off. He'd therefore miss the next three games. Two soft, gift goals gave the game to Doncaster; the first when the ball ballooned off Carlisle's head as he misheaded it with no-one near him. The ball nicely plopped at the feet of a totally unmarked Doncaster player who said thank you very much and neatly slotted the ball home. Other than a few minutes in the second half, Burnley were never in it, second to every ball, reverting to Cotterball; worryingly lethargic, slow and sluggish, Eagles in Bambi mode, ineffective, and lucky not to be sent off for a kick at goalkeeper Sullivan. McCann anonymous, only Jensen, maybe Paterson and Blake emerging with any credit; Duff, another deserving credit, showed again how good he is in the centre of defence. Carlisle slow and ponderous and gave the ball away time and again with long punts upfield. Paterson scored the solitary Burnley goal after a long, mazy run from Elliott who moved into midfield as part of the ten-man shuffle around. For just a few minutes it looked as if the adrenalin might have prompted a second-half come-back but it was not to be and everything just tamely fizzled out, leaving the faithful away support with a Christmas hangover. Previous good work was undone in two dire games with questions asked about team formation and selection. Still fifth and still in the Carling Cup semi-finals but optimism had been replaced by doubt as suspensions and defeats kicked in. The team had lost its way and January could be a poor month we reckoned. Carry on stumbling and mid-table and Carling Cup disappointment beckoned.

And the new Doncaster stadium: typically new, small, neat, tidy, but featureless; one of those identikit stadiums that litter the football leagues. It made me think of those Swedish timber house kits you can buy that you assemble by numbers. Just yards away is the lakeside retail centre, and yes there really is a lake complete with birdlife over the road. At halftime we enjoyed the restroom facilities – and not a red bucket in sight in any corner. The ground is smaller than most new-build stadiums. You don't find crowds of 30,000 at Doncaster; 15,000 at the most. If there is one plus it is the acres of car-parking space but the downside is the time it takes to get away. There is the obligatory keep-fit centre, a glitzy club shop and a large social centre. You could walk round the whole building in minutes. It cost £12million to build and also hosts rugby league. In the shop we were easily identified by our colours and several of the old-timers broke into friendly conversation with us as we looked around. Tell the truth, they seemed rather in awe of a visit from the mighty, high-flying Burnley riding high in the Championship and having despatched Chelsea and Arsenal from the Carling Cup. Little did they know that three points were coming their way.

The stumbling went on for three more league games. But everyone knows and remembers how the season was recovered. In the board room by the time of the fifth defeat there were accusing looks at Brendan Flood and much grumbling at the money that had been spent

Legendary figures in the history of Burnley FC. Clockwise from top right: John Haworth, the first great manager until his untimely death, who guided the club to the 1914 Cup Final triumph and the Division One title win of 1920/21; Billy Watson; George Halley; Bert Freeman, scorer of the 1914 Cup Final goal; Tommy Boyle, possiby Burnley's greatest ever captain, who suffered with mental ill health in his later years

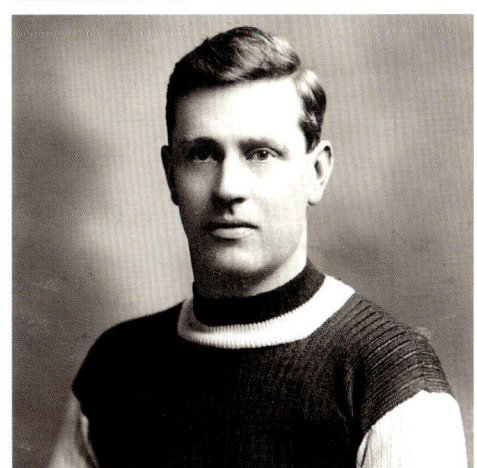

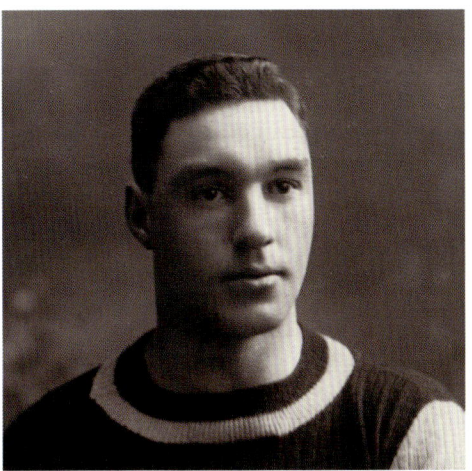

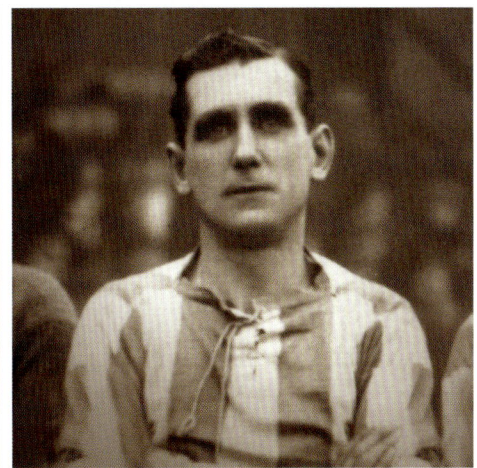

The 1914 cup winning team shown above and (below and right) back in Burnley after the Cup Final. The players are sporting flat caps that would almost serve as umbrellas and shown parading the trophy for the jubilant fans in an open-topped horse-drawn charabanc

'Robbed' was the general verdict and certainly Bob Lord's after the cup-tie at West Ham in which Gordon Harris (below) walloped West Ham's John Bond

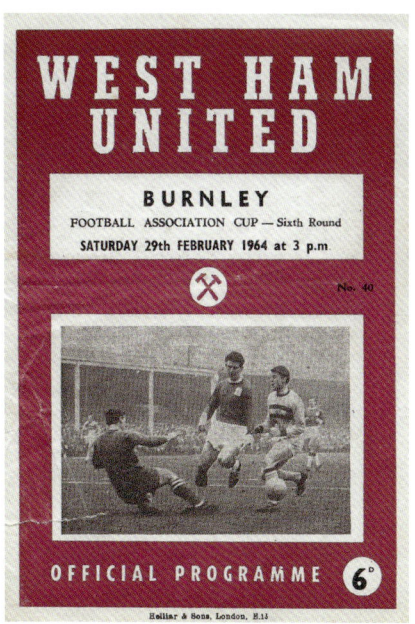

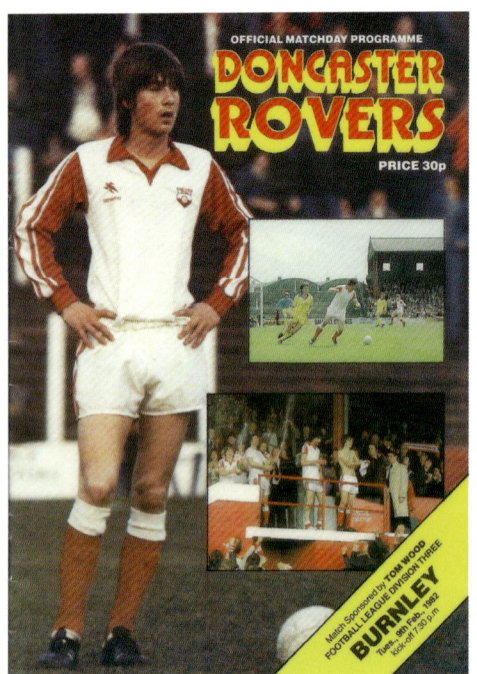

1982, Martin Dobson (below left) the skipper of the side that won promotion with Trevor Steven (below right), one of the stars of that team, and Steven Caldwell (above right) who was sent off in the Doncaster game of 2008/09 but pictured on a happier day at Wembley in the 2009 Play-Off Final

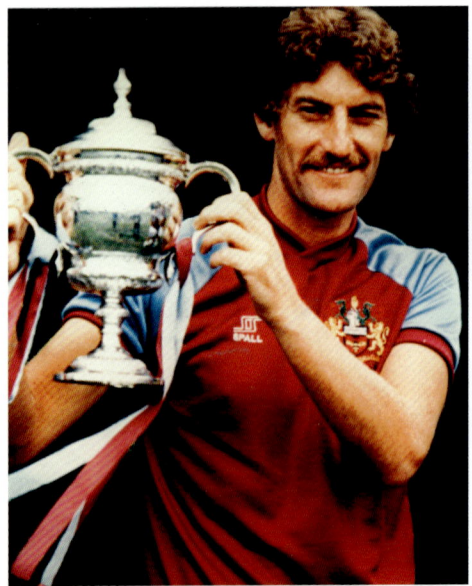

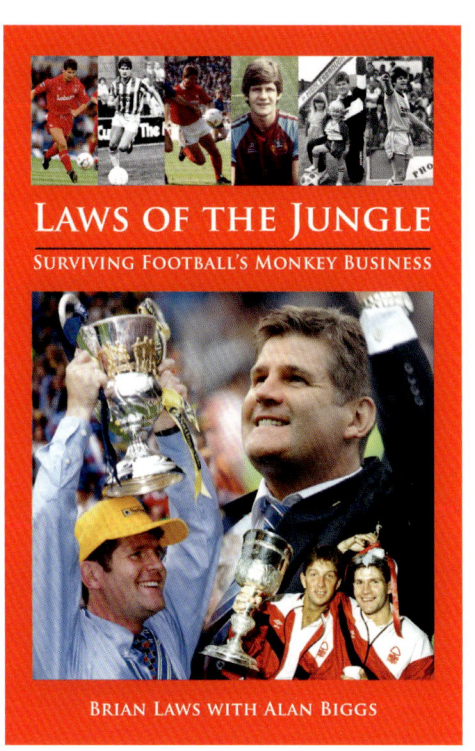

Brian Laws, pictured above as an apprentice, was a key member of the 1981/82 promotion team but was sold by John Bond. He went on to play for Brian Clough at Nottingham Forest and eventually returned to Burnley as manager in the ill-fated 2009/10 season, taking over from Owen Coyle who was subject to the ire of the fans when he returned with Bolton Wanderers

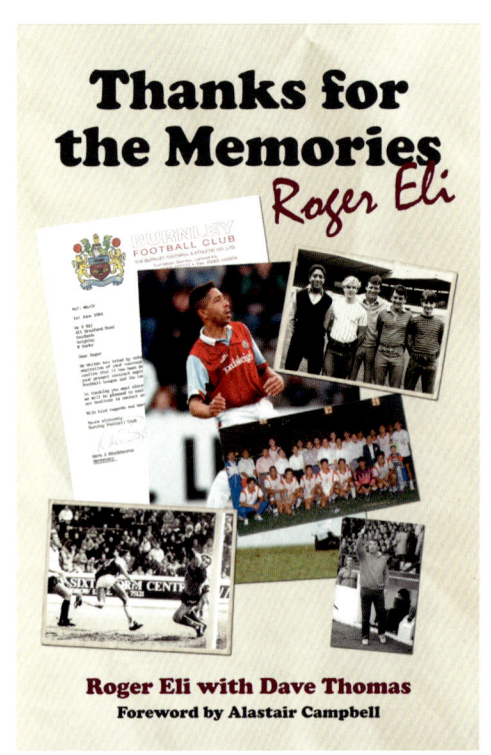

Roger Eli battled with injuries through most of his playing career but had a glorious season in 1991/92. He's shown above scoring a bullet header past Peter Shilton in the FA Cup and giving his usual one-hundred per cent commitment below

Sean Dyche and the famous gable-end mural that is no more. The mastermind behind two Burnley promotions, the fans are shown celebrating the team's return to the Premier League after playing QPR in May 2016

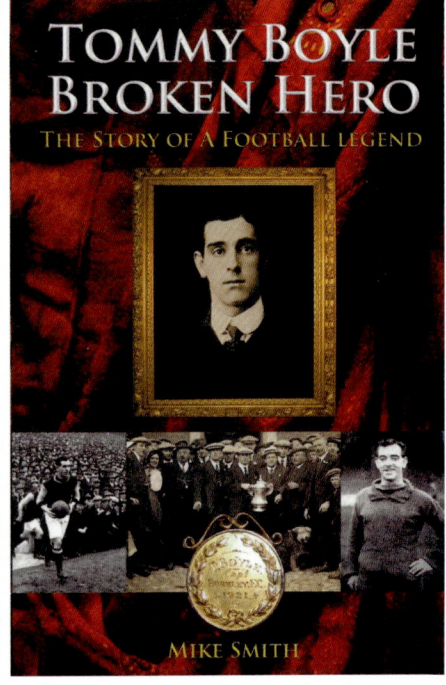

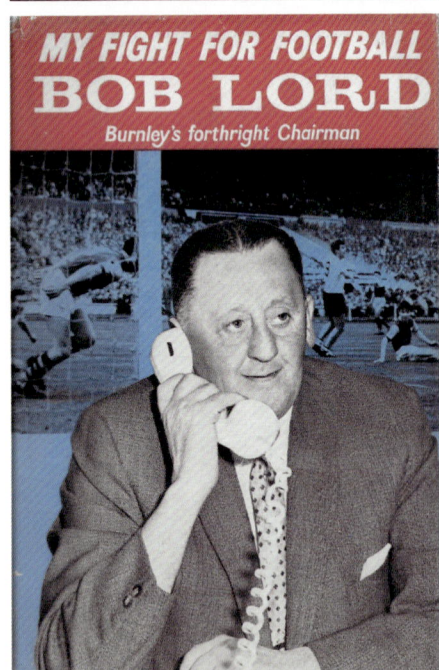

A treasure-trove of publications featuring Burnley FC

1982 And So to Doncaster

as the team floundered. At that point too, they would have known what the fans didn't, that the money was running out as Brendan Flood's business was hitting the skids.

But recover they did, despite a transfer embargo and by April, near insolvency. The wins began again and key games away at Blackpool and Plymouth got the club back in contention. The final games seemed like a dream. The Carling Cup semi-final second leg game was one of the great games of all time at Turf Moor. Recovering from a three-goal deficit, the Clarets pulled it back to 4-4 on aggregate. If away goals had counted double they would have been through to the Final at Wembley. As it was, the rules favoured Tottenham who scored two very late goals in extra-time to go through.

And Doncaster? I haven't been back since 2008.

6

From the Big Time to the Bad Times

When Dave Roberts and his wife took the huge decision to move to the USA, Dave naturally assumed that his treasured collection of 1,134 football programmes would go with him on the 'plane. He was wrong. In no uncertain terms Dave was informed that space was at a premium and he would have to whittle his precious hoard down to what would fit into a Tupperware box. How could any rational fan do this? How could I do it? How could you sift through your lifetime collection of football programmes and choose the most important 32?

In truth I'd once been through this process. When we moved house in '99 I had cupboards filled with programmes. I had cupboards filled with all kinds of stuff. We downsized from an old, cavernous, early Victorian house in Headingley to a smaller more modest place in the suburbs. Car trips to the tip were never-ending. Trips to charity shops unloaded the rest. The programmes, bar just a few, were unceremoniously dumped into carrier bags and boxes and then binned. This was before we had resumed regular trips to Turf Moor. It was four years before the first book appeared. Nowadays I look back on that time and see it as madness. And here I am buying the same programmes from eBay when I need them for a new book.

Dave Roberts relates the story of the 31 programmes (yes 31) he selected. Each stirred memories significant in some way, evoking bitter-sweet reminders of all his life's journeys. From the excitement of his first game as a young boy, through crushing teenage disappointments both on and off the field, to the strange places life and football can take a man; his football fan's world was never simple.

Dave could never have predicted the chain of events that would lead to the final, 32nd programme and a homecoming that would bring a lump to the throat of even the most hardened midfield destroyer.

32 Programmes is a book that you think, now why did I never think of that? Brilliant, funny, heart-warming and all about the obsession that many of us football fans share: saving our programmes. It's about the things that we keep, are important to us and remind us of things we've done and places we've been. They remind us of the passage of time and the meaning of family and friends ... and football.

Of Dave's precious 32 programmes, two of them are from games that involve Burnley.

I am indebted to Transworld Publishers and to Dave Roberts himself for permission to use the two Burnley chapters.

***

This was the season at the end of which Burnley were relegated. Jimmy Adamson was manager having usurped Harry Potts as Bob Lord's adopted son. Potts, meanwhile, was still at the club in a meaningless role as general manager, a job without any real kind of job-description. While Adamson, in a flush of optimism, had declared that the young lads at the club along with people like Martin Dobson and Ralph Coates would be the 'Team of the Seventies.' Alongside them were people like Frank Casper, Colin Waldron, Mick Docherty, Dave Thomas and Steve Kindon.

It took them until October 31st to win their first game and the next one was then promptly lost 4 – 0. Prior to all that, the season had begun without Dobson who suffered a broken leg, and Brian O'Neil who was sold to Southampton. The loss of those two was pivotal. Bob Lord confessed that O'Neil was one of his favourite players. O'Neil never did find out whether he was sold because of his alleged indiscretions in the town, or whether Adamson was happy to get rid of a terrific player who pretty much answered to no-one but his own flair, spirit and single-mindedness, once he got stuck in on the field. Adamson wanted the discipline of controlled team-work but O'Neil was a terrier-

The Best of Burnley

like free spirit who could not relate to having any shackles put on him. Today, a player like O'Neil would fetch millions. At Southampton he just got better and better, so much so that Manager Ted Bates was adamant that he should be picked for England.

By the time Burnley went to Highbury in April 1971, they were pretty much doomed. A win might have delayed the inevitable. Could they possibly win against Arsenal – up there at the top? Alas no – and Arsenal went on to win the Double.

***

32 Programmes by Dave Roberts (Bantam Press)
From Chapter 7: Arsenal V Burnley 20 April 1971

Top of the league – eight wins in the last eight league games and 15 goals against one – a great tribute to the skill and enthusiasm of the whole team – we hope you will drive them on this evening by your enthusiasm. (From the official programme)

I had been off school for the best part of a week with a cold and had got thoroughly used to the lifestyle. Lying in bed with bottles of Lucozade to keep my strength up, peanuts to snack on, and Ribena and aspirin to keep the fever at bay seemed infinitely more preferable to double maths, chemistry and biology. And to make sure I had even less motivation to recover, my parents had moved their colour TV into my room and brought me the *Guardian* every morning when they'd finished with it.

I would have been happy to stay like this forever, if it hadn't been for the lure of football. Although Bromley (my first love) didn't have a game, I'd agreed to go to Highbury with Dave to see his beloved Gunners in action against Burnley, despite what was, in truth, a mild cold. The added bonus was that most of the time skinheads from school would be there and my credibility with them was at an all-time high following my programme-buying excursion to Nottingham on their behalf the previous Tuesday.

Tonight's game had taken on an added significance following what

From the Big Time to the Bad Times

had happened at the Leeds v WBA match on the Saturday. Leeds had needed a win to stay two points ahead of Arsenal but had gone a goal down early on before one of the most bizarre incidents I'd ever seen on a football pitch took place. I'd watched it unfold on *Match of the Day* and shared commentator Barry Davies' astonishment from the comfort of my sickbed. A misplaced pass from Norman Hunter had hit Tony Brown, the Albion striker, and rebounded into the Leeds half, where Albion's Colin Suggett was standing around 20 yards offside. The linesman dutifully raised his flag and Brown strolled to a halt as he waited for the inevitable whistle. It didn't come.

'The referee's waving him on,' screeched Davies in disbelief, the injustice he was seeing clear for all to hear.

'Brown is going straight through ... taking on Sprake!' Davies then temporarily lost the power of speech as Brown passed across the face of the goal to Jeff Astle who put the ball into the unguarded net.

'And the goal to Astle!' he finally spluttered as a sheepish Astle raised his arm in triumph.

Davies wasn't going to sit on the fence with this one. 'And Leeds will go mad,' he shouted. 'And they've every right to go mad because everybody stopped with the linesman's flag.'

And go mad they did. The players surrounded the referee, Ray Tinkler, pleading with him to change his mind. Manager Don Revie in his trademark blue gabardine coat, rushed onto the pitch, inexplicably clutching a tartan blanket. And a heavily whiskered Leeds fan in a mustard-coloured Burton's blazer with blue tie was grabbed by two burley policemen before he could inflict any damage on Mr Tinkler.

The protests were to no avail and Leeds eventually lost 2 – 1. This meant that if Arsenal could beat Burnley tonight they would almost certainly win the title. I was desperate to go, but despite my best efforts to explain, my parents didn't seem to grasp the distinction between being too ill to go to school, but not too ill to go and watch a football match. The only way they'd let me go was if I promised to go back to school the next day. In a bizarre twist, instead of pretending to be ill, which was something I'd done on so many occasions I'd lost count, I'd have to pretend to be well. After announcing my miraculous recovery, I phoned Dave and arranged to meet him at Bromley South station after tea.

As soon as I saw him, my feeling of general unwellness was replaced by one of resentful envy. He was wearing a purple and black Budgie jacket – the same one I'd had my eye on since we'd seen it in the window of Top Man a couple of weeks earlier. I knew the faux suede would make him irresistible to sorts, while I was stuck wearing the faux sheepskin I'd got for Christmas a year and a half ago, back when they were fashionable.

I sulked for most of the train journey, but my spirits started to lift as we approached Highbury, despite coughing a lot and suffering from a mild headache. Dave diagnosed me as having 'caught exposure' which I wasn't convinced about. He had to lend me 40 pence (we were struggling to get used to decimal currency) to get into the ground as I'd already spent my pocket money. I had no intention of paying him back. *(Trust me: 40p was a fair bit of money back in 1971, and not to be sneezed at. DT)*

We went to what we called 'our usual place' in the North Bank, even though we'd been there only once before, and found a good spot near the front. My cough was getting worse, so I put a Victory V lozenge in my mouth to stop the irritation in my throat. They were so hot and fiery that only North Bank hardmen like me could put up with the chloroform and ether taste without spitting them out.

Trying to ignore the burning sensation on my near-numb tongue, I glanced through the programme. The only major absences from the Arsenal team were Peter Storey (mysteriously dubbed the 'fridge kid of this jet-aged soccer' in the morning's paper) and Bob McNab, who had both been called into the England squad for their game the following night against Greece.

Suddenly, a familiar voice came across the Tannoy. It was Arsenal's manager Bertie Mee, urging the fans to make themselves heard on this crucial night for their title chances. 'We need more vocal support,' he pleaded. This wasn't what someone with an agonising sore throat wanted to hear, but the fans responded by bursting into song. To the tune of 'Rule Britannia', 'Good old Arsenal, we're proud to say that name, and while we sing this song we'll win the game' was repeated over and over again, as these were apparently the only words the song had. On the plus side, it didn't take me long to learn it. The lyrics, Dave informed me, had been written by Jimmy Hill after he'd held a contest on *The Big Match* to compose a song for Arsenal and couldn't find a winner since all the entries were so rubbish.

As the sole verse was being sung for about the 50th time, the players appeared and Burnley's albino goalkeeper ran out in front of the North Bank. We gave him a huge ovation, which he acknowledged gratefully. It was his first league game for four months and he couldn't have picked a bigger one for his comeback. If Burnley lost, they'd be relegated.

After 20 minutes of not much happening, during which I got through about five Victory Vs, Mellor gave a fair indication of why he'd spent so long out of the first team. He went to catch a John Radford long throw and fell over, leaving Ray Kennedy to head the ball in the direction of the goal. Left winger Eric Probert made a diving save, tipping the ball away with his hand, and the penalty was duly awarded by the referee, Mr T W Dawes (Norwich).

I looked around for penalty king Peter Storey, and then remembered he was on England duty. Charlie George, whose every touch was greeted with frenzied shrieking from Dave, stepped forward, sent Mellor the wrong way and it was 1 – 0. The goal seemed to release Arsenal's tension and they started to play the way I'd seen them so often that season on TV. I was really starting to enjoy watching an outstanding team at the top of their game.

Then my legs gave way and everything went black.

The next thing I was aware of was an intense bright light and the sound of trumpets. Was I in heaven? No, I was lying on a bed and a St John Ambulance man who bore a strong resemblance to the actor Oliver Reed was peering intently at my face and was shining a torch in my eyes.

'Where am I?' I asked groggily.

'You're in the first-aid room at the Arsenal,' he explained, before adding somewhat unnecessarily, 'You fainted.'

I wanted to go back out but he wouldn't let me, insisting I stay there and drink a cup of sweet tea first. If there are two tastes that don't mix, it's tea and Victory V residue. But since it was the only way

The Best of Burnley

I'd be able to get back to the football, I gulped it down.

He then escorted me down the corridor, where I finally discovered why I'd heard trumpets. The brass band was warming up for their half-time display and was running through a selection of songs from *Mary Poppins*. We walked past them and out onto the cinder track surrounding the pitch. A glance at the giant clock at the aptly named Clock End confirmed that there were still a few minutes of the first-half left. The score-board showed an unchanged scoreline. Arsenal were still one up.

It was a thrill being so close to the players and I walked as slowly as I could to make the most of the opportunity, even though I felt everyone was watching me. When the Oliver Reed lookalike opened the gate and let me back into the North Bank, I thanked him and then scoured the packed stand for a shortish, slim, long-haired figure in a Budgie Jacket. Despite spotting dozens, none of them was Dave.

I watched the second half on my own. Burnley looked a team resigned to relegation and Arsenal were by far the better side, without really threatening to add to their solitary goal. But, to the North Bank, the score was irrelevant. The two points were all that mattered and the roar that greeted the final whistle signified that they knew the title was now within reach.

When I got home I immediately rang Dave to find out what had happened. According to him, he was talking to me while he was watching the game. When I didn't say anything he turned round to demand a reply and I wasn't there. Someone nudged him and pointed to a couple of St John Ambulance men carrying me around the hallowed turf (as he called it) on a stretcher. He had no interest in finding out if I was feeling any better, but was desperate to find out what it was like under the East Stand.

It didn't take long to get to sleep that night and I woke next morning with my throat no longer sore, which I attributed to the Victory Vs. After breakfast and a quick read of the *Guardian,* where I learned that George Best had once again gone missing from the Northern Ireland squad, I bravely went to school, confident that this would prove how hard I was.

The playground had already been the site of one of my most

humiliating moments when I attempted the Willie Carr free-kick in front of dozens of people. The idea was to grip the ball between the ankles and flick it up in the air for the person standing behind to volley. This is what had happened when Coventry played Everton earlier in the season, Carr and Ernie Hunt combining for one of the goals of the season. What happened when I tried it was that the ball remained on the ground and I managed to kick myself ferociously in the nads with both heels, before collapsing in a screaming heap. And now that same playground was about to be the scene of something even more embarrassing.

As I walked into it the day after the Burnley match, I didn't quite get the hero's reception I'd been anticipating. Instead, one after the other, the skinheads (including the one I thought liked me) collapsed to the ground laughing, pretending to faint. This then spread to several other boys who took their turns to fall to the ground. The humiliation rose inside me but I was determined not to show them how devastated I was.

It was clear my skinhead days were over, but football showed no sign of loosening the grip it had on me. I was spending more and more time at Hayes Lane, home of Bromley, a team that won about as frequently as Arsenal lost. Expectations were always low – until one perfect day that autumn.

* * *

Dave Thomas continues:

In the press the following day Peter Mellor claimed that he had been fouled when he went up for the throw-in that led to the penalty. 'I was definitely pushed when I went for that throw. I don't think the referee saw it. Arsenal are very strong and they were really going in hard for those centres.'

Norman Giller reported on the game: 'Arsenal dumped Burnley into the Second Division last night as they lifted themselves two points clear at the top of the First and it was that man Charlie George again, whose 26th minute penalty put Arsenal in command of this tense, double-edge game.

'Burnley had to win to keep alive their hopes of clinging on to First Division status. But Arsenal were too involved with keeping up their title tempo to spare any sympathy. Burnley, with 25 points from 39 games, can only draw level with West Ham who at present have 31 points and a vastly superior goal average.

'Arsenal failed to produce champion style football last night. But with one game still in hand, they have the laugh on Leeds, who are still smarting under the circumstances of Saturday's home defeat by West Bromwich. Arsenal are now poised to take away Burnley's best player as well as their First Division future. They are preparing to open negotiations for Burnley schemer Ralph Coates – who missed the match – a transfer transaction that could relieve Arsenal of £180,000 from their massive profits this season.

'Burnley boss Jimmy Adamson had brief talks after the match with Arsenal manager Bertie Mee and Spurs chief, Bill Nicholson, but then said: "I expect all my players to re-sign for next season."

'Arsenal defenders Peter Storey and Bob McNab were also on England duty with Coates and both were missed.

'Manager Bertie Mee had appealed before the game for the Arsenal fans to make themselves heard. "We need more vocal support," he said. But, quite frankly Arsenal gave their supporters little to sing or shout about in the opening 25 minutes, during which Highbury was as quiet as a monastery. They showed plenty of industry but little invention against a Burnley side that refused to lie down and die.

'Arsenal's lone goal was a personal disaster for goalkeeper Peter Mellor who was making his first appearance for four months. Mellor stumbled as he moved to collect a long throw from John Radford who powered the ball into the middle from near the left corner flag. Ray Kennedy stepped forward to head the ball down towards the net and Eric Probert became an instant understudy for Mellor as he dived to push the ball out with a hand. With penalty king Peter Storey unavailable Charlie George was elected to take the spot kick. He coldly studied a position to Mellor's left but drilled the ball into the opposite corner as the blond 'keeper shuffled the wrong way.

'The goal released a lot of Arsenal's tension and they began to stitch together passing movements that explain why they are sitting

From the Big Time to the Bad Times

proudly at the top of the table and within shooting distance of the First Division title.'

With Burnley's fate settled, the angry letters poured into the local press. Great player he may have been with a string of accomplishments to his name, nevertheless this was a bad time for Manager Jimmy Adamson. His brand of football at this stage was far from popular with supporters. There was widespread dissatisfaction with him on the terraces and indeed with the way the club was being run. This letter was typical from R D Kippax:

'First, Mr Lord's statement when admission prices were raised – "if they don't like it they can lump it." Mr Lord, the lumps are in our throats now.

'Next came "most footballers couldn't manage a fish and chip shop." I wonder if he would like to add as an afterthought "and not too many can manage a football club."

'Mr Lord's frequent reference to our backroom boys has come true with a vengeance. They could only have led us one place further back.

'On TV, the statement that Brian O'Neil couldn't command a first-team place was true. Neither could any other player. Since Mr Adamson took over one could only surmise that the team had been chosen by means of drawing names out of a hat.

'Then there was Mr Adamson's statement about widening the goals. In most games this season we wouldn't have scored if the goal posts had been where the corner flags are.

'When Mr Adamson said he had sent Dave Thomas home because he was jaded, he didn't mention the 15,000 other people at Turf Moor feeling the same way. These people were thanked by him for their loyalty. They are gluttons for punishment.

'I hope the manager does not think he was being witty when he had said on TV that Burnley had a great bunch of lads, but they couldn't play football. Mr Adamson should go and stand on the terraces and hear the comments about his management. He would soon discover that there is not much praise for him.

'Burnley haven't been relegated; they have been sacrificed.'

R D Kippax a supporter for 60 years

Alas it was to get much worse for Adamson during the next two seasons, until at last he found the blend of players and the winning formula that would so very nearly produce 'The Team of the Seventies.' From the time of his departure from the club, there was a steady decline in results and attendances. By 1980, the time of Dave Roberts' next programme piece, Burnley Football Club was very much a spent force with real financial problems. Bob Lord was still chairman but that would come to an end in 1981.

Harry Potts had been dismissed and replaced by Brian Miller. The club was in Division Three after relegation at the end of 1979/80. Things were drifting along with no sign at all that the following season there would be a promotion with a mix of kids and older experienced players, led by the incomparable Martin Dobson. By then, Bob Lord had passed away and the chairman was John Jackson. The story of that season is in No Nay Never Volume 2 *making use of the diaries of then director, Mr Derek Gill.*

***

From Chapter 21: Burnley Versus Plymouth Argyle, 20 December 1980

Traditionally today is the worst day of the year for clubs to attract spectators. (From the official programme)

We'd left Manchester early for the Burnley v Plymouth Argyle game as bad weather threatened to make the drive slow going. On the plus side, the snow covered the 'THERE ARE TWO BIG REASONS WHY I MARRIED CAROLINE' graffiti which was now a permanent feature of the rear window. Another worrying aspect, on top of the weather, was my doubt over the car's ability to get there. I had a distinct feeling that the rattling and thumping that had been coming from under the bonnet recently might be a bad sign. I'd been so worried that earlier in the week, I'd joined the AA Relay, just in case.

I wasn't really expecting the Viva to make it to Burnley, even though it was only around 35 miles away, so I hadn't allowed myself

From the Big Time to the Bad Times

to get excited about the prospect of seeing Plymouth Argyle again. But when we reached the outskirts of the town and started seeing well-wrapped fans in claret and blue making their way to the ground, the familiar feelings of anticipation started bubbling up inside me.

We got there with an hour to spare before kick-off. This was just as well since Caroline suddenly expressed an urgent need to find a newsagent, so we drove around until we found one. She dashed inside, came out with a paper and seemed to be stuffing something else under her coat. We then found a car park near to the ground and made our way in, taking extra care not to slip on icy pavements.

I had a soft spot for Burnley. They were in Division Three for the first time in their history and I remembered seeing them on *Match of the Day* the previous season, when they were relegated, losing 7 – 0 at QPR. Their young reserve goalkeeper Billy O'Rourke made his debut and the cameras had caught him going off in tears that day. It was one of the saddest things I'd seen in football and I was pleased to see that not only was he still with the club, he was having an exceptional season for the reserves, conceding a goal only every two games or so.

You know it's not going to be your day when you scald your mouth biting into a pre-match pie, and that was exactly what happened to me. And that wasn't the only sign of impending doom. Caroline had picked up a copy of the Burnley Express at the shop, and there was a small piece in it about how the home gaffer, Brian Miller, was on a streak of incredible luck. Not only had he picked up £1,000 in last Saturday's weekly lottery, he'd also won a colour television in the club's Christmas Draw. Things were not looking good for Plymouth.

The crowd was on the small side, but as the programme pointed out, that was the fault of the Football League for making them play on the day when everyone was doing their Christmas shopping. It was good for me and Caroline though, as it meant we got really good seats. As she sat down, her mind seemed to be elsewhere so I tried to get her interested in what we were about to watch, by quoting statistics from the programme. It was not a success.

Both sides were challenging for promotion, although Plymouth had recently gone off the boil. The game began with Burnley looking the more threatening and Billy Hamilton, the Northern Ireland international, tormenting the Plymouth defence. At least David The Kemp, The Kemp, The Kemp was looking his usual brilliant self. He was already on 19 goals for the season, despite shockingly going on a streak of nine games without scoring. Presumably he had an injury he was keeping from everyone. I kept ringing the Plymouth hotline from work, desperately hoping Manager Bobby Saxton wasn't going to drop him, and so far he'd kept his place.

The 13th minute was always a time for increased anxiety for me at a football match, because 13 had been my unlucky number since I conceded as many when keeping goal for my Boy Scouts team. This is why I wasn't remotely surprised when Burnley opened the scoring after exactly 13 minutes. From a corner, 18-year old Vince Overson out-jumped the defence to head the ball back across the goal, and top scorer Steve Taylor placed a nice header just inside the far post. Brian Laws nearly doubled the score a minute later but his shot was brilliantly saved by Geoff Crudgington.

Moments later, David The Kemp, The Kemp, The Kemp had a shot blocked on the line, and then referee Trelford Mills (Barnsley), who had until then been frozen out of the action, went on a yellow card waving spree, booking Plymouth's George Foster for sulkily throwing the ball away, Forbes Phillipson-Masters for an innocuous foul, and Burnley's Laws for an over-enthusiastic challenge on Murphy.

Things got worse for Plymouth after the break, when Taylor beat Crudgington from just inside the area to make it 2 – 0. If I'd been a fair and impartial observer, I would have said that the second goal was well deserved and that the scoreline was an accurate reflection of the game so far, but to me it was an act of gross injustice.

But as anyone who knows anything about football knows, you didn't keep David The Kemp, The Kemp, The Kemp quiet for long. He made a brilliant run into the box before being chopped down and falling flamboyantly to the floor. Mr Mills pointed equally dramatically to the spot, and Donal Murphy pulled the score back to 2 – 1. Caroline, who had been a bit distracted the whole game, didn't even seem to notice. It was as though she had something else on her mind.

The game was end-to-end action and it was no surprise when David The Kemp, The Kemp, The Kemp's perfectly placed header eluded Stevenson in the Burnley goal to level the scores. I was so busy hugging Caroline in celebration that I failed to notice that the referee had disallowed it for a push on a defender. It was 13 minutes before full-time. That was the last time Plymouth looked like scoring and Burnley could have made the margin bigger on the stroke of full-time when Potts had a great shot tipped round the post by the impressive Crudgington.

We walked back to the car park, a little despondent. It had been a day when nothing had worked out and it didn't get any better when Caroline told me to wait in the car as she suddenly realised she'd forgotten something. I asked her if she wanted me to go with her but she said it was fine. And then, for the second time since we'd arrived in Burnley she went off to do something she wouldn't tell me about.

I was so thankful that I had the programme to keep my mind occupied while she was gone. I put the interior light on and eagerly started to read it. The Puzzle Page had a unique way of ensuring that no-one walked away with the prize of two tickets for any league game. 'Today's puzzle competition should not be too difficult for you soccer fans to solve,' it announced. They were right. It wasn't difficult. It was impossible. Alongside a picture of Peter Mellor, the former Burnley goalkeeper I'd once seen at Highbury, were the words: 'Take a look at the photograph and let us know who the two former Burnley players are,' with the helpful addition: 'We'll give you a clue – both players have appeared at Wembley.' However hard I looked, I could only see one player.

I then had the luxury of being able to read through the list of ball sponsors for the entire season, study every advert in detail (my favourite was a cartoon cow dressed in a superhero outfit to advertise Super Beef from Peter Todd Meats Ltd) and even attempt the clarets crossword with my newly acquired souvenir pen. I was stumped by the crucial one-across which was: 'scoring the second most vital goal.'

I wondered if Caroline would be interested in hanging around for a bit so we could see 'LYNNE ALLAN – vivacious young female artist' who was appearing at the Centre Spot Social Club in the main stand. This was a club that was famous throughout the north-west for attracting just three people for a televised England game. So I hoped

Lynne Allan's expectations were low.

I'd been so engrossed in the programme I had no idea how long Caroline had been gone. It couldn't have been that long, but when she got back her eyes were gleaming with excitement. She made no attempt to explain why she'd kept me waiting in the freezing cold. It would be five more days before I found out.

The journey back was notable for being the last one we made in the Viva. Somewhere along the M65 the thumping sound from under the bonnet started getting worse and I announced that I was stopping at the next AA phone box, adding, 'I reckon the big end's gone.' I didn't actually know what this was but I'd been in a friend's car when a similar thing happened and that was what he said.

After finding an AA box by the side of the road, I rang and was told they'd be there within the hour. The snow was getting heavy and the temperature couldn't have been far above freezing. I kept the engine running so we could keep the heater on. While we were waiting, Caroline got so bored that she started reading the programme. It was at times like this I was always glad I bought two. It meant we could have one each to study.

Less than an hour later, as promised, the AA tow truck pulled up and a man got out.

'What's the problem?' he asked, adjusting his peaked cap.

'There's a noise coming from the engine, he thinks the big end has gone,' Caroline replied, with touching faith in my mechanical knowledge. I felt my face reddening.

'Right,' said the AA man, opening the bonnet. 'Let's have a look shall we?'

After poking around for a few minutes, he re-surfaced with the news that the engine mounts were loose and we were unlikely to make it back to Chorlton. And this was when joining AA Relay suddenly paid off. The idea was that they towed your car either home or to the garage of your choice. And, they gave you a lift at the same time. It felt quite humiliating being dropped off outside the house by a tow truck, but luckily it was dark.

There was no point in getting the Viva fixed. It was a rubbish car anyway, especially with the impossible-to-remove TWO BIG REASONS graffiti, and we managed to find someone who would tow it away and use it for parts. I'd already found a replacement: a friend of mine was selling his Mini Van and I was assured that it was a good deal. Fortunately we'd done all our Christmas shopping so we didn't need a car until Boxing Day, when we'd be driving down to Devon. This gave us the perfect excuse to spend the next few days at home, eating and watching TV, starting with a magnificent Saturday night double bill of *The Little and Large Show*, followed by *Dallas*.

On Christmas morning, before opening our presents (I hoped mine was the full-size football game on metal legs from House of Holland that I'd been lusting after), we opened our cards. Most were for both of us, but two of the envelopes had my name on them and I recognised Caroline's writing on both. But only one was from her. I tore open the other one and pulled out a card that said 'Happy 9th Birthday' on the front with '9th birthday crossed out and 'Christmas' scribbled in its place. Inside, it read:

The gayest birthday (birthday was crossed out and Christmas written in) greetings.

The best of wishes too, for happiness and lots of luck. In everything you do

It then said 'Best wishes from Plymouth Argyle' and was signed by the entire team, John Sims, Forbes Phillipson-Masters, and the rest of the side currently sliding down the Third Division table. I stared at David The Kemp, The Kemp, The Kemp's signature. He only signed it with one 'Kemp', a little longer than was strictly necessary. His handwriting was as flamboyant as his football.

The newsagent we'd stopped off at had apparently run out of Christmas cards, but Caroline hadn't let that stop her. As for the age discrepancy, apparently she was so embarrassed about getting the players to sign a card for a 25-year-old that she'd had to invent a nine-year-old nephew. As I stared at the card, that routine Third Division match between Burnley and Plymouth Argyle was suddenly elevated from instantly forgettable to one I'd always remember fondly. Even after the disappointment of a defeat that had put the club five points adrift of the leading three, every single one of the players had still managed to sign a Christmas card that had been passed round the

Plymouth dressing room – just for me. I wondered if that would happen with one of the bigger clubs.

Arranging to get it signed was one of the nicest, kindest, most thoughtful things anyone had ever done for me and showed that there were a lot a more than just two big reasons why I married Caroline.

7

Roger Eli's Glorious Season

What a pleasure it was to write this book with Roger Eli, a book that isn't about money, or glamour or European competitions. Nor is it an expletive filled story of recovery from gambling, debt or depression. It is just the story of a lad from Bradford who had his dreams but never made the big-time and met no end of hurdles and injuries along the way. It's a story about life, the crossroads that we meet, the choices that we make, and the way in which the decisions that other people make will impact on our own lives.

Roger Eli's career was influenced by several managers: Brian Clough at Nottingham Forest, Eddie Gray and Billy Bremner at Leeds United, and then Frank Casper and Jimmy Mullen at Burnley. There are others who appeared fleetingly in his story; a story of struggles, determination and bravery, and then brief success before the man that mattered, the man who picked the team, decided he was of no further use.

Roger Eli was one of those pioneer black players of the early 90s. He was Player of the Year at Burnley in season 1991/92 and scored the goal of the season. It was an iconic season and took Burnley out of the old Fourth Division where they had stagnated for seven years. After several years of knock-downs he eventually tasted glory in this season, but then yet another injury saw him lose his place. He never regained it and made only a handful of further appearances after that one glorious season; a season in which he became a cult hero and a genuine Burnley legend. It was a promotion season but he missed the final games and the joyous night at York City. Burnley's slow rise to where they are today can be traced to that one season.

The Best of Burnley

His story is one of what lies at the heart of football; about how cruel football can be and how success is so fleeting, and above all how a manager can determine the path of a player's career. For every galactico and millionaire footballer, there are scores of other players lower down the pecking order that never make the headlines and just about make a living from the game. Many of them could write a manual on how things can go wrong, about the pitfalls and obstacles that lie along the way.

Yet some of them retain good memories and leave the game to find success afterwards. Roger, now a successful businessman, is one of them. His story is almost a textbook on what is needed to stay in the game despite all the setbacks. One review described it as a book that every parent should read with a youngster who wants to make it in the game.

Roger and I met regularly at the Potting Shed café at the Woodbank Garden Centre, Harden, near Bingley, eating breakfasts and talking football. The result is this book: Thanks for the Memories. *The stories and recollections spilled out as the season was re-lived. Some stories were happy and others not, but all of them had lain dormant waiting to be told.*

His story ended too early and this book tells why. Today he runs a thriving business, Ventura Office Supplies, based near Bingley. He still plays in charity games. Many footballers fall by the wayside when they leave the game. Roger didn't.

Copies of this book are still available from Dave Thomas at beehivethomas@aol.com

***

***Thanks for the Memories: The Roger Eli Story* by Roger Eli and Dave Thomas (Vertical Editions) From Chapter 8: A Season to Remember Begins**

One of the items I have in my collection of old bits and pieces from my playing days is the pennant we received before one of the 1991 pre-season games in Russia. I looked at it and couldn't help smiling. My career had touched a few depths since the days at Leeds United and in the most depressing of those depths Russia was the last place I ever imagined I'd play. For sure it was a hell of a long way from Bury and Northwich Victoria. But there it was; the pennant and it must have been 20 years since I'd last bothered to look at it. With the pennant was a copy of the programme from one of the games. I've no idea what it says. It's in Russian.

Then there are the three programmes for the Derby Cup games. They were memorable games, one of them especially so when Peter Shilton could only blink in astonishment when my header flew past him at 90 miles an hour. And at the end of the season there were two programmes when the club printed FOURTH DIVISION CHAMPIONS on the front cover. The first was against Wrexham. Life is funny sometimes. We lost it. Then there was the end of season friendly against Ajax, Dennis Bergkamp, Van der Saar and company. I was never a great collector of such things but just these few found their way into my box. My boys can have them all one day; my memories of a great season and the old Fourth Division.

Frank Casper was still manager when the new season, 1991–92, began; the Torquay disappointment forgiven if not forgotten. Frank Teasdale, battling against disgruntled fans, was still chairman, putting up with abuse and threats and demonstrations. Who'd be a chairman?

But, even though we'd blown it against Torquay, there was still a little bit of optimism, the kind of optimism that exists at every club in the land at the beginning of a new season when there is a new start and a clean slate. One or two players left as is always the case at the end of a season. One was the late Ray Deakin, a great fans' favourite. His epic long-distance clearances were accompanied by the fans uttering a loud and sustained 'whoosh'. But he was not unskilled and supporters remembered his wonderful performance in the 'Orient Game' when the club avoided the drop out of the Football League. Fans were very disappointed when defender Steve Davis Mk1 left. He went to Barnsley for £180,000, a lot of money back then that no doubt enabled the club to pay our wages. He was a good, solid defender and it left a bit of a hole at the back.

The Best of Burnley

My strike partner Ron Futcher moved on and this was all to do with a new contract. Jimmy Mullen was desperate for him to stay. This much travelled striker was 33 when Burnley signed him for £65,000. Burnley became his 13th club and four of these had been in America. He was joint top scorer in his first season at Turf Moor with seven goals. In the 'nearly got promotion' season he'd scored 18. Despite those 18 goals he never quite managed to become a cult hero which was a surprise. Of all the many players I played alongside he was a real professional and really thought about the game. He had an exceptional knowledge of football. But he was also a joker or the one who was first to say, 'That's not right,' to Frank Casper or Jimmy Mullen. We respected him for that because his opinions were based on his vast experience in the game. But at the same time he was the first to groan when it was time to do a long distance run.

In his place Frank bought Mike Conroy. By the end of the season supporters would know who Mike Conroy was alright. He was a striker at Reading where he'd ended up playing at full-back. Ron went to Crewe and Mike came in from down south, although in fact he was Scottish and up there he'd apparently done OK. Mike says it was Jimmy Mullen who was behind the move. He knew him from when he was assistant manager of Aberdeen and Mike played for Clydebank. Mike always seemed to score against Aberdeen and Jimmy filed that away in his memory bank.

But then Frank pulled off a masterstroke. Out went Steve 'Swede' Davis and in came Steve Davis Mk2. The Swede got his name because he looked like a character in a Clint Eastwood film of the time. The replacement Steve Davis had been to Burnley already, on loan from Southampton. Back he came to Turf Moor and became one of the outstanding players of the nineties and bedrock of the team right up until the Stan Ternent team that won promotion in 2000. He was voted an official Burnley legend a few years ago. He cost Frank just £60,000 and it was money well spent.

There was a summer tour to Russia. We never knew how this came about and wondered if a Burnley director had contacts over there. It seemed an odd place to go and the travel was draining. There was a 1 – 1 draw with Stavropol and another with Asmaral which is something I thought you got from the chemist to cure piles.

It was the charms of Rotherham for the first proper game; God it was a dump back then against a backcloth of a giant scrap yard where old steam engines were broken up. Surprise, surprise Burnley lost to two late Rotherham goals. I didn't play because of an Achilles problem. Mike Conroy became an instant favourite with a goal and a celebration that saw him leap at the away end fence and cling to it for dear life. It was so insecure and flimsy it was a miracle he didn't come crashing down and break his neck.

There were quite a few fans at the away Wigan League Cup game. In those days few people actually ever wanted to go to Wigan. It was a place most people wanted to get away from. This was the Rumbelows Cup in another ramshackle place that a light breeze might have brought crashing down. The only Rumbelow I knew so far was Mr Rumbelow in *Are You Being Served*. I half expected to see him there somewhere. Behind one goal there was no terracing, just a grassy muddy bank where the Burnley boys gathered. We lost and I only mention this game because I played and it was an example of no matter how poor the ground or the conditions I always loved playing.

At last a win over Aldershot. I missed this one ironically not with an injury but because of 'flu. But the game counted for nothing as before the season ended Aldershot were wound up. They were in their death throes when we played them. Remember the Monty Python sketch 'This parrot is dead'? It was a bit like that when we played them. Officially the game never happened; the two goals were never scored. The crowd who watched were never there. But by now Mick Conroy was looking a bargain. Funny how a change of club can kickstart a career; it had happened to me as well a year earlier.

An old crumpled newspaper can bring back moments and bits and pieces of your career. There are a few odds and ends in my loft; just a few things I can show the boys one day to let them know who I was and what I once did. There's a report of the Doncaster game.

Big Billy Whitehurst still played for them. Ask anyone what it was like to play against him. I'd already played against him once the season before. He made Kenny Burns look like a kitten. In his pomp he was a striker and battered centre-halves mercilessly. It was funny. When I realised he was in the Doncaster team I thought this was still his old position up front, but to my horror he now played centre-half. In his old position he was big and terrifying. In his new one he was still big and still terrifying. Now I'd be directly up against him. You could hear my knees knocking from 20 yards away down the corridor as I got changed. There was real apprehension on my part. The thought of him coming through me if I had my back to him was worrying. The old faded newspaper has all the details. It wasn't exactly a walk in the park, but it brings a smile when I read about it now.

It was Doncaster 1 Burnley 4 and who was there managing them but Billy Bremner again. The clock in my head turned back a few years I can tell you. I looked across to him and knew he'd remember me. I was determined he wouldn't forget my performance that day. This was a game when I was playing not against Doncaster Rovers but against Billy Bremner. What a game to have a blinder. I didn't score. How good would that have been? Up and down, in and out; headers, brought down for the penalty, shots and tackles and passes galore; sometimes you play a game and you want it to go on forever. You're in the zone, can do no wrong, the ball sticks to your feet; shots are on target and Billy Bremner was there in the Doncaster dugout. 'Are you watching Billy?' I thought as I came off with a huge grin on my face. I went to see him afterwards to say hello. Yes he was sitting in his chair in his office. I'd love to remember exactly what we spoke about. I know there was some small talk. I'd love to think he said, 'Roger you should have stayed with me at Leeds'. But he didn't. I still went out feeling well pleased.

Doncaster were down to 10 men when Billy Whitehurst was sent off. He'd already clattered me in the penalty area and given away the penalty. It was hilarious how he was sent off. On the halfway line he was caught in possession by me and Mike Conroy. Setting off after us must have been like watching two sleek greyhounds being chased by a lolloping Rottweiler. Somehow, landing on all fours he stumbled over the ball and began a juggling act with it to stop us streaking away. He walked off the field before the red card was even out of the ref's pocket.

At my best they called me 'psycho'. Stuart Pearce wasn't the only one. There was one game when even with a damaged rib I showed what I was all about. Maidstone I think it was. There was a ball there to be won. If it was within reach, it was mine. I went in with one hard tackle and won it. It squirmed away. I went in with a second tackle as the next opponent came in for it. I went in and won it. Somehow it rolled away again and for a third time I went in hard and won it. It was gladiatorial. It was epic. Three tackles with three different opponents one after the other in quick succession. It was like a moment when a boxing crowd are up on their feet urging on their favourite as he batters someone. That's how it was. A crowd will recognise bravery. I had it in buckets. Years later you realise that this kind of daft bravery was the very reason you ended up on the treatment table so often. But I also had skill and knew more than a few tricks that I would always spend time practising, and before a game I'd often go back to my old school and practice touch and passing against the wall, imagining myself to be in different situations on the pitch. If it was a Tuesday game I'd go on a Monday night. If it was a Saturday game I'd do this after training on a Friday under the stand. I just had to play with a ball before every match.

This book is no parade of every goal I scored but there was a hat-trick against Chesterfield in the very next game. John Francis and I still argue about it. Footballers do that, especially strikers. The one that John and I still laugh about was the third one that gave me the hat-trick, and soft goal that it was, there was no hesitation in me claiming it.

'Hitman Eli Does Trick For Clarets' said the local paper: 'Hat-trick hitman Roger Eli was the hero of the hour as Burnley moved comfortably into second place in the Fourth Division at Turf Moor last night. But without taking any glory away from the Claret's sure shot striker, Eli was merely the final cog in a well-oiled goal-scoring machine that's netted seven times in two games.

'Manager Frank Casper promised: "We can play better," after Saturday's 4–1 away romp over Doncaster. And so they did. From number 1 and goalkeeper Andy Marriott through to number 11 Mark Yates, everyone played with gusto and determination that's been inherently lacking in so many teams in recent years. The balance of the side looked better than anything Casper has had charge of since he returned to the club two and a half years ago. So much so that the Burnley boss never appeared to consider tinkering with substitutions. From the first second to the last Burnley's sole objective was to attack. Five, six or seven goals would not have flattered.'

In all honesty it was a strange hat-trick. The first came when Mike Conroy surged forward with the ball. A linesman's flag went up for offside. The ball was slightly behind me but somehow my leg hooked round it and turned it into the net. Offside or not, it stood even though the Chesterfield players were not happy. Goal two came in the second half. A long ball from defence, flicked on by Conroy; it took me a couple of steps to catch up with it and then slam it, but alas straight against the goalkeeper. Sometimes your luck is in. The ball came back and I curled it inside the far post and in it went. Goal three was 20 minutes later. A corner, a defender's boot, another corner, the next cross only partially cleared, Johnny Francis lets fly from 20 yards. The ball brushes off my leg and in a second it's in the net. John Francis claimed it, but no way was he having it. The ball came off me, this was a hat-trick moment; this was my goal and nobody else's. It was me that went on the celebratory run that lasted the longest; but to this day John says it was his goal.

Afterwards I hung on to that match-ball and talked about the third goal. The quote is there in the paper to this day: 'This is my first ever hat-trick and I feel brilliant. John Francis fired in a shot and I had my back to goal. The ball just brushed my leg and took a deflection into the net. But whether John's shot would have gone in or not I don't know. But I'm claiming it.'

I read these two reports now of how well we played at Doncaster and then home against Chesterfield and I wonder how we managed to mess things up for Frank Casper. We were brilliant in those two games; so why not in the games to come when it went so badly wrong and Frank eventually resigned?

Meanwhile Frank had signed another goalkeeper, Andy Marriot, from Nottingham Forest. He was class and was to have a huge impact. After this there was optimism and cheerfulness. Doncaster was another ramshackle ground but when you've won 4–1 you don't care. It was the kind of ground where the 'Ladies' was a bucket in a brick shelter in the corner of the ground. It doesn't get more basic than that.

Supporters told me it was the first Burnley hat-trick since Kevin Hird in 1885, sorry 1985. I was a hit, my popularity now secured. It was a wonderful feeling. It gave me energy and determination to give 110% in every game. I got the match-ball signed by all the players; it was a ritual set in stone that a player got the hat-trick ball, even if the club was hard up.

'For me,' wrote one fan Andrew Firmin, 'this was the first claret hat-trick I had ever seen. For that, Roger Eli will always have my thanks.'

Frank Casper played three central defenders and two wing backs. This was novel back then and Frank was keen to take credit for the masterstroke. Why not, he'd had plenty of criticism like all managers do, so when something works grab the credit. We all do it whether we're footballers or not. The win took us to second.

A glorious September sunny day and Ron Futcher was back with Crewe for the next game. He got plenty of stick which was disappointing. He had served the club well. Instead of merely smiling and absorbing it as all his years of experience should have enabled him to do, he got himself all worked up and lunged at Steve Harper. The referee found it very easy to send him off. With them down to ten men the way was clear for us to win. Alas, football never works like that. Yes Franny put us in the lead but then our own David Hamilton was sent off. He'd had an awful game anyway and was probably pleased to be heading for the bath. We all have games like that sometimes. Crewe had equalised by then anyway so the game petered out into a draw. Nearly 10,000 people went home disappointed, unless they came from Crewe. Yes there were a few of them, just enough to fill a taxi and a tandem. Before the game Dario Gradi had come over. We shook hands and he said he was pleased that my career was now heading in the right direction.

The wheels began to fall off at Hereford. The rot set in with a vengeance. Hereford is a beautiful place set on the River Wye. This ancient, historic town with its old charter dates back to 1189. The football ground looked like it was built the same year. Famed for Bulmers cider production and the Weston Brewery, some of the

The Best of Burnley

boys felt quite at home. The game was lost 0–2. David Hamilton was stretchered off. John Francis was sent off. John was a tough lad from a hard background and he allowed nobody to take liberties with him as one Hereford player discovered. If he'd ever discovered the name of the member of staff at Burnley who was giving a young and talented Asian lad a hard time he'd have separated his head from his shoulders.

From hoping to go top, the slide took us down to eighth and this was what was depressing to supporters. They thought Burnley Football Club was better than having to go to places like lowly Hereford – and losing.

There was even worse to come. Rochdale came to Turf Moor. Burnley goalkeeper David Williams had been allowed to go to Rochdale on loan. There was nothing wrong with that except he was then allowed to play against us when Rochdale came. Sod's Law decreed that he had the game of his life. He had never played like this before and never did again. He was unbeatable and stopped everything we could throw at him. So when Rochdale scored, yes, they won. A total of 8,630 Burnley fans were furious. The three Rochdale fans were incredulous. Fans asked by what daft lack of sense was Williams allowed to play? Probably because nobody in the Burnley admin or management team ever thought he could play like this so didn't think it would matter. That was why they had got Andy Marriott instead. The Rochdale fans loved it. They were minnows and remembered how the once great Division One Burnley fans had looked down their noses at little clubs like penniless Rochdale. They remembered every jibe and act of football snobbery committed over the last six years when Burnley came to Rochdale and took over the ground and had been so supercilious. Now they were on level footing. Oh how the mighty were fallen. Frank C and Frank T were screamed at by the angry crowd. Supporters were wildly seething. The mood was sour, bitter and vitriolic. The two Franks became public enemies one and two. Burnley had plumbed the depths with this result and oh how the Rochdale fans loved it and rubbed the Burnley noses in it. For Burnley fans it was a humiliation.

Frank Casper was on borrowed time. The next game, away at Scarborough, was lost 3–1. God it was a desperate game in wet, wild and windy conditions at a ground that had become a graveyard for Burnley. Frank Casper described the whole thing as 'horrible'. Fans who were there said it was appalling. And this was in spite of Scarborough being reduced to 10 men. I'd burst through, the way to goal was clear and I was a yard ahead of the nearest marker. An arm reached out and a hand nearly ripped my shirt off as a defender held me back. A goal then if I'd broken away would have changed things. Maybe even saved Frank's job or given him something to help him change his mind about resigning. We were his team; he had gathered us. We could play a bit, and we'd shown that earlier only a few weeks ago. But the howls of abuse at Scarborough affected us. The louder it got the worse we played. Fans should realise that they do affect the players both in positive and negative ways. At Scarborough it was all negative. The longer the game went on I just wanted it to end so we could all get in the bath. And the fans thought I was one of the good guys. It was exactly how Frank described it: 'Horrible.'

In the dressing room after the game we sat numbed by the scoreline and the direness of the game. We could hear everything as the fans left the stadium, every bit of abuse, every bang on the walls and the doors, every catcall, all the boos and jeers. At a time like this you look to the skipper maybe, the manager, or the bubbliest players, for some sort of pick-me-up. But this time there was just silence.

Fans went home angry, resigned to more years in Division Four. Another bright start had descended into yet more dross. What we could hear so loudly was the result of the frustration, the bitterness and the fury at the prospect of another season in Division Four. But what they, the fans, or we, the players, didn't know was that this game marked the end of an era; the era of being not good enough. The pattern of failure was about to be shattered. Salvation was just round the corner. If only players and fans knew that this season would end with success, oh how much more we could all have enjoyed it.

We were shocked when Frank called us together on a pleasant sunny day at the Gawthorpe training ground and told us very briefly that he was leaving. We'd no idea why we'd been gathered together and this was the last thing we were expecting. There was no great long speech; he just said he'd get straight to the point and he was resigning.

He was clearly choked and the meeting lasted only a few minutes. He thanked us and with huge dignity wished us luck. Moments like this are emotional. We were stunned. We were his players. Burnley had been his life. He was a Burnley man through and through.

This was the third time as a player I'd been part of an occasion when a manager had called his players together to tell them he was leaving. When it was someone you respected it was all the more hard to feel unaffected. First it had been Eddie Gray at Leeds, then Brian Little at Wolves and now Frank. Jimmy Mullen said that he had spent the previous couple of days trying to get Frank to change his mind. More than just a few of us looked at each other in surprise when we heard that.

We learned later he'd been deeply upset by the death of a good friend of his, Gordon Clayton, who had once been his assistant, and I'm pretty sure the funeral was the same week. Football can be a heartless, savage business and takes its toll on mind and health. As a player it's enjoyable. As a manager it's pressure and more pressure. And when you lose too many games and the supporters are on your back then it's just all stress and utterly thankless. Frank simply re-appraised his life and what he wanted to do. I guess he didn't want to go the same way as his friend. And who could blame him for that. He said it wasn't just the abuse he endured at Scarborough. To this day I regret that we didn't do more for Frank. Footballers don't play badly on purpose or not try. At Scarborough fans might have felt that was the case. The previous season Frank had got to 79 points and that in another season would have been automatic promotion. Fate, then, kicked him in the teeth.

Speculation abounded about who would be the next manager and don't forget that when there is a change it's a trying, uncertain and nervous time for a footballer. Martin Dobson had just left Bristol Rovers a couple of days earlier. It must be him, we thought. Other names were thrown into the hat, Mick Docherty, Stan Ternent, Brian Flynn and Leighton James, but it was Jimmy Mullen who was appointed caretaker-manager. We were not surprised.

His first game was at home to Carlisle and a quiet 2–0 win. It's the same at every club when a new man comes in. You wonder what he's going to do, who he's going to drop; what he's going to change. His training methods were nothing radically new. But they were simple and effective. We did plenty of possession work and teamwork. Mind you we'd done that with Frank. But everything was kept as simple as possible. Full-backs were ordered to get the ball to the wingmen as quickly as possible either to their feet or down the channels for them to chase and turn the opposition. He played with two quick wide men and me and Mick Conroy in the centre. Mick flourished with this service. But the start was a quiet one and there were no radical changes. No one on this day would have thought something big was to happen by the end of the season. It was a dour game but a welcome win. It was the same players and a return to 4-4-2 and in came a young lad Graham Lancashire who was to be a massive instant hit, in place of injured Conroy and suspended Johnny Francis. Graham would score a hatful of goals in his first few games but then his career would unfortunately fade. The ball in this game squirted to Lancs and he pounced from close range to score a predator's goal. Did it feel like a new dawn? A couple of thousand people from the previous game thought not and stayed at home.

Steve Harper was fit again. The club had issued a statement that he had broken his arm in training. In fact what had happened was he'd broken his hand when he punched a wardrobe door in Cheltenham where we were staying one weekend. There'd been a heavy drinking night and more than a few lads were the worse for wear. Back in the hotel there was some larking about which included someone trying to shave Steve's eyebrows off while he was asleep. Steve was not best pleased when he woke up and discovered this. Punching the wardrobe door so hard was not the best thing to do.

A new manager comes in and in the second of his games, away as well, against Wrexham you win 6-2. This was an incredible score and it was even after Wrexham had taken an early lead. But then our goals started going in and the first was that new man again – Graham Lancashire. He was only 18 and he went on to get two more for his hat-trick. His third was an audacious piece of skill, lobbing the ball over the keeper's head. (But hey, the assist was mine thanks very much). When you play well you enjoy everything. The sixth was me, chesting the ball down and sliding it in. Maybe not quite Jimmy Greaves but a goal is a goal and this was the season that was to be special for me.

The Board apparently did interview other candidates for the manager's job but after a 6–2 win away from home, and a new fighting spirit, Jimmy Mullen got the job on October 17th. They weren't to know it but history was being made. Graham Lancashire celebrated his 19th birthday with yet another goal in the third consecutive win. There was a definite buzz developing. 'A cocky little so and so,' said Mullen when asked about Lancs.

We continued with the Autoglass Trophy. No matter what the competition, I loved being involved and playing. A win was always good for morale and self-esteem. There seemed to be so many games in this tournament just to get to the regional finals. By the time you'd got there you'd played so many games that no-one seemed to care. But I cared. I scored twice. But there were only just under 3,000 there to see my two masterpieces. Lincoln, another wonderfully old city steeped in history with its castle and cathedral, were thumped next at Sincil Bank. Lancs scored again when I was taken off and he came on.

That night, back in Burnley I was collared by a supporter. 'Hi Roger you were rubbish today,' he said. Such moments certainly kept your feet on the ground.

So far we had won every game under Jimmy Mullen. In Burnley, away from the gaze of the media, people were starting to get just a little excited. The shape of the team was beginning to emerge. Marriott was damned good in goal. The defence, Measham, Davis, Pender and Jakub, was ominously hard to beat. Andy Farrell and John Deary were skilled and competitive in midfield. Steve Harper and John Francis played wide. Up front was Mike Conroy, scoring all the time, the prodigy that was Lancashire, and me. Me, bustling, all action, head going in where it hurt, chase everything. They said I even chased the crisp packets that blew across the turf. I could do no wrong. Fans made comments that reflected the way Mullen had taken the same players and got them winning. The next games couldn't come soon enough. It was becoming a side that people wanted to watch. Roll on November. But why hadn't we done this for Frank?

When you'd won, the dressing room was a great place to be. As we got back in after every game there was jubilation. Hugs, high fives, shouting and towels being tossed around, huge smiles and Jimmy Holland scurrying round trying his best not to show his delight, tending to the players' cuts and bruises. I'd grab him in a headlock and ruffle what hair he had left. Secretly he enjoyed all the players' banter. The gaffer would bounce in feeling pleased and want the attention of all the players to go briefly over the game. He'd raise his voice, the first words: 'Take a seat.' His voice would fall on deaf ears; you were still on a high, in a daze, thinking about the game, your own game, and if you'd scored re-living the sweet moment of scoring.

Nobody was interested in any negative aspects of the game if it was a win. That could come on Monday. The three points were the most important thing. In that dressing room the euphoria and adrenalin still pumping meant you didn't bother about a bad pass, the time you nearly let them score or falling out with a teammate on the pitch. A win was a boost, a shot in the arm, as satisfying as an addict getting his fix but then only until the next time. Scoring goals is like a drug. You need the elation again. Once is not enough. A win is the ultimate collective high in the game. The group is everything. For a little while it's like reaching the moon; the supporters are pleased, the manager is pleased. Everyone is buoyant. You are a star, for a day at least.

Some players would want to get out of the dressing room as quickly as possible to get to the bar and let off a little steam. Others wanted to soak and relax in the white-tiled bath where you'd let the pressure of the last 90 minutes disappear and gather your thoughts. And then Jimmy's last words as we left: 'Enjoy the victory tonight without going crazy, we are bang at it again next Saturday.'

Halifax and the Shay; round the perimeter was an old speedway bike track. The gravel and cinders used to fly up from the track and land on the pitch. A sliding tackle and you could end up with a cinder stuck in your leg. This was a club so hard up that one year the winter ice was so thick they used the pitch as a skating rink and charged folk to use it. This was the world I lived in; places like Liverpool and Man United were in another galaxy. But yet another win took Burnley to third. Halifax had two players sent off. Pundits say that sending-offs spoil a game but the other team thinks good, that's a bonus. And if it's a foul and a sending off in the penalty area, it means you're doing something right and they can't handle it. Halifax normally had maybe a thousand spectators and a few pigeons up on the stand roof. Burnley took a phenomenal 3,000 fans with them. It was six wins in a row, officially the best start ever by a new Burnley manager. It was a game when I embarrassed myself before it had even started. Both teams lined up ready to come out but I was so focused, oblivious to everything around me, and had this habit of looking down at the ground when I came out. I followed the Burnley colour socks out that my eyes focussed on. Out I came. But it was the Halifax team I came out with; their socks were so like ours at Turf Moor. John Francis and Ian Measham were creased up laughing.

I had my trademark hairstyle, shaved to the skin round the sides and back so that only on top was there this mop of black hair. I must have thought it made me look hard, fearsome on the pitch but cool when I was out and about. I've had a few hairstyles in my time.

Make that seven wins on Bonfire Night against York. John Deary was having the season of his life and got a deserved goal; then Graham Lancashire again because I was injured. It was the day tycoon Robert Maxwell died. Funny the things you remember. Nobody will ever know if he fell overboard off his yacht or was pushed. There were plenty of people who would have been willing to help him over the side. The win set Burnley up for a top of the table clash against Mansfield. Nearly 12,000 people turned up. Chairman Frank Teasdale was by now beaming and the abuse previously hurled at him was silenced. I'd played in a new pair of boots that I was unused to. I remember that because I missed a golden chance and blamed the boots.

I'd drive to the ground from Bradford with loud music roaring away. I'd have had a pasta meal the night before and would always arrive early before a game; park the car and then walk along Harry Potts Way to the players' entrance. If it was a night game I'd have a sleep in the afternoon. At home I wasn't the easiest of people. I'd be irritable, anxious and tense. Andrea understood. She'd once worked at the Alhambra Theatre in Bradford and saw how short-tempered some of the 'stars' could be before a show. She knew all about pre-show nerves. Walking along, maybe someone would stop me for a chat and always: 'We gonna win today Roger?' Even an hour early there'd be people there waiting to get autographs by the entrance. The atmosphere and focus gradually built up.

The walk down to the dressing room at Turf Moor is down a long, narrow corridor under the Cricket Field Stand. The noises of supporters above your head up in the stand would be starting. I was usually the first in. The kit was there ready waiting for us in the small dressing room. Back then though you didn't get all the staff and subs that try to crowd in today. There was a brief period of quietness on my own. I'd read the programme and then begin to focus on what lay ahead. Jimmy Holland would be around getting his gear ready. One by one the other players arrived with their chat and gossip, banter and jokes; some of it nerves.

My boots were special to me. Nobody cleaned them but me. Other members of the team let the apprentices do theirs. This was a season we rarely lost at home, a season that was driven by the crowd as expectations grew. Jimmy Mullen would go round the players individually. I can't remember him being any kind of Churchillian orator before a game. But after a game he could dish out the hairdryer treatment when called for. Close to time and the referee would come in to inspect and check boots and studs. A bell sounded when it was time to go out – warriors, gladiators; psyching each other up, battle cries, hand-shakes, shouts: 'Come on lads, come on …' And then out into the light, the amphitheatre, the Coliseum, the wall of noise, eleven of us, one thing in mind.

It was a brilliant game against Mansfield, said to be one of the best Fourth Division games ever. The win, the eighth, was a tribute to a galvanised team with a never say die spirit. A bunch of lads comes together every so often and for some reason at some point they just gel. They win and win again and then a momentum builds up so that eventually they just assume they will win the next game, and the next, and the idea of losing just doesn't happen. You can't underestimate the confidence factor. When it goes you lose but when it's high you expect to win. If I related in detail the story of every game this book would be the length of an encyclopaedia but this one was a hell of a game. Andrew Firmin's diary tells the story of this one:

'In front of a crowd huge by the standards of the division, Burnley took on the leaders and beat them. We opened the scoring with a deserved early penalty. John Francis ran into the box where he was scythed down by a clumsy tackle. It was a clear penalty. Conroy made no mistake with the penalty sending the keeper the wrong way. One of the reasons it was such a good game was that Mansfield could play a bit too. Deservedly they made it 1–1. In the second half Burnley regained the lead from a fine Jakub corner and Steve Davis rose above everyone to head powerfully home. But five minutes later they were level again. It came from that rarest of things, a mix up between the two central defensive colossi. Davis and Pender banged into each other going for the same ball. It aimlessly looped into the box and in the confusion it fell nicely for Wilkinson to blast in his second goal.

'Mansfield could have won it after that. They had chances, none better than the shot headed off the line by Joe Jakub. It summed up a heroic performance by the little 5' 6" Scot. This was the moment the crowd warmed to him. He hadn't been popular before and had laboured under the less than flattering nickname of 'Cabbage'. But at left back under Mullen, this 35-year old produced a string of terrier-like performances. Before long the 'Cabbage' taunts were shelved and the crowd was singing, tongue in cheek, "Scotland's number three". It was from another Jakub corner that Pender scored the winner. The corner was long and high and was met by the captain lurking close to goal. Conroy characteristically whooped it up at the Cricket Field End. We all did.' (Andrew Firmin)

Joe had got the name 'Cabbage' because he'd once called the fans cabbages. It was on the coach in private to another player. Unfortunately it became public and it took a long time for the fans to forgive him. They frequently abused him after that and even used to knock on his door at home and then run off.

It was a barnstorming game; the win was a hard-fought and valiant one with relentless attacking and determination. It was one to send everyone home happy. 'We're on our way,' everyone thought but Jimmy Mullen tried to dampen the growing expectations. 'I'm not making any promises to anyone. This game has a knack of kicking you in the teeth.'

The wins wouldn't stop. The County Ground at Northampton was famously shambolic. Those who have been there still talk about it. It was where George Best scored six times in one game. Somehow Northampton went all the way up to the First Division ... and back again. With the score at 1–1 they pressed and obviously fancied their chances of all three points. But they didn't take into account our attitude. As they pushed up they were punished by a superb goal. Farrell cleared a long ball forward to Mick Conroy. He controlled it and laid it to Steve Harper whilst he himself charged through the middle. Harper played the ball in front of Mick; he controlled it on his thigh and then buried it in the net. You could only stand back and admire his skill. And this was the player who was so unsuccessful at Reading they played him at full-back. He was on 10 goals already and it was only November. The goal showed everything that was good about us. When Steve Harper brought the ball forward, three Burnley players raced into the box against one of theirs. We were never beaten, always looking to attack, fast and skilful, imaginatively looking to use the wings. Another huge away following erupted.

But there was a downside. It was Andy Mariott's last game. Brian Clough wouldn't sell him to Burnley so supporters spilled onto the pitch and chaired him off the field. It was emotional and touching. When he got back to Forest he said something remarkable: 'I think of Burnley as my first club and Nottingham Forest as just somewhere I train.' It was an extraordinary thing to say. What Clough's reply was is not known. I can't imagine he didn't blast him to Kingdom Come. But later in the season he broke into the Forest first-team and even played at Wembley in the League Cup Final. He was a damned good keeper, and a great lad. We called him 'Beaver'.

Jimmy Mullen was rightly awarded the Manager of the Month award. He'd overseen seven wins and a draw during the month. Northampton was the ninth consecutive league win. He tried to be modest about it in public. The crowd chanted 'Jimmy Mullen's claret and blue army' long and loud. They thought they and we were invincible.

He had taken over a club when it was on a downslide. The

remarkable thing was he still had to sign a new player. This was the same squad of players that Frank Casper had managed. All he had done was tweak the formation and tactics. There were no great sweeping changes and he had stuck by the same players.

But what was disappointing was that the phenomenal Graham Lancashire didn't really get the chances to develop further. If Mike Conroy was injured, then Graham was in the team. When Mike was fit he dropped to the bench. So the appearances and goals dried up. You wonder if that talent should have been nurtured just a little better. After his wonderful start, he never produced anything like it again and he slid down the familiar northwest slope, from Burnley to Preston, to Wigan, Rochdale and then non-league. If you'd seen one young kid in any team in '91 you'd have put money on Graham to make it to the big time.

Nothing lasts forever and the league winning run finally came to an end. Not away to one of the top teams but at home to Scunthorpe. It wasn't a defeat but a 1–1 draw. It had to happen sometime and this was after nine astonishing consecutive league wins. Scunthorpe were no mugs and hard to break down. Having taken the lead, we assumed the win would come. I had a hand in the goal, my saved shot prodded home by Andy Farrell. The equaliser was bad luck for big John Pender, sometimes called 'Penderdog' by admiring supporters. To us he was 'Bison'. He went for everything, and doing that yet again headed into his own net. The bigger disappointment was not going top which a win would have secured.

The club were meeting a firm refusal from Forest in more attempts to sign Marriott. Jimmy Mullen clearly had little faith in Chris Pearce and now brought in yet another loan goalkeeper Mark Kendall who had previously played for Wolves and Spurs. It sounded impressive enough. If we'd known Aldershot would be wound up by the season's end maybe we'd have chosen to stay in bed on 21st December. All that way for a result on a day that was beset by a howling gale, a win that was eventually expunged. But on the day Mansfield the leaders lost, and Burnley went top. Lancs scored again but it was to be his last for Burnley.

Going to a place like Aldershot was a lovely example of the quaint places in which we lower league players plied our trade. Supporter Tim Quelch described it beautifully:

'We will miss Aldershot with its quaint park entrance and herbaceous borders. You expected to pick up your crazy-golf clobber and your raspberry split as you squeezed through their turnstiles. Once you had climbed up the winding path up to the pitch, you were actually quite disappointed not to find a boating lake and a few ducks. When kept behind after an evening game you half expected them to ask you to turn off the lights and put the cat out as you left. Steve Claridge told us in his book *Tales from the Boot Camp* that one 'Shots' player qualified for a disabled sticker. Forget your Nou Camps and San Siros; this was a club with true class.' (Tim Quelch)

Maybe it was struggling clubs like these, and the Rochdales and Torquays and Herefords which were at the heart of the game. These places were filled with the little people of football, the people filled with genuine heart. Half-time collections at Aldershot games had helped keep them going and pay the wages. This was the reality of Division Four football and not that many years earlier it could well have been Burnley.

Despite this rise to the top, Mullen was careful. 'We have to keep our feet on the ground and make sure we don't get smacked on the nose.' This was ironic. The after-match interview was delayed because Jimmy had a nosebleed, probably because we were so high in the table.

Unfortunately, we got smacked on the nose in the very next game. Boxing Day at Turf Moor and some of the laws of football transcend all others. Regardless of the circumstances, however well Burnley are doing, Burnley always seem to lose on Boxing Day and Burnley duly lost against Rotherham United in front of nearly 14,000 people, most of them filled with turkey, mince pies and stuffing. Fans used to say there was always a magic atmosphere on Boxing Day with the aroma of cigar smoke and the tang of brandy from hip flasks. Try doing that today. This one was the day that the 16 game unbeaten run ended. I remember us being below our best; this was so disappointing in front of such a big crowd. Fans said it was typical of Burnley to screw up when the pressure mounted and now that we were top was it this pressure that was invisibly weighing us down? No, we said, you can't stay unbeaten forever. However good you are, a defeat will catch you up one day. And we were still top because all the top four teams lost so there couldn't have been a better day to lose. People went back to their turkey sandwich suppers. We went back home thinking there was another game just two days later. We'd actually been in the day before on Christmas Day for a training session. Footballers don't get a Christmas. There was even one Christmas when we stayed overnight in a Burnley hotel and I took a voluntary breathalyser test down at the local police station to see if I was fit to drive. If not I would need to ask Andrea to drive me.

The last game of 1991 and it was back to winning ways. For the fifth time it was against Doncaster Rovers. Bremner was no longer there. The score in this game never reflected how well Burnley played and how dominant they were. There were so many chances one after the other. I cringed when I managed to miss in front of an open goal. It was total one-way traffic; we were always on them, always at them, pressuring and outplaying them. Mick Conroy scored early and then yours truly atoned for the earlier miss, latching onto a long pass and then chipping it over the goalkeeper. Lovely stuff but somehow they pulled one back nearer the end to make it a daft scoreline and leaving supporters chewing fingernails in a game where we might have had six. But we hadn't lost and at the end of the year there was Burnley at the top of the Division, leaving supporters blinking and Frank Teasdale and the directors dreaming of triumph.

Jimmy Mullen set a target of not losing two in a row. Do that he said and promotion is possible. We didn't lose two in a row. Promotion was possible.

8

Owen Coyle Returns

Daniel Gray's book is one of those classic football odysseys where after a decade's exile in Scotland, Gray, an Englishman, sets out to reacquaint himself with England via what he considers to be its greatest asset: football.

Hatters, Railwaymen and Knitters is an affectionate search for the essence of England and its national game, even if that means finding a Burnley fan who claims that local butterflies support his team. Gray paints a picture of a curious England, as he watches teams from the Championship to League Two and aimlessly wanders round towns from Carlisle to Newquay. Observing more than just the actual matches, he discovers how the provinces made the England that we know today, from Teesside's role in the Empire to Luton's in our mongrel DNA. Moments in the histories of the teams come together to form football's story – starting with the Sheffield pioneers and ending with fan ownership at Chester. Gray's stories and discoveries show how the game unifies an England that is changing all the time and dominates the towns in which it is played. They are a wry look at England and its football and a ramble through the towns that make the country.

When he alights at Burnley he could not have known the significance of the occasion and the game he was about to witness. It was the first game of the season on 18 August 2012 against Bolton Wanderers. Their manager was Owen Coyle. To the delight of most, if not all Burnley supporters, they had been relegated at the end of season 2011/2012. It was seen as Coyle and the Bolton chairman, Phil Gartside, receiving their just comeuppances for the way that Coyle had been poached from Burnley in January 2010 when they were in the Premiership. It further amused the good Burnley folk that Coyle, as is the way of all managers, had heaped blame on bad luck, refereeing decisions and injuries.

Shortly after his departure to Bolton, Burnley had to travel to The Reebok and lost 1 – 0. Since then there had been another game between the two clubs when a relegated Burnley, at Turf Moor, had eliminated Bolton from the League Cup in front of a bumper crowd that hurled incessant abuse and fury at Coyle. At that point Bolton were still in the Premiership.

But the game on August 18 was different. The two clubs were now on a level footing. Coyle had suffered the ignominy of relegation and Gartside had egg on his face. Burnley fans were delighted and filled with anticipation. There were also rumours that a 'plane had been hired to fly over the stadium with a banner.

I am indebted to Daniel Gray and the publishers, Bloomsbury, for permission to reproduce the Burnley chapter.

***

Hatters, Railwaymen and Knitters by Daniel Gray (Bloomsbury)
From Chapter 10: Burnley

First day of the season, five words that mean the world, five words that let us breathe again. Five words that radiate hope and radiate optimism; the sun is out, our shirts are new and anything can happen. We say we would be happy with mid-table, but secretly we think that promotion is possible. It matters not that our best players have left since relegation; we like the look of youth. This is August, our month, one whose dictionary definition in our minds reads 'noun, start of new football season.' Even just rolling the word around in our mouths conjures first days gone by and the fiery glow of chance.

Our Saturdays are back. If we are not at the match, we can listen and watch; 5pm is the day's pinnacle again, not just another time on another long day. Even if the football man or woman still has things to do, chores to complete, he or she can do them with the commentary on. From now until May he or she will be a happier or a sadder person, exultant like a baby with a balloon one week, inconsolable when it bursts, the next.

This particular August I feel defensive of us football people. After Hinckley and all that, England were ritually ejected at the quarter-final stage on penalties; which was comfortably familiar if nothing else. Then came the Olympics. People were allowed to enter that mesh hamlet I saw before the Orient game. Gold, silver and bronze made its grey heart blaze, a thawed mammoth. British achievement captivated. The Games as a whole captivated a nation. Watching handball at midnight suddenly seemed like a national activity. In itself, that was fine, delightful in fact. Then they went for our sport.

The people and the press gassed lyrical about the evil of football and footballers compared with the Olympics and Olympians. Here were Corinthian titans running, throwing and rowing for the love of the sport, spurred by joyous and positive congregations of wholesome families in Union Jack hats. Set against them were voracious footballers, injury-feigning and philandering, berated by boozy hoards with bellies seeping from nylon. All athletes were smiling, gorgeous role models like Jessica Ennis, all footballers were brag-traders and fist wavers like Joey Barton. In the *Guardian,* Geoffrey Wheatcroft wrote of 'the incurable social disease known as Association Football'; which 'sometimes looks like a game owned by crooks and despots and played by racists and rapists.' Today, as I travel to Burnley I read the same newspaper's letters page. It contains the following: 'Geoffrey Wheatcroft reminds us that football is back. So is wife bashing. Our women's refuge had no requests for space during the Olympics. We had six by Tuesday.'

If I believed that football was a game played by rapists and watched by wife-beaters, it might dampen my August enthusiasm somewhat. But when Wheatcroft et al write of 'Association Football,' they are writing of top-end Premier League, of multi-millionaire players. That is a faraway outpost of the sport, one bruised fingertip. That is not my game. It is not the football that unites post-industrial towns when so much else is lost to them and it is not Chester FC running themselves.

The Best of Burnley

Neither is it the football that acts as a social lubricant when I am at a wedding or in the workplace, straining for common ground. I could go anywhere in the world, a dusty African village or Sydney, and find a game or a bar-room debate to join. Rowing and equestrianism incidentally, are none of these things. Yes, I can do class prejudice, too.

These thoughts are jangling as my train passes through the Lake District, its speed smudging Wordsworth's England. Luckily August conquers all. Burnley versus Bolton Wanderers at Turf Moor on 18 August is a compelling, history-scented proposal. I change at Preston where hordes of lads await their carriages to the new season, sampling the poetic delights of the timetable boards: Corkickle, Dove Holes, Flimby, Langwathby, Poulton-le-Fylde, Ramsgreave and Wilpshire. My route to Burnley fares well in the romantic stakes too, encompassing Pleasington, Oswaldtwistle and Rose Grove.

On the train, the heating blares and the windows are glued shut, which at least keeps the gossip in. Behind me two ladies in their sixties are nattering in heroically foggy Lancastrian accents: "e smokes too much, 'e smokes on 'oliday, in that liddle room upsturzs. Mind, 'e never smoked in Australia, smoked when 'e got back, mind. It's no life.'

'You're not wrong luv. I sez to 'im last time I was thur. I sez: "Kenneth, you 'ave got to stop," but 'e teks no notice.'

We skirt Irongate, the neat wee home of Bamber Bridge FC tucked between tracks and houses.

'I sez you'll get nowt for that at car booter. Give it ter charity shop.'

The land is lush, peaks and troughs up to Accrington. We curve towards Blackburn's red bricks and towers of old churches, mills, then minarets, a visual history.

'I sez to Roy, I sez, "There's a sale on."'

'E sez ter me, "You never buy owt anyway. Let's spare t' bother 'n stay at 'ome. Yer can watch t' shopping channel if yer like," 'e sez.'

After they leave the train at Hapton, I miss the rattle and hum of their conversation and hope Roy has put the kettle on. The train jolts into Burnley, above us the motorway, below us the canal, further topographic context. Burnley Central station is a bungalow with an added aura of 1960s asbestos and more recent moss on gravel. I take in its facilities – a fence and a bin – and leave. Ahead is the abandoned wreck of the Adelphi Hotel, a grand haunted house with its eyes patched by chipboard.

In Burnley's 1950s heyday, fans would splurge from the train and into the Adelphi. Wearing their claret and blue scarves over Saturday corduroy, they would gather here after steaming in from Colne, Nelson and even Skipton, over the border into Yorkshire. Ale necked; those supporters would walk downhill into town, sweeping hills above and beyond, choking chimneys in the middle distance. As they crossed an iron bridge their clogs and boots would clop and clank; many had come straight from the morning's shift in mill or mine. On Yorkshire Street they passed under the nobbly bolts of the Leeds-Liverpool Canal viaduct and filed to their 2pm destinations. Some went for a pint in the Miners' Club, some into Fitzpatrick's herbalists for a sarsaparilla, some into the butcher's for strips of tripe, eaten from a greaseproof bag in the street. If they did not live in the town they probably worked in it or at least knew its every nook and cranny, past and present.

During the Industrial Revolution Burnley grew from a market town backwater into the earth's largest producer of cotton cloth, and from 10,000 people to 110,000. Pitted in the dungeons of a valley, its damp air provided perfect conditions for making cloth, and the Empire's growing markets invited exploitation. There was innate artisanship among Burnley's people, cultivated by centuries of spinning wool from the sheep that loitered on the hills above the town. Before breakfast, mills supplied the home market and for the rest of the day, the world, went the legend. In their hundreds, chimneys speckled the skyline like giant stone trees. Those who did not work in the mills mined the rich carbon beneath their clogs. A number of Burnley's mines were in the town centre. The Leeds-Liverpool canal with its wondrous Straight Mile, shunted supplies in and exports out.

The work of the spinners, weavers and miners should not be glorified from distance, though its effects deserve to be lionised. The harm they put themselves in the way of, helped make Britain rich, contributing the revenues with which Teesside steel built the Empire's infrastructure. Their lives were hard. While the sun was still up in some part of that Empire, the workers of Burnley would be woken by a 'knocker-up' man. His job was to 'rat-ta-tat-tat' with a cane on bedroom windows and stir the dirty-nailed sleepers within. Mines we know were dangerous, but mills too. Thunderous machinery bred a staff of lip-readers and turned many deaf. Oily machinery, air clouded with dust and wooden floors that meant fire spread wildly and tragically. Burnley was predictably filthy on land and water, with bronchitis in children, as common as nits. The same damp air that made it a boom town withheld smoke and sulphur, concocting gritty smog that reduced visibility to five yards.

When the First World War finished, boom times turned to hard times in Burnley. During the 1920s Depression, unemployment hit 50% and unrest bubbled. Cheaper foreign markets had taken jobs away. Then, the Second World War saved Burnley by driving employment upwards and, when it finished, mill modernisation and pit nationalisation continued the trend. When Burnley won the league in 1959/60 though, decline had again begun to claw at the town. There was still the kind of work that had merited those clogs on the way to the match – over a dozen working chimneys remained – and coal was still being wrought from the earth, but Burnley knew it must change or die. That same 1959, the one in which Luton lost the FA Cup Final as Reginald Dwight looked on, the town pinned its hopes on familiar redevelopment plans based around a shopping centre, bus station and ring road.

Four days before the 1959/60 season kicked off, a faraway August with identical hopes and themes, the closure of the Benjamin Thornber and Son Mill was announced. Thornber's had been in Burnley for over a century, but was now to become another statistic among the 6,000 looms scrapped in Lancashire by the Conservative Government's concentration plan. Burnley's players will have known all about this grumbling malaise; most lived in the town and travelled by bus to games. Over the next nine months they produced football that made the entire town suspend its woes. That town backed them in force. The average Turf Moor crowd of 27,000 meant that a third of the town's population attended matches. The First Division average was 12%.

Owen Coyle Returns

Burnley had long cherished its team, residents of homely old Turf Moor since 1883. The club had a significant early role as leaders in the charge for pay and professionalism; they signed waged Scots and threatened to break away. In a town like Burnley, all labour had to mean a wage. The link between work and club was strong. Most Burnley players were miners or millworkers through the week and when they won the FA Cup in 1914, thousands of workers went on strike to join the victory parade. Seven years on, Burnley won their first League Championship, going 30 games unbeaten along the way. Then as the team slid, so did the town. The pair have often mirrored one another. Burnley's population declined dramatically, falling to 80,000 when the league was won again in 1960. That year seemed to mark the last of 'old Burnley' with mill and coal work still sprinkled around by the magic dust of the post-war boom, as such representing a final pinnacle for town and team.

The latter went out in style, renowned as they were for their princely play. Jimmy Greaves referred to Burnley's game as poetry and 'smooth, skilled soccer that was a warming advertisement for all that was best about British football.' Indeed, only Greaves' Spurs matched Burnley in their swift passing, possession-oriented game, modelled on the methods of Italy, Spain and those Hungarians who destroyed isolationist England and instigated our identity crisis. It was a Burnley man, Jimmy Hogan, who instilled 'push and run' football in Hungary, the nation dedicating its 6-3 victory to him. The Claret and Blues were best friends with the ball, happy in possession and fluidly exploiting space when not.

Burnley's football pivot was Jimmy McIlroy, a sumptuous and languid centre-midfielder who seemed to stop all the clocks and find a pass. When no player was ready to receive, the ball was his hostage, and as the opponents stormed the kidnapper he released it into the captivity of pitch room. The Wolves captain, Billy Wright, admired the Burnley way, 'every man searching for space.' Theirs was an early version of Total Football with rigid roles melted away into a loose arrangement of barnstorming full-backs and centre-halves that could play a bit. Freedom was injected into their DNA. This team and their style left an indelible mark on those who saw and read of it while young. My own dad, then a young Leeds United fan, can still recite Burnley's line-up of Blacklaw, Angus, Elder, Seith, Miller, Adamson, Connelly, Robson, Pointer, McIlroy and Pilkington. What a shame for today's young fans that huge squads and high player turnover will kill the future joy of recalling notorious XIs, lounging over every syllable.

Each tier of Burnley's team played in the same way, youth to reserve, training and matches. It was part of a progressive approach to training encapsulated in the club's belting training ground, dug from nothing by players in search of a summer wage. Then Manager Alan Brown recalled in Arthur Hopcraft's classic *The Football Man* how, 'The players got down to it, famous ones like Jimmy McIlroy and Adamson, and dug ditches with me.' These of course were maximum wage days, days of scarcity for some players, and days when Davids like Burnley could compete with the Goliaths of wider Lancashire, Merseyside and London. Training was intense but pioneering, coaching advanced but clear. It fostered fiddle-fit players with speedy minds and super quick feet, whizz-kids from the moors. Squad additions needed raw qualities that could be built upon, and they needed to be good lads. This was a close-knit team that won and drank together. Their wives were a collective force to be reckoned with, influential and well known across the town.

Two key figures built this Burnley, a club from an unfashionable Victorian town playing advanced football, the scarecrow in a spacesuit. Harry Potts had arrived at Turf Moor in 1937, a 16-year old centre-forward who soon became the club's number 10. He became manager in 1958, quickly building on football principles laid down by his predecessor Alan Brown. A fatherly track-suited tutor through the week and a firebrand when Saturday came, Potts was loved by his players. The manager, who moulded his team on the training ground and quietly encouraged each player in turn at quarter to three, was transformed by the whistle. On the touchline he headed and kicked everything, a bonkers street mime act. This could overspill: during a European cup-tie in Rheims, Potts became incensed at the home side advancing free-kick positions. He ran on the pitch and retreated the ball himself.

Potts' chairman was Bob Lord, according to Kenneth Wolstenholme a 'fair man' who worked the sort of day that would make younger men wince.' And to Danny Blanchflower 'a self-made man who worships his creator.' Lord was elected in 1955, a lifelong fan and successful butcher, the paternalist Victorian town chairman after his time. Despite the time warp, many of his ideas for Burnley and football were undoubtedly progressive, or at least foretold much of what was to come. It was his idea to upgrade the training ground and put emphasis on a youth programme. He supported the professionalization of referees and abolition of the maximum wage, a rare trait in a chairman, and presided over the gradual upgrade of Turf Moor. He even flew his team to some away games. Yet Lord resented supporter input saying: 'We don't recognise any supporters' associations. My ambition is for the club to function completely without any money coming through the turnstiles at all. That is the road to Utopia.'

His labelled 'bluntness' was in reality often plain offensive once saying: 'We have to stand up against a move to get soccer on the cheap by the Jews who run television.' Lord's humourless demeanour and habit of banning journalists for criticising his club meant he was, wrote Hopcraft, 'the Kruschev of Burnley.' He even sold Jimmy McIlroy and that behind Potts' back. McIlroy's sale was the first of many. Lord's stands, with their heated floors, were subsidised by the departure of talent.

If Lord's words were often, in modern political parlance, regrettable, his and Potts' results were wonderful. In the red-hot summer of 1959 they pokered Leeds 3-2 and scorched Everton 5-2. 'Stand in with us for all you are worth,' wrote Potts. Champions Wolves were destroyed 4-1 at Turf Moor. 'The ball was on our side,' said McIlroy afterwards; but only because he made it so. The FA Cup holders Forest were given an 8-0 seeing-to; Bolton just the four. At aristocratic Highbury, the mill boys beat the posh boys 4-2. Soon, top of the league Spurs visited Turf Moor. The pass-masters were turned past-masters, two nowt to the Burnley boys. Still, Potts' men were not perfect. Flexible football meant open football. Gaps at Molineux meant a 6-1 defeat and the Clarets faced a must-win game at Manchester City on the final day.

Win they did, 2-1, on fierce Moss Side. Back home in Burnley, Potts danced on the Town Hall steps and the hordes cheered Bob Lord. Their men had lifted a town that knew it was on the precipice of decline. Potts and McIlroy had set out to see the people smile again. It was mission accomplished.

***

The Adelphi's old wooden sign swings in the breeze today, its faint pastels of two Fauntleroys ghostly. Behind this dead inn is Sainsbury's where men wearing claret and blue shirts push trolleys; shopping first, then the match. I walk downhill into town, my modern office-boy shoes registering no noise. Old mill chimneys still mark the sky like disused parentheses and beyond them are motionless wind turbines. The turbines are set on gentle hills, the kind of which surround Burnley on all sides, giving a secluded feel, as if the inhabitants are the inmates of an organic prison. Though placed similarly, it feels more isolated and secretive than Sheffield, as if it could not care less whether you knew it was there or not. I arrive at St James' Street and the first buildings I see are humbly pleasant and intact Victorian shopping blocks with flats above. Their shops have kindly wooden fronts whose names swither between museum piece (Empire News) and modernity (Bibi's Kebab and Pizza House). Behind the main row and about 100 metres apart are more mill chimneys, emphasising just how physically central industry was here. The last town centre mine only closed in 1971, the final steam-powered mill in 1982. All of these buildings are in chunky stone the colour of dirty straw.

This quiet grandeur masks high unemployment and poverty levels. Burnley has finished mourning but is still suffering. Its population level remains in decline and those who stay often work elsewhere. Rather than the refined and refurbished mainstays of lower St James Street, an abundance of dirt-cheap shops at the highest end tells Burnley's truths. As I walk around I see children holding yellow and blue balloons pronouncing the opening of the new 99p shop. Its competitors will include Poundland, the original Mega Pound Superstore and Wacky Pound, among others. Today they offer DVDs, games consoles and furniture for rent. *Furniture for rent* in the world's seventh richest country!

I sit on a bench, surrounded by hanging baskets, last night's hardened kebab onions crunching under my feet. There is calmness here and a soft happiness that will always triumph over rented furniture. That, a thousand times more than the Union Jacks that line St James' Street, makes me feel patriotic. These people have had everything hurled at them but will stop in the street to laugh together about last night's telly. Not that much has changed. Burnley is a perfectly decent place because of these people.

There are shirts of claret and blue everywhere in Burnley today. The club belongs to the town as it did in 1959 and to support anyone else is an act of treason. New shirts in August, bare arms before winter, are all part of the gleeful first-day ritual. When I see a child in full kit (including shinpads) I know everything is grand in the world. In the Charter Walk shopping centre one such shirted man tells a flock of old ladies of his NHS woes: 'There's going to be a helluva lot of suing going on, I can tell you.'

Here occurred one of Burnley's rebellious episodes. In 1842, the Plug Plot Riots, a general strike across Britain inspired by Chartism, reached Burnley. One report recalled how: 'All the shops in the neighbourhood were demanded of their contents. The crowd made a special design on Horatio Hartley's butcher shop. Being well-stocked with meat, he and his brother armed themselves with knives and kept back the plunderers. The mob deemed it prudent to leave his shop alone.'

Today in the market hall the butchers shops are being demanded of their contents again, albeit politely and from queues of nattering locals. One's window stickers offer 'Black puddings, hot or cold,' another boasts 'Tripe sold here, honeycombe seam, dark and roll.' Burnley Market contains the usual bright menagerie of sweet stalls, grocers and poster/print/flag stands, and a lively fancy dress emporium. It is busy. Most units are occupied and the packed booth-like side cafes leave the air heady with gossip and chip fat. In a side hall an old-boy artist paints the Burnley he remembers and 60p VHS videos linger unloved on a table.

Back on St James' Street my nostrils guide me to Oddie's Bakery, my ears towards the brass band. Whoever is in charge of my *Truman Show* life is doing it again: a brass band. I sit, look and listen. They are a bit cheerier than a Yorkshire brass band, knocking out sing-alongs for the blue rinse crowd. A band member shuffles among us offering lyric sheets and the conductor tells the story of each song. One involves an extended anecdote about 'Ben', a Michael Jackson record. An old man in a Disneyworld T-shirt heckles something derogatory about that 'oddball Jackson'. Beyond the bandstand, more claret and blues swarm into twin pub corners, nodded in by Robocop bouncers. I potter down backstreets and eventually reach the lapping waters of the Peace Gardens, complete with Princess Diana plaque. Every time I read or hear her name, I think not of tragedy and the People's Princess, but of football being postponed. In 1981 (that year again) as dewy eyes watched her royal wedding, Burnley responded to a Conservative Government edict asking councils to spend money on civil defence by declaring itself a nuclear-free council. The Peace Garden is a monument to their defiance. It is surrounded by serious Victorian buildings, built to enable the working class and keep secure its streets. The library, building society and police station assert civic order in a reassuringly deep northern voice. As I stand and admire them I catch the bass of Bolton fans arriving from Burnley Manchester Road railway station. 'White Army' they bellow. On Manchester Road stand the pillars, porticos and frills of the Mechanics Institute and the Town Hall, further glorious stone elegies to Burnley's buzz town years. At the Weaver's Triangle the worm-brown canal shimmers briefly before turning still again. More claret and blues stare at their reflections in it and sup pints.

I walk from the peak of Manchester Road, hundreds of claret and blues, peppered with whites, lumbering towards the match in front of me. It feels as if this town exists today for the football and football only. Everything else is a side matter. It is a football town in which every road leads to 3 o'clock. Me and the August shirts reach Yorkshire Street and cross under the bolted viaduct like millions before us. On this road of yellow bricks Turf Moor comes into view, a hazy emerald city. There is no eating of tripe today; just burgers

Owen Coyle Returns

snaffled quickly in-between swift ales at the Brickmakers' Arms and the Turf Hotel. Off the main drag I walk through the guests' door of the Miners' Club and pay my 20p entrance fee. By the pool table is a monument to 'Those who worked and died in the darkness, still loved the light,' 19 miners who lost their lives in the Hapton Colliery disaster of 1962.

I order a pint of bitter and a 'Bene 'n' 'ot'. This is a Benedictine liqueur with hot water. More Benedictine is sold in Burnley's Miners Club than anywhere else on earth. It was a taste cultivated by the East Lancashire Regiment in the trenches of Normandy during the bitter winter of 1918. Today, their great grandsons and daughters lap it up. A proud barfly reels off the story for me and tells me how 'We've had them, all here, Sky, BBC, even a Canadian film crew the other week. That's one of the only two gallon bottles of Bene in't world. Other's in't monastery.' The Bene smells ever so antiseptic and is the colour of a 'sample'. Despite these unpromising medical beginnings it tastes marvellous. Sweet menthol meets a brew made by Nana. Here's to the Burnley boys in the trenches making their best of a bad lot.

The first day sun beams invincibly as I cross from Yorkshire Street on to Harry Potts way. Both sets of fans are mixing easily despite the presence of police horses which always seems to heighten tension. Many supporters stroke the gee-gees fondly as they pass. 'I've got a tenner on you, cock,' smiles a tubby Boltonian. The noises of matchday stoke up once more, a routine soundtrack blown and dusted down like a photo from a loft.

'Programmes, programmes, get yer programmes,' then something intelligible from a half-time draw salesman in a bib, and solo male voices growling away at the frustrations of Pools-free Saturdays. Those fans that have not seen one another since May shake hands and sometimes embrace in the street. Names are not always known but once you have had a season ticket next to someone for a decade it is too late to ask.

I walk around the outside of Turf Moor, the ground that Bob Lord built. Only two of his stands remain, one named after him. Lord died a week before I was born, not living to see Burnley go up as Division Three champions in 1981/82. That was a temporary reprieve;

far had they fallen since their halcyon days. In 1987, only a last ditch defeat of Orient preserved league status. Although the enclosures and food kiosks are named after Burnley greats, there is a strange lack of football's former world for such an old ground, save for the painted scars of a disused turnstile wall at the far end of the David Fishwick Stand. That, though, is by design; Lord was, remember, a modernist. The innards of the Jimmy McIlroy Stand host 'UCFB' which offers, apparently, 'university degrees in football business.' It is probably what our Lord would have wanted.

I turn a corner and spot a queue. Hundreds are waiting patiently for beer from the canteen hut of Burnley Cricket Club, whose ground neighbours Turf Moor. The far boundary brushes against the stand behind one of the goals; these Siamese venues were a Victorian entertainment complex. The whites of Bolton have commandeered the sizeable pavilion and a youths' game played to parents this morning is now cheered riotously by the visiting hundreds. The roar that goes up when a wicket is taken inspires jubilant scenes in the slips, a glimpse of the big time long to be cherished.

Passing new stewards meeting for the first time I heave a turnstile into the Bob Lord Stand. At the John Connelly Bar I wait for my pint of Thwaites to settle and note that they too stock Benedictine which beats even Mr John's Portman brandy as a football ground catering exercise. Youth team players hover in official tracksuits, their first team fantasies intact for now at least. I perch on a wall while two bulky Burnley fans born with plastic forks in their mouths pick at chips and talk about holidays. 'You've been to that Sharm el Sheikh, haven't you Steve? She fancies it but I'm not going over there while it's like what it is. They wouldn't leave our lass alone over there; blonde haired isn't she?'

From the dark of the concourse I climb over into the wide-open light of the new season and am transfixed by the varnished wooden seats that pack the stand. They are working antiques, with their ornate brass joints as close to arts and crafts as stadium seats go. The brimming Bolton end has them too, although most in there stand up and glare distractedly at the lush pitch.

The lull before the players enter the pitch is filled with songs from both sets of fans. This is all too perfect until the man in charge of the PA responds by blasting everybody with some unwelcome Foo Fighters. Thankfully, when the claret and blues and the whites stroll on, even he turns things down. The players' tunnel is located behind the goal, so the bench battalions must cross the pitch to reach the dugouts, situated in front of our wooden wonders. This allows cacophonous barracking of the away manager, once of this parish.

'Jooooooooodas … Jooooooooooodas,' sing the boys and girls and men and women of Burnley. Loyalty remains prized among supporters. To move to another Lancashire club is like shacking up with the tarty girl next door.

The sun climbs higher, visor arms move to foreheads and the season kicks off. From home and away the noise rises, amplified by the end of non-season boredom and the swagger of new season hope. The Wanderers fans in particular are strident, which they never seem to be at The Reebok. It recalls for me early 1990s trips to intimidating Burnden Park and highlights that the best noise is now often made by the away fans; and often the best place to watch your team is somewhere else. The racket transfers straight to the hearts of the players who begin frantically, passing quickly, tackling sharply and shooting widely. It is all very English and very enjoyable. Wanderers, newly demoted from the big time try to slow things down and engage in the artful. A delicately chipped free-kick intended to be ornate backfires momentously, trickling out of play. The Burnley mobs jeer as one. Welcome back.

The treacherous away manager moves to the touchline, causing those around me to rise and bellow biblically. Not one of them looks harmful or readily violent and I reflect how, if they saw him in the street, they would probably engage in polite conversation. This kind of hostility seems more traditional and theatrical than the needless vitriol I have seen elsewhere, though perhaps the hands of my moral compass are looser following a summer far from the madding crowd.

Wanderers have an implacable mountain up front. Born in Sheffield, he is built for the days of shove the keeper and Ernest Needham. For nigh on a decade he has been the peak at which team-mates have cast long passes and crosses like picks on ropes thrown into the snow.

If he had played for Graham Taylor's Watford he would have been a superstar. He was born after his time, but simply by refusing to change has earned opposition respect. It is not a deferential respect (this is football), but one detectable in the jubilant celebrations that greet the floppy-blonde Burnley left-back who clatters him. Footballing respect is grudging, perverse and will never be admitted. Though his team do initially try to pass the ball on the ground, when no joy is found they seek his head. Burnley, with two narky ferrets up front, keep things concise. This is in contrast to their supporters, who in song manage to wring three syllables from the word 'Burnley.'

Things become niggly as players wheeze in the heat which reminds them that the beach is only a few weeks behind them. Fitness does not yet match intention, making for late tackles and one or two circus moves. Two opposing midfielders try to outmuscle one another and end up resembling a pantomime horse without a costume. Short hit passes are seized on and possession veers quickly between the sides, ending usually in a fit of pinball rebounds that serve to keep the crowd cooing and being unfeasibly grateful that football is back. In the neon frenzies of football's first day, there is nowhere else to be. This is heartfelt football in which ability does not always meet idea and the ball is not always taken before man.

Burnley begin to find their range, firing in a succession of long-range shots. One swerves, and reminds me of the heat you see on continental airport tarmac. Somehow the Wanderers' goalkeeper gets both wrists to it and bats it over for a corner. One of Burnley's ferrets irks Wanderers lanky centre-half, snipping at his ankles and sniffing for crumbs. The home side are tenacious. When they shoot they follow after the ball and sometimes seem to overtake it. Such forcing and hunting brings them a 1-0 lead.

'Jooooooooodas, Jooooooooodas what's the score, Judas what's the score?' sing those around me.

Wanderers kick off but Burnley set about them again. Away shoulders drop and most in white become guilty of propelling missiles in the direction of their big man. I look at their loyal army behind the goal. To a man and woman they are stood, many with arms folded. Last year's tepid relegation stretches out behind them, the

Owen Coyle Returns

long season ahead, in front. The half-time whistle goes and they are not sure whether to boo or clap so in the main keep silent. The man in front of me rises, revealing on his seat an ancient remnant of floral carpet. I imagine he has had this since Burnley were champions. He reaches for his flask because it is never too hot for tea. Ahead of us, substitutes thrash footballs at one another and on a pitch within a pitch school-kids play the game of their young lives. In the gents, half-time analysis is curt.

'They are utter shite,' says one man.

'I think we might go up,' says another.

The second-half begins with two free-kicks each in the opening 30 seconds and a purple butterfly hovering around us. 'Even that bugger is Burnley,' says carpet remnant man. Burnley force the pace again, though Wanderers strive to remind us that they are alive with thudding challenges. The home keeper indulges in a short spot of keep-ups before floating a pass straight to an opposition midfielder. He has a clear run on goal and is bawled on by those behind the goal whose noise reaches a crescendo as he reaches the penalty area. Their sound crescendos like that of the paddock as an outside bet nears the finishing line. Wanderers will equalise, go on to win it and probably be top from now until May. He falls over the ball. A few minutes later Burnley make it 2-0.

The second comes when a cross is hoiked in and Bolton's centre-halves and goalkeeper stare at the ball as if it is a difficult Japanese puzzle. A Burnley player nods it in to the gaping net. The new season is only an hour old and the claret and blues have promotion in their nostrils. To the tune of Wild Rover they chorus: 'No nay never no more/ Will we play Tranmere Rovers.' *(As well we know this should read Blackburn Rovers but we can forgive Daniel Gray one tiny hiccup. DT)*

Across from us in the stand-edge nearest the away supporters, hundreds are turned towards their Lancashire brethren, jigging and jibing. A few twirl their shirts over their heads revealing expansive stomachs. Jooooooooodas creeps forward from the bench to be met with cries of 'sacked in the morning/you're getting sacked in the morning.' His instructions make no difference as Burnley continue to probe when on the ball, and harry when not. Wanderers have lost their map to the penalty area and instead shoot implausibly. When anything looks like it might be on target, a Burnley leg, chest or head, blocks it. It makes the away side lose heart and even when they keep the ball; their forays seem more like contractual obligations than investigative experiments.

Burnley inhale the pressure and strike Bolton on the break. Full-backs and wingers overlap and swap roles, the living ghosts of 1960. Their left-winger runs with one shoulder lower than the other as if pressed to the mill. As he labours three step-overs and lands another cross on top of the net, those behind the goal ponder the away fans' dilemma: stay to boo and see who claps, or leave and make the earlier train? Today's Man of the Match is awarded to Burnley's number 8 who celebrates with a crunching centre-circle tackle that puts hairs on the chest of his opponent. By the referee's third and final peep, an almighty roar fills the air. Happy Clarets drift off into the evening sun and before long I am left alone in the wooden seats.

Litter blows across the players' car park and the wind carries a scent of ageing burgers and police horse manure. Just after Yorkshire Street I cross high above a small stream and waterfall, church bells chiming a street or two away. I begin an uphill walk to my hotel for the night, passing the Duke of York pub, centrepiece of riots here in 2001. What were initially reported as race riots turned out, according to an official inquest, to be drug gang turf wars exploited by racist groups external to Burnley. Scapegoating and mythology allowed the British National Party to crowbar a divide. In 2002 they made their first breakthrough into British politics in Burnley, winning three council seats. They were able to paint a town flooded by foreign invasion and bursting at the seams. In fact, this is an emigrant town whose population decreases every year. In council elections three months before my visit, the BNP lost their remaining token seat.

Along Colne Road, Asians and whites inhabit the same space without mixing. Sharing social class and geography, they are silently bonded by having nowt. Some rows of terraces remain, some are boarded up and four or five of the streets have been bulldozed, rendering a crater of a community. Any sadness I feel is tempered by the sight of young kids of every colour hammering a ball about in the rubble.

The main drag is a mix of Burnleys and Englands, old and new, both still breathing. On one side of the road are Byerden House Socialist Club and then paradise WMC; on the other are sari shops, halal butchers and a Polski Sklep. I imagine there is still tension, but there is a pact of silence that is hopefully a welcome stepping stone to future integration rather than simmering resentment. Ten minutes uphill, I cross a road and things change. The houses are gradually larger and farther from the path. Eventually I reach mill-owner mansions now inhabited by tanned Lancastrians and multi-Mercedes Asians, both of whom have left their people down the hill behind. If one road on my travels is an exhibition of England's narrative, then this is it. At this end, no one ignores his neighbours because of race, but because isolation is what middle-class people do. In this strange way does becoming bourgeois, unwittingly fight racism.

In the hotel bar, dregs of a wedding party slur their disapproval of the modern world. A Lancastrian businessman of 63 sits with his Mauritian wife of 37. I am not guessing this. He tells most that enter the room.

'There will never be another generation like ours,' he says to a Cockney man of similar age who sounds and looks as if he once managed Status Quo. 'We pulled ourselves up by the bootstraps; worked our backsides off. Not like this lot today.'

Quo replies: 'I have this saying – you get out what you put in.'

I am not sure that is strictly his idiom, but I let it go. The conversation turns to which cars they let their wives drive. Quo says: 'I don't let her near the Bentley now; £3.5k of damage the bitch did.'

I leave hoping that my generation is not like theirs and reflecting how, despite 1981 and all that, we are not Thatcher's children. They are.

The bus into town redeems my mood. First, we pass a horse and cart, then, a man in a flat cap gets on and tells the driver jokes that we can all hear. I walk by the Keirby Hotel, a dreadful concrete hive and the showpiece of the 1959 ring road renewal plan. It resembles a decrepit block of flats wearing a conservatory as a tutu. Outside the Bier Huis, Claret sleeves raise toasts to 2-0. I seem to have arrived during clientele shift changeover, as all-day drinking husbands swap with dolled-up wives. They complete their substitutions, a peck on the cheek instead of a high five. Ales are abundant in the Bier Huis, but even hops and oats do not fill my stomach. For some time I walk the streets of Burnley in search of food. The polished cobbles and thudding chain bars of Hammerton Street are empty of people. A small mill at the road's end has been smartly converted into nightclubs called Lava and Ignite. Next to the canal, a rat runs over the shining night-out shoes of a man smoking outside a bar. I remember a conversation I had with my mother.

'You've been to Burnley before love.'

'Have I ... when?'

'On that canal holiday, there was a dead sheep in the water, or a cat, I forget.'

I end up eating my first McDonald's in well over a decade. In my lifetime McDonald's went from the height of exoticism (everyone my age remembers their first, mine was in Milton Keynes) to a hated symptom of all that was wrong with the world. It is now somewhere in-between apparently because it sells salads and tells you how pleasantly its cows are killed. It is bright, just as I remember it, and the servers still smile even though they would rather be anywhere else. I pity the young girl that serves me; the end of the drinking shift has brought the hunter gatherers in nylon claret. After chips that taste just how I remember, a not unpleasant sensation, I return to the hotel feeling a bit grubby.

The next morning I cleanse my soul with a walk high above Burnley. I pass through an estate where children kick a flat ball in the road and one two-up and two-down has a St George's Cross painted across its entire front. As I glance down this unique little place of bold stone, foreground chimneys and background hills, I see that Turf Moor is almost at the centre of the landscape ahead of me, which feels like its natural place. The club matters today as much as it did when it was founded. It matters even more than it did in 1959; it, and football, are things worth belonging to and believing in.

The significance of the game that Gray writes about was enormous to all Claret fans who remembered Coyle's walkout. Football is cruel and most if not all Burnley fans rejoiced in the relegation that Coyle suffered, not just because of Coyle himself, but also because of Phil Gartside's role in it. It is just possible that although he sussed out the dislike for Coyle, Gray didn't fully grasp that significance and probably didn't fully appreciate the origin of it. He would probably have had little knowledge of the circumstances of the move to Bolton Wanderers. The absence of any mention of the 'plane and banner that was hired is surprising; but seated where he was up in the Bob Lord stand he might not have seen it circling the ground. Many people knew in advance that something had been planned. It was a sight to behold and I was one of thousands who loved it.

***

For a number of years I have written a diary/blog of each season. This was the first entry for season 2012/13.

Where Did Summer Go, August 2012?
Burnley 2 Bolton Wanderers 0

And so to Turf Moor for the Bolton game; you could hear the collective gasp when this first fixture was announced earlier in the summer. What a scandal that it was not on live TV. It was a Leeds game on TV, who else? The game was not a sell-out but the club had set new prices that meant pay on the day fans had to break the £30 barrier. Plus the football of the season before had hardly been riveting or rip-roaring stuff that would bring the crowds back.

But more of the same from this opening game of the new season and they certainly would come back. We drove over from Leeds, me working out that it now costs my old banger £1 to do 6 miles. The summer had gone by quickly and this first game almost caught us unawares leaving us thinking: 'Gawd there's a game tomorrow.'

A 3-0 win for Burnley had a nice ring to it, we thought as we journeyed across the Pennines. In fact it was the next best thing and 2-0 was richly deserved. Bolton could not have grumbled had it been double that going by the number of chances made and the times

Burnley got the ball in the box. Anything other than a win would have been an injustice, although Bolton had one cleared off the line in the closing minutes. They looked crisp and smart in their black and white outfit, but this smart appearance belied the poverty of their play. Where were the pass and move, the old-fashioned wing play, and all the pleasing on the eye stuff so beloved of their manager? As long as Davies was on it was mostly just kick and lump it up to him. Sadly it looked time to put the old warhorse out to grass.

Once the game began it became clear that Bolton were a mixture of carthorses, one-trick ponies and one donkey. Meanwhile our brave lads looked like sleek, thoroughbred racehorses for much of the game. Once the first tentative ten minutes were over when football was at a minimum and get-rid-of-it-quick was the only thing on offer, the game settled into a pattern which consisted of Burnley getting the ball, passing it around, creating swift incisive moves, making the openings and chances and deservedly taking the lead.

Shackell and Edgar were giants. McCann surged forward imperiously, just like in the old days. Peterson was just electric and ran himself into the ground, Marney was absolutely everywhere, Wallace was tireless in support, Austin was a real handful, Trippier had Petrov in his pocket, Grant caught everything and was guilty of only one goof that could have been costly. Mills was superb and Stanislas made Austin's goal with a cross that just begged to be bundled in for the second goal. His blistering shot was the catalyst for Burnley's first. And all this was in what seemed like 90 degrees.

And the Bolton manager? We debated whether or not it was time to forget Owen Coyle and what he did. Was it time to move on? Clearly not in the cauldron of abuse that was Turf Moor that day. The 14,000 Burnley fans in the bumper crowd had no intention of being impartial; they would not forget the classic lines such as: 'I'm here as long as the club want me.' They would not forget the departure of a complete coaching staff. And the irony was he was now in no better position than when he had left Burnley following Bolton's relegation under him.

Forget the spin and honeyed words; Bolton were now millions in debt and relegation had hit them with the weight of an articulated truck. It could only get worse and if Coyle did not bring an instant return to the top division he would be sacked, just as Megson was before him. There is no sentiment in football. Coyle had worked a miracle at Burnley but on this scorching Saturday there was no sign that he would do anything similar at Bolton.

And so the boos and jeers rained down on him mercilessly as soon as he appeared and walked to the dugout. The catcalls and jibes were strident, ear piercing, ceaseless and filled with bile. When he had left in mid-season he had truly hurt the good folk of Burnley, and if he ever thought that time would heal, he was mistaken. What was demonstrated was the fact that whenever he brings a team to Turf Moor he will be assailed by the voices of those people who felt so let down. If you kick one person in Burnley, the saying goes, everybody hurts.

Overhead was the 'plane that appeared. Not just once but several times as it circled the ground with the banner that read: JUDAS COYLE YOU REAP WHAT YOU SOW. Quite frankly we rejoiced in Bolton's relegation. We refused to believe that Coyle could have sat in that dugout and not seen it and heard the hostility of the reception he got and been unaffected by any of it. And then at 2-0 down came the pièce de résistance as cries of 'you're getting sacked in the morning,' rang round the ground.

His Bolton fans gave it large in the opening minutes but the verbal exchanges were soon quietened. Coyle had taken them to relegation and the unpromised land of the Championship. In 2009 they had called for Megson's head on Boxing Day at Turf Moor. They would soon be calling for Coyle's. 'What goes round goes round,' Stan Ternent had once said.

After the game, I looked over at one or two of the Bolton fans' websites. Most of the posts agreed that Bolton had been lucky it wasn't more than two; that Burnley had wanted this result far more than Bolton and more than a few were already unhappy with their manager. Karma, we thought. And yes, his services were eventually dispensed with by Chairman Gartside. Of course the Burnley fans were on a delirious high on the way home and in the pubs and clubs after the game.

The Best of Burnley

After the glorious summer we'd had in Greece, basking in the sun, watching the Euros in the Boom Boom Bar in Meganissi, we were back home to the nitty gritty of the Championship. And what a start it was.

9

Sean Dyche

This chapter is reproduced from Michael Calvin's excellent 2015 book Living on the Volcano *a study of a host of managers. One of them was Sean Dyche and I am hugely grateful to Michael Calvin for his permission to use the Dyche chapter. Calvin also worked with Joseph Barton on the acclaimed Barton book* No Nonsense. *Both should be on the shelves of every football fan. These are two books that stand out from the crowd.*

The title of the Dyche chapter is hugely significant. Seeing through the noise is the way we focus on what we are doing. Other things going on around us we ignore, we concentrate on where we are heading and tolerate no distractions. Sean Dyche likens it to walking into a crowded and noisy room but over there in the corner is the person we want to see. We make for and hear that person and ignore the noise and clutter of the surroundings. Getting to the end of a game with a win is much the same. Getting to the end of a season with all its myriad commotions and disturbances and retaining focus is very much the same. It is about single-minded and dedicated application.

***

**Living on the Volcano: The Secrets of Surviving as a Football Manager by Michael Calvin (Arrow Books)
From Chapter 16: Seeing Through the Noise**

It was the sound of the first cuckoo of spring, shrill and self-regarding.

Jose Mourhino condemned 'criminal' challenges, citing four incidents in a home draw with Burnley to support his latest conspiracy theory. In so doing, he traduced a team he evidently considered to be at the knuckle-dragging end of football's evolutionary scale.

Sean Dyche did not get mad. He got more than even in a ten-minute 47-second monologue into the lens of a single camera. It was a masterly point-by-point rebuttal of the Chelsea manager, in which repeated assertions of respect were as acidic as his rationality, professional insight and forensic analysis. He protected his players and, for good measure, concluded his case with a video clip which exposed the champions-elect as cheap and faintly nasty.

Anyone with Dyche's shaven head, sculpted goatee beard, piercing eyes, furrowed brow and pebble-dashed voice gets used to lazy stereotyping. He is routinely compared to a nightclub doorman or the sort of 70s detective who imposed order by fitting up the manor's villains. He demonstrated a QC's ruthless articulacy and sensitivity to the human condition.

He added to his lustre as an emerging manager of the highest quality. It was one thing to get Burnley promoted into the Premier League on one of the lowest budgets in the Championship, entirely another to keep them there while spending the equivalent of a string of shiny beads. His group were mainly English, prodigiously hard-working, impeccably organised and imbued with a spirit of Churchillian defiance.

This was his idea of a day off. He had arrived home in Northampton at 2.15 a.m. after a game at Turf Moor. He was up for the school run five hours later and apart from a brief diversion to sort out the builders as they installed new windows, spoke engagingly and knowingly until it was time for a return trip across town to pick up his son, Max, at 3.30 p.m. Then he went to watch his daughter, Alicia, ice-skate.

His intensity was leavened by moments of self-deprecation. He was no glib propagandist; he thought deeply about what he was saying and was unafraid of screaming silence. He combined the components of a journeyman's playing career with experiences as coach and manager at Watford. They sacked him in adopting the business model developed by their new owners, the Pozzo family.

That was not the sort of dismissal to deface a CV. He was the first of 12 candidates to be interviewed for the Burnley job when Eddie Howe returned to Bournemouth in October 2012. He impressed with his respect for the club's ethos and was called back for confirmation that the caricature of a Rottweiler centre-half could not be further from the truth.

He understood: 'You look like me. You've had a career like me. Everybody thinks I was this mentalist as a footballer. I was only sent off twice, only once for a straight red, when I was 36. I was never suspended for bookings; the most I got in a season was three. Now, either I was the cleverest hard man in the world or I actually played quite fair, quite tough, and gave out body language that I meant business.

'I was a tricky centre midfield player as a kid at Nottingham Forest, a passer. The lower leagues moulded me into what I became because you have to learn to fight. They were more brutal than they are now, I can assure you. Here's the other thing about perception against fact. When I left Watford, I started doing SKY. I was on the panel there. Very quickly things started turning.

'I'm not up my own arse about it but people started going, "hang on, there's more to this ginger skinhead. He's got some good thoughts on the game. He's actually thinking." We do question the media at times but the power of the visual media was invaluable to me. People see how you say things. They see your authenticity, see you care.

'The term I use is seeing through the noise. That may not make sense to some, but imagine this scenario. You walk into a bar and your mate's on the other side of the room. It's hectic, mental. You can't hear yourself think but you still catch eyes and know what's going on. That kind of analogy works well in football management.

'There's all this stuff on the outside, media talk, internet sites, perception against misperception, fact against fiction. Your job is to see through all that and even see through the results at times. We are arguably the biggest underdogs the Premier League has ever seen. Maybe Blackpool were similar but I don't say that for effect. We have nowhere near anyone else's resource base.

'We didn't win for the first ten games so one reporter asks, "Will you ever win a game?" I said "what, ever, ever again?" You know just scoffing at him really, having fun with him, not trying to be offensive. Then someone else said, "They'll only win a game when they get relegated," and everyone gets involved.

'You have to look through that noise. I'm looking at the players' performances. I'm looking at the analytics. I'm looking at the facts. It's about being a motivator, an organiser, being empathetic, sympathetic, and psychologically strong. It's about being a developer, an innovator, though I'm not keen on that word because it implies you're re-inventing the wheel, which I'm certainly not. This game has been going on for 150 years so you pretty much find that every tactic, every trend has been used before.

'People re-brand it, re-package it, sell it again but that's not really my bag. I'm currently trying to get everything to work at once because we can't touch what we really need. Experienced Premier League players are out of our world financially, not just the fees but the wages.

'Seven of the clubs in the Championship have got a bigger wage bill than we've got in the Premier League. You'd be amazed at some of their numbers, amazed. They have players on 35-grand a week and then some. I've got to try and build a club for the future. I believe in what we do because I'd describe myself as a custodian. My job is to look after the club.

'Other managers have been saying, "Why don't you go out and get all the money you can and spend it?" But I was brought up a certain way by my parents. My dad was in business. You don't risk what you've built unless it has to be done. People forget Charlie Austin was sold a year ago to allow the club to move forward.

'Are you really going to throw all that Premier League money on the pitch and keep your fingers crossed, knowing that in two years' time you're going to have to sell someone to pay the electricity bill? Because, believe me, there aren't any sugar daddies at Burnley. They're wealthy, but not football club wealthy where you can throw away 20 million a year. That's what it takes now.

'The board, the club and myself have a realistic way of working. If that alignment goes, that's when you see trouble. When the manager starts saying, "Why are we doing this?" the board start saying, "He should be doing that." Then the players will say, "Where do we fit into all this?" It's not helpful to anyone. I can't see how that is healthy.

'My parents had good moral fibre. I put a lot of my way of working down to that. I was brought up in an era when if your job was to clean the floor, you'd make sure it was the cleanest it had ever been. If your job was to paint the fence, it was painted properly. If your job was to do your schoolwork, you didn't just do the basics. I still insist on those standards even now.

'My team is built on respect, honesty, desire, will, demand, self-demand, pride, passion, all the things that are seemingly unfashionable in this country. I feel quite strongly about it because I see some ridiculous things going on with our youth footballers, and nobody seems to want to stop it. I've never seen anything like it.

'Parents need to be educated. I'm not getting on my high horse about how they bring their kids up, but I'm referring to football education. Some old-fashioned beliefs are absolutely relevant to the modern game. We've got so drunk on technical detail that people have forgotten about moral fibre, about what it takes to walk out in front of 78,000 and deal with it.

'There are thousands of young, lovely-looking footballers who can receive on the back foot. They can pass, but when the ball's coming into the box, I'm not seeing so many centre-halves who want to head it. They want to block it, kick it. I don't see so many wide players who want to take the risk of dribbling past someone and beating them.

'I don't see so many centre-forwards who want to head it like their life depended on it. I see lots who want to score a trendy goal. That seems to be the in-vogue thing. I just like people who score goals. They can score them however they want. I'm not trying to be a dinosaur here but in the old days you had to earn the right.

'I left Forest, to go backwards to go forwards. I played 200 senior games before I earned a contract that you would recognise as being decent. Now, there are players in youth systems earning more than I ever earned as a player. And they're probably never going to kick a ball in the first team. I find that astonishing.

'There are a lot of players whose desire has gone by the time they're 21. Basically they're confused. They've been paid a hell of a lot of money almost to the point of being life-changing but they've never played in the first team at their own club. There are some really conflicting messages out there.'

Don't run away with the idea that here is one of life's regimental sergeant majors, pining for the return of National Service and the brain-numbing conformity of square-bashing. Dyche is inclusive by nature but uses freedom of expression in a subtle, educational manner. His first act as Burnley manager was to give his players a questionnaire, to gauge individual and collective character.

'It was very simple. They had complete anonymity. I wasn't interested in who said what. I wanted them to be respectful of the process, but if they wanted to be flippant, they had the right. I just told them, "Fill it in, and bring it back. I'm interested in knowing what your thoughts are." You can quickly tell the ones that take it seriously by watching them disperse around the room.

'You immediately see the ones looking at someone else's answer like when they were at school. You see the one who has his arm covering his sheet because he might be saying something he doesn't want the others to see. You see the one who has his shoulders back telling you, "I'm prepared to say it all."

'You watch for those tiny nuances, those little idiosyncrasies. You get them in and feed it back. You say, "Right, this is where you've told me where we're at. These are the things you want changing. These are the reasons why." You then go through the negotiables and the non-negotiables. The non-negotiables are really basic things.

'We work hard at all times. We show respect. Honesty and endeavour are a given. Show enthusiasm or say goodbye. We won't have people wandering round with headphones on. That might change in the future because it's fair to say there are certain cultures where that is important. As Brian Kidd once said, you can have a fight every day; it's which fight you want to win.

'Don't get me wrong. This is not set in stone because if I went into a different group with a different culture I might have to be flexible. I try to debate, to nurture. I try to get them to open up in small groups. Then we'll put ideas and views to a bigger group and build it into a collective voice.

'There are different kinds of leadership. I was deemed a leader as a player because I've got a big mouth and I can shout instructions. David Beckham wasn't a big voice but he delivered by example. His stats were phenomenal. His message was: "I will do it for you. I am willing to run for you. All I expect is for you to do everything you can to deliver." It's almost subliminal.

'I've learned over the past six months how quickly people become affected by success and change. I don't think I have. I've learned there's no magic answer and that people can't wait to drag you down. It's almost a jealousy thing within football managers and coaches. It creeps in from the outside, which is strange. I enjoy people's success and I tell them so.

'I don't do envy. I've known John Still for a while from when I was at Watford. He'd bring his own team over and we'd play. I send him texts now: "Hi mate, brilliant what you're doing." I do that a lot to people because I know how hard it is. It's my personal choice but I don't do de-branding of managers. I don't do slagging off of other teams.

'What do I mean de-branding? The favourite way to de-brand another manager is to comment on how they play. It's like a vicious sting; if you kick a ball more than 30 yards, they tell you that you play direct. We had that all last year so I don't even bother with it. I can show you the pass notes. I can show you the stats. But what's the point? We got promoted. I choose not to get involved.'

It was tempting to close my eyes, to kill the image of this physically imposing man, edging forward to make his points. A cold page can strip words of their warmth, their life force. This was a process of greater sophistication than a settlement of scores; it was someone searching within himself to share the truth of who he was and how he worked.

He was ahead of me: 'Psychology says that within four seconds of meeting someone you've formed an opinion without even speaking. So it's fair to say, if you walk into a group of footballers you are immediately scanning the room. There is no definite answer to this but I'll give you a feel of it. If I walked into a dressing room, I reckon within a morning I could go back to the manager and say, "Right, he's that, he's that, he's that." I reckon my strike rate would be pretty good.

'Loads of managers and coaches could do the same. You can sense it, smell it. Just by a very few conversations, watching and listening to a group, you'd know the leaders, the followers, the alpha males. You'd know the fraud, the one who thinks he's the alpha male but if you scratch the surface he's got nothing. It's amazing.

'One of the biggest achievements in management, because it has changed massively, is softening egos, getting rid of agendas, getting them to understand that the group will sort out everything. I sell that to players all the time. When the group achieves, even if you're out of the team, you'll be looked on differently.

'I'll give you an example. We were top of the league last season, doing great. Some of our subs moved on. The reason they got another club is because people thought, oh, they were part of a really good team. Think of what happens when the group underachieves. You're at the wrong end of the table, you're not in the team, and you've got your agenda. You're giving it big ones and you're mouthing off. Trust me, no manager is going to be looking at you when you are let go.

'It's rare that you get a group that aren't giving their all but you do get it. I've been in a couple where, to use that favourite expression, people have downed tools. It comes and goes; it's strange, Clive Woodward talked about "sappers" and "energisers". Paul Sturrock called them "crows" and "pigeons". Others speak about "terrorists" and "mavericks", or "assassins" and "mavericks".

'It's bizarre, you can remove three individuals from a dressing room and the whole feel changes. Sometimes you only need to remove one. I was talking to another manager about this the other day. Every one of us would take the maverick touched with a little bit of genius but nobody wants the terrorist, however talented, because he will quickly change the dynamic of the group.

'You know when you're in a good group. I went through the divisions, played at a few clubs and you can sense it, very quickly. There are a few in the middle, where it's good, but not going to get you where you want to go. I've had four promotions as a player and one as a manager. Every group has been right for that season. And I've seen it quickly turn.'

Some questions accelerate time; others make it stand still. When I asked him to consider what Sean Dyche the manager would think of Sean Dyche the player, he paused for what seemed an eternity. He puffed his cheeks out, gazed into the middle distance, and then allowed a small smile to play on his lips.

'Full on, opinionated, not tough to deal with, but I'm going to have to deal with him at some point. I'd very quickly say, he's going to have to stand up and do it for me. If he moans, I'll take that because he will still get it done whether he thinks it's right or wrong. If he has a fall-out he's going to sort it. The dressing room's going to be good because he'll make sure it's good. Underneath any edges he's got, he knows the fundamentals of how the group should operate.

'I went to Crystal Palace for a trial as part of a swap deal. I was on a real low when I went there but they wanted to sign me. That was a great boost because they were at a higher level but the money didn't work, so I had to go back. I delivered really good performances, and do you know why? One day John Duncan had me in and actually asked my opinion. It was about defensive positioning.

'That's all I really wanted, that little moment to be heard and rationalised. I didn't even need to be agreed with. I just felt, I can't get through to these people. They see me as this cocky Herbert who's got a lot to say for himself. He's a young player and should do what he's told. To be fair to John, he thought, he's got something to offer here. It was almost like the flick of a switch.'

Tellingly, Dyche still regards Duncan as a mentor. A pivotal personality in Chesterfield's run to the FA Cup semi-finals as a third tier team in 1997, he earned what seemed an ideal move to Bristol City. He made only 17 appearances and underwent another unseen rite of passage.

'There was a hard core of about five or six players who were the daddies of the dressing room. They were getting a bit older, a bit cliquey. I was 26, had a great season with Chesterfield the season before, and it is fair to say I was not backward in coming forward, without being disrespectful. I was a strong character and they immediately thought, hey, he's a threat.

'Off the pitch it was difficult and I kept on getting injured. The mix wasn't right. I'd started thinking about coaching, management, team modelling, team thinking. It formed me as a manager without a shadow of doubt because it gave me an understanding of the realities of the ugly side of football.

'I went there as quite a big signing. The fans didn't take to me. I learned about the human element, how you should and shouldn't treat people. I learned about dealing with media spin because Bristol City is quite a big club in that neck of the woods. They saw themselves as massive which was interesting in itself because they were in the third tier of football at the time. It was intriguing because I had an insight into support systems for injured players. I thought it was going to be hand in glove but they were not getting me and I wasn't getting them. It was a big shock, really odd to have this feeling of "me and them". That's why, as a manager, I've tried to keep a handle on the balance in my dressing room.

'Players speak to the staff and they make it clear to them I don't want tit-for-tat stuff. They know they only tell me something that really needs influencing because it could hurt the group. Footballers moan a lot. There's moaning for moaning's sake when we all know it's flippant, and a damaging moan. It sounds ridiculous but you fathom the difference very quickly.

'It's the difference between a maverick and an assassin. Mavericks moan but you know they're going to go out and do it. I was a bit like that, I suppose. Not in my skill level, but I would have a moan at the manager, which he accepted because I dealt with things in the dressing room. I could work players out, even the cute, clever ones who say all the right things and do all the wrong things.'

His growing stature led to an invitation to address candidates on the FA's Pro Licence course in March. They included fellow managers Jimmy Floyd Hasselbaink, Dave Flitcroft, Mark Warburton and Andy Awford, in addition to his assistant at Burnley Ian Woan. His treatise on leadership – 'I'm not here as a guru, I'm not here as the font of all knowledge and I'm not here to pontificate' – contained insights from the original maverick, Brian Clough.

He knew Dyche as 'young Ginger', an apprentice whose year-long growth spurt made him five inches taller and two stones heavier. Clough expected his garden to be tended, but would invite him into the first-team dressing room, where his unorthodox approach intensified the clarity of the message.

'There's an art to delivering information in a dressing room. It has to be done in a manner that, even if it's theatrical, it's believable. Brian Clough was the best because he could do it in very short blasts, in the most surprising ways. It wasn't always about tactics. It was the mood, the feel, the timing, the love, the hate, the power, the anger, all at the right time.

'I remember distinctly seeing Forest come in three-nil up at half-time and he absolutely ripped them to bits. I've seen him at three-nil down saying, "Well done, you're doing a terrific job lads. That's how we play at Nottingham Forest, we keep playing like that." They then go out and get a 3-3 or something. He used to say, "Hey, young Ginger, go and sit next to someone who plays in your position."

'One day, me and Steve Stone, who's a big mate of mine, were in there with another lad, Craig Ball, to get a feel of things. I'm not kidding; Cloughie got on his hands and knees with a towel and crawled over to the middle of the dressing room. He curled the towel up, put a ball on top of it and went on his hands and knees back to the benches.

'It was quiet. They didn't have ghetto blasters in those days. He simply started pointing at the ball. When the referee's bell goes, he keeps pointing and says, "There she is, look after her, all the best captain." That was the team talk, done. The players get up, line up, get out there and win 2-0. Now imagine me going home and telling my dad that story about the legendary, mystical tactician, the brilliant manager.

'My dad's going, "You're kidding me." And I'm going, "No dad I swear." The simplicity of it was genius. The hardest thing as a manager is to say a lot in not many words. At half-time for example, when there are a million things going through a player's brain, you can lose them with too much information. Psychologists say go for three points they will remember, particularly three buzz words. But can you imagine

The Best of Burnley

what I'm thinking as a youngster: wow, what is going on here?'

His influences are eclectic. Lennie Lawrence re-ignited his playing career at Luton. Mark McGhee and the late Ray Harford made him think at Millwall. Aidy Boothroyd's acerbic honesty in releasing him as a player at Watford and re-employing him as a coach two years later was cleansing, for both. Brendan Rodgers, Boothroyd's successor at Vicarage Road, remains a friend.

When we piece together the jigsaw of what makes a successful manager, it contains shards of bone, scraps of sinew and slithers of grey matter. Dyche's sensitivity may not fit the stereotype. His assertiveness does not translate easily. Yet he appreciates the mechanics of getting the best out of himself. He has developed the confidence to change.

'If you want to be brutal, if you're going to bullshit people, you'd better remember your bullshit. But if you're going to be honest, you don't have to remember anything because you've just told it how you see it. That's why I won't project to my players about honesty or authenticity without delivering it. I don't spin. I'm not trying to work an angle.

'Five years ago I was typical. I came out of the game with a bee in my bonnet. I'm now not afraid of money being someone's key driver. It's not mine, but if it is someone else's, fine. Last season we were saying to the players they had every possible means of fulfilment within their grasp. We told them, "If you want money, go for it and you'll get money. If you want kudos, you'll get kudos, if you get this job done. If you want local fame, you're going to get it. If you want national fame, you're going to get it. If you want to nick a bird, you'll get a bird on the back of what you're doing now. If you want the car, you'll get the car. And if you just want old-fashioned winning and success, you're going to get that as well."

'So, I've got no problems as long as the player is stimulated to drive forward and get what he wants. Like most, I used to go, it's disgraceful; all they want is money. Well, so what! As long as you're giving everything to me, the team and the cause, you go for your life. My personal thing is winning. That's what I do it for, that's my buzz. Get that right and everything else will come anyway.'

He is not keen to amplify recent praise from Sir Alex Ferguson, since your peer group go, "Oh do me a favour, what are you doing, you egg." He is though, quite happy to rationalise his habit of cold-calling fellow managers, if he hears they have been at a Burnley match.

'Friends will tell you what they think you want to hear. Family will tell you what you roughly want to hear, but managers tell it as it is. You can usually get a number for them in this business, so I ring them: "Hi, Sean Dyche, what did you think? Tell me the brutal truth." It is important to get that outside view. It can help if you are emotionally or physically stretched. Sometimes you've been working so hard, you can't see the wood for the trees.

'I'm lucky because I have a hard core of mates. We've known each other since we were five. Quite frankly, they don't particularly give a toss about me and football, they never did. They like football but they're not of football. They are my go-tos, for my ups and downs, ins and outs. Hopefully they are always going to be there for me.

'We have a curry night now and again. All the stories come out. The fish gets bigger, the bird gets uglier, we drink more, we tell the same stories a thousand times over and wet ourselves laughing to the point where our wives do that face thing that women do, like, what are they on about, idiots? I don't think my mates realise how important that is to me.

'This job is intoxicating. You can morph into something different. I'm 43, pretty young to be doing what I'm doing. Imagine if my future keeps going on an upward curve and I end up at what you'd regard as a really big club, with no disrespect to Burnley. You might meet me in four years and think where's the geezer who was popping home to see the builders and get his hands dirty and then coming out for a coffee?

'I'd like to think I won't change but I can't guarantee it. This isn't about management but about life. I really like music and saw a Kasabian show the other day. We were in a small room, maybe thirty feet square. There were friends, family, people they've known for years. There's drink, and the stereo goes on. No lights, just a big speaker with a phone.

'For three hours it was mayhem; laughter, dancing and joking. These guys are going to be regarded as rock legends, yet they know the world they live in is false. I'm the same. I take great pride and enjoyment in some of the doors that open because of football, but I know where I live, that's my point. I go off home to my kids, my family, that's my number one priority – bar none.'